WATERGATE'S LEGACY AND THE PRESS

Medill School of Journalism
VISIONS *of the* AMERICAN PRESS

GENERAL EDITOR
David Abrahamson

WATERGATE'S
LEGACY AND THE PRESS
THE INVESTIGATIVE IMPULSE

Jon Marshall

Foreword by Bob Woodward

MEDILL SCHOOL OF JOURNALISM

Northwestern University Press
Evanston, Illinois

Northwestern University Press
www.nupress.northwestern.edu

Printed in the United States of America

10 9 8 7 6 5 4 3 2 1

Library of Congress Cataloging-in-Publication Data

Marshall, Jon, 1963–

    Watergate's legacy and the press : the investigative impulse / Jon Marshall ;
foreword by Bob Woodward

      p. cm. — (Visions of the American press)

    Includes bibliographical references and index.

    ISBN 978-0-8101-2719-7 (pbk. : alk. paper)

      1. Investigative reporting—United States—History—20th century. 2. Investigative reporting—United States—History—21st century. 3. Watergate Affair, 1972–1974—Press coverage. 4. Bernstein, Carl, 1944– 5. Woodward, Bob, 1943– I. Title. II. Series: Medill School of Journalism visions of the American press.

PN4888.I56M37 2010

070.4'3097309045—dc22

                           2010024052

To my parents, Maxine and Jonathan Marshall, for sharing their love of journalism, books, and politics, and to Laurie, Justin, Andrew, and Zachary for bringing joy to every day.

CONTENTS

FOREWORD

Bob Woodward

In the fall of 1972, Carl Bernstein and I stepped away from the *Washington Post* newsroom so we could talk one-on-one in private.

We frequently met inside the canteen not far from our desks for a cup of vending machine coffee. Since the break-in of the Democratic National Headquarters at the Watergate office complex that June, these were our moments to strategize about a story that had evolved well beyond a simple burglary. Our 1974 book *All the President's Men* featured some of these conversations. But not this particular one.

By that point, our reporting showed that Richard Nixon's Committee to Re-elect the President (CREEP) had used a secret cash slush fund to pay for the Watergate break-in, in addition to other acts of espionage and sabotage.

After several days of aggressive interviewing, we knew that John Mitchell was among the five who controlled the slush fund. My anonymous source known as Deep Throat—who after thirty-three years of silence revealed himself to be former FBI associate director W. Mark Felt—confirmed Mitchell's involvement.

Mitchell was an intimidating and imposing figure, almost as close to Nixon as you could get. He had been Nixon's attorney general from 1969 to 1972, having resigned to manage the president's reelection campaign. But Mitchell had controlled the slush fund while serving as attorney general.

As Carl slipped a coin into the coffee machine, he thought

about this and said to me, "Oh, my God. The president is going to be impeached."

"Jesus, I think you're right," I said, and cautioned, "We can never use that word"—*impeached*—"in the newsroom." It was a year before Congress began impeachment proceedings and almost two years before Nixon's resignation.

Our evening interviews in parking garages and homes, relentless phone calls, and late nights were not designed to get a president impeached. Our approach was empirical. What were the facts? What really happened? How could we verify? We wanted at least two independent sources, if possible. It involved the occasional stumble. We were fitting the pieces of a puzzle together, following through a story by getting answers that only led to more questions. Chief among them was why, a question we could answer much better after several years.

We now know far more about Watergate and the resulting cover-up, courtesy of the 750-page Senate report on Watergate and the gradual release of Nixon's secret White House tapes. New tapes and transcripts are being released to this day. They repeatedly prove his crimes, abuses, and motivations.

Nixon used government power—the FBI, the IRS, the CIA—illegally, the record now shows. A seething rage, a catalog of personal vendettas, and a sense of self-pity consumed him. He declared a covert war against his perceived enemies. He ordered Mitchell to investigate the big Democratic contributors, those who might pose a threat to him. And when the Watergate burglars were arrested, his orders were to buy their silence. "They have to be paid. That's all there is to that," Nixon told his chief of staff on August 1, 1972, six weeks after the break-in, according to one tape.

When I had information in April 1973 that Nixon himself would be implicated in the Watergate scandal, the president told his spokesman to send me a very specific message. "Tell him he better watch his God damn ass," Nixon said, his words preserved on tape. "They're going to attack the president's men, but they must not attack the president."

With those tapes, Nixon unwittingly provided history with evidence of both his mindset and his deceit.

The nature of journalism itself has changed since Watergate. Much of it is now based on urgency and speed, rather than the details that emerge from weeks of hard work and strategizing by the coffee vending machine. Financial pressures have caused the number of news organizations that can sustain this level of commitment to dwindle.

But the principles of investigative reporting outlined by Jon Marshall in this volume remain the same. It takes an inner drive instead of an editor's suggestion. It is detective work, full of frustration, false trails, and dead ends. It involves messy desks and sleepless nights. It means a penchant to challenge authority. Carl and I were fortunate to have an editor such as Ben Bradlee at the *Post,* and Katharine Graham as the publisher.

All of that came together on the Mitchell article about the slush fund. We filed it at 6:00 P.M. The reelection committee issued a denial statement five hours later. Carl phoned Mitchell for elaboration, reaching him at his hotel in New York City.

When he asked about the slush fund, Mitchell responded, "JEEEEEEEESUS" and personally threatened Graham. This was a primal scream, a visceral response because he had been found out. After all the official investigations of Watergate by the Senate, House, and a special prosecutor, and the decision by the United States Supreme Court that Nixon had to turn over his secret tapes, the dots were connected. The clarity and proof of criminality were now fully on the record.

PREFACE

More than two hundred reporters and editors filled a Washington, D.C., hotel ballroom one afternoon at the 2007 convention of the Society of Professional Journalists. Usually skeptical and irreverent, the journalists murmured with excitement as they waited to hear three of their heroes talk about the Watergate scandal thirty-five years earlier. When Bob Woodward, Carl Bernstein, and Ben Bradlee ascended to the podium, audience members surrounded them, shaking their hands, requesting autographs, and maneuvering to get their photographs taken with the three famous men. Other renowned journalists and Watergate experts participated in that afternoon's panel discussion, but they did not receive the same adoration. Unlike Woodward, Bernstein, and Bradlee, they had never been portrayed by Hollywood stars. Nor had their names become synonymous in the public's mind with Watergate and the best of investigative reporting.

Woodward, Bernstein, and Bradlee have attained near legendary status because of their work uncovering key parts of the Watergate conspiracy that led to President Richard M. Nixon's resignation. After five men carrying bugging devices were caught inside the Democratic National Committee's headquarters in the Watergate office complex on June 17, 1972, Bernstein and Woodward pursued the story more tenaciously than any other reporters. They received staunch support from their bosses at the *Washington Post,* including executive editor Bradlee, managing editor Howard Simons, Metropolitan Editor Harry Rosenfeld, and publisher Katharine Graham. Woodward and Bernstein's stories revealed that the burglary had been plotted at the upper levels of Nixon's administration and reelection campaign. They proved the break-in was part of a secretive, illegal, and widespread attack on Nixon's political opponents and the democratic process.

Thanks largely to Bernstein and Woodward, the popularity of investigative reporting soared during Watergate and its immediate aftermath. Their book *All the President's Men* and the subsequent movie by the same name epitomized an era when investigative reporters were seen as courageous fighters of corruption and injustice. As media scholar Michael Schudson noted, "No other story in American history features the press in so prominent and heroic a role."[1]

Nearly forty years later, Watergate continues to influence American journalism, government, and politics. It certainly influenced me. Watergate seemed to fill the air during my middle-school years. At dinner my parents discussed the shenanigans of the Nixon White House, and my family watched the Senate Watergate hearings on television with rapt attention. After I won my school's fifth-grade presidency, the movement to impeach Nixon inspired my classmates to impeach me as well (even though I was not accused of any high crimes or misdemeanors). I did not take my impeachment personally and was reelected a few weeks later. That summer my friends and I read the recently released transcripts of Nixon's Oval Office conversations and substituted our own creative curses for each "expletive deleted" uttered by the president. Watergate also had a more serious impact on my life by encouraging me to become a reporter. As I researched this book, I talked with other journalists who were similarly influenced.

Watergate's legacy for the press, however, is far more complex than a simple tale of inspiration for young journalists. It shaped the way investigative reporting is perceived and practiced and how political leaders and the public respond to journalists. While investigative reporting has improved in many ways since the Nixon era, Watergate unleashed forces that fed a growing public mistrust of journalists. The very aggressiveness that made Bernstein and Woodward successful—and which was imitated by legions of journalists—produced a long parade of exposés that an increasingly cynical public greeted with dwindling outrage. Investigative reporting began to have less impact as the economic and legal environment became more treacherous for journalism and the political climate more poisonous. Bernstein and Woodward raised the journalistic bar by writing stories that contributed to a president's resignation. No other reporters have been able to jump quite as high since, at least in the public's estimation.

Even if Nixon himself was crushed by Watergate, the sort of contempt, intimidation, and subterfuge that shaped his approach toward the press has survived and at times flourished since he left office. Each new presidential administration has looked for ways to better shield itself from prying reporters. Like the Nixon administration, the White House of George W. Bush strengthened the power of the executive branch as it responded to the September 11 terrorist attacks and prepared for war in Iraq. Like Nixon, Bush displayed open disdain toward the press and shrouded the workings of government in a veil of secrecy. In contrast with the Watergate era, however, the press response during much of Bush's time in office was more impotent than heroic.

Although investigative reporting remained in the spotlight following Watergate, it was not a term commonly used during most of American history. And yet the impulse to challenge authority and expose wrongdoing appeared in the days of the first printing presses in colonial America and has endured to the current era of Internet exposés. Journalists and their critics have given this kind of reporting different names: "muckraking," "watchdog journalism," and "the journalism of outrage" among others. The terms have different shades of meaning, but they share in common the pursuit of facts hidden from the public.

For the purposes of this book, I will use the definition of investigative reporting developed by legendary reporter Robert Greene of *Newsday:* "It is the reporting, through one's own work product and initiative, matters of importance which some persons or organizations wish to keep secret."[2] This definition was adopted in the 1970s by Investigative Reporters and Editors, better known as IRE, a nonprofit organization that became the leading promoter of investigative reporting in the United States. IRE eventually broadened the definition to include digging up facts on important issues that had never been pieced together, even if no one was trying to hide the information.[3]

Some journalists argue that investigative reporting should not even be considered a separate craft. Typical of this sentiment is a comment made by renowned reporter I. F. Stone: "All journalism is investigative."[4] Stone's career, however, exemplified how investigative reporting is different from most stories we see in the press. Stone spent his days combing through documents to find countless instances of government lies, while many other reporters of his time were content to repeat official pronouncements. Most news stories are not investigative in nature and never have been. Investigative reporting is often controversial, difficult, expensive, and time-consuming. For example, more than two-thirds of the stories entered in the IRE annual contest between 1979 and 2007 took longer than two months to complete.[5] In contrast, most stories we see in the news—the president's latest speech, the car crash that injured three people, the upcoming art fair, last night's big storm—have nothing investigative about them.

Through the years, the investigative impulse has inspired American journalism at its powerful best. This book explores Watergate's role in that history. Each chapter answers a basic question about Watergate and investigative reporting:

1. How did investigative journalism become a powerful force in the United States by the start of the twentieth century?

2. How did investigative reporting evolve in the twentieth century, even when it was largely ignored by the mainstream press, to the point that journalists could uncover the crimes of Watergate?

3. Why did Nixon's anger toward the press start him on a path that led to Watergate?

4. What role did journalists, and in particular Bernstein and Woodward, really play in the unraveling of the Watergate mystery?

5. How did Watergate help investigative reporting flourish in the years immediately after Nixon's resignation?

6. Why did investigative journalism begin to struggle in the 1980s and 1990s even as reporting techniques improved?

7. What led to the backlash against the press during the presidency of George W. Bush, and why did journalists fail to adequately investigate Bush's case for war?

8. How can new technology and economic models give investigative reporting a renewed opportunity to flourish as the journalism world struggles through a time of crisis?

While answering these questions, I will describe the work of journalists whose determination to dig for the truth has made our government more honest, our workplaces safer, our economy fairer, and our environment cleaner. This is their story.

ACKNOWLEDGMENTS

I am forever thankful to the many people who helped me with this book during its long gestation. My colleagues at the Medill School of Journalism offered tremendous support throughout the research and writing process. David Abrahamson, the editor of Medill's Visions of the American Press series, has been a kind and wise guide from start to finish. I cannot thank him enough. John Lavine, Mary Nesbitt, Frank Mulhern, Michele Bitoun, Janice Castro, and Richard Roth provided the time, resources, and encouragement that I needed. Douglas Foster, Loren Ghiglione, Rachel Davis Mersey, and other members of the Faculty Book Group shared useful advice and motivation. Judy McCoy and the staff of the Northwestern University Library helped feed my insatiable demands for more books.

One of the joys of researching this book was the opportunity to interview journalists who played important roles in the history of investigative reporting. Scott Armstrong, Donald Barlett, Ben Bradlee, Sarah Cohen, Andrew Donohue, Leonard Downie Jr., Seymour Hersh, Brant Houston, David Kaplan, Philip Meyer, Deborah Nelson, David Protess, Gene Roberts, Rhonda Schwartz, James Steele, Barry Sussman, Steve Weinberg, and Bob Woodward generously shared their knowledge and insights with me. I am also indebted to the dozens of scholars whose research informed my work. I especially appreciate the contributions of James L. Aucoin, who provided valuable advice on my original proposal.

Gail Goldstein, Laurie Goldstein, Maxine Marshall, Robert

Marshall, Melissa May, Susan Witz, and C. Adam Wren read early versions of my manuscript and shared terrific advice. My research assistant, the talented Florent Blanc, tenaciously tracked down journal articles that I needed, offered valuable analysis of the research, and shared thoughtful suggestions on early drafts of the book. Graduate assistants Melissa May and C. Adam Wren spent many hours transcribing interviews and double-checking facts. Medill students Philip Taylor, Gary Cohen, Hamsa Ramesha, and Phil Kaplan also contributed to the research. I deeply appreciate their help.

I am grateful to my parents, Maxine and Jonathan Marshall, who always encouraged my writing and introduced their children to the drama of Watergate during our dinner table conversations. Their spirit fills these pages. Most important of all, I want to thank my wonderful wife, Laurie, and fabulous sons Justin, Andrew, and Zachary for their loving support and understanding when I would disappear into my office to work for hours on end. This book is for them.

WATERGATE'S LEGACY AND THE PRESS

ONE

STARTING TO INVESTIGATE

I have at least the satisfaction of knowing that the poor unfortunates will be the better cared for because of my work.
—Nellie Bly, "Ten Days in a Mad-House," 1887

When Bob Woodward, Carl Bernstein, and other journalists began investigating Watergate, they challenged the country's most dominant men—President Richard Nixon and his top aides. How could the reporters risk their reputations and their careers to doubt the truthfulness of these authorities? More than three hundred years earlier, John Davenport of colonial Massachusetts faced a similar question. In 1663, he wrote "Another Essay for the Investigation of Truth," a pamphlet disagreeing with the colony's powerful Puritan leaders on how to properly baptize children. There was one big problem: the only available printing press was controlled by the same people whose policies he was attacking. Davenport worked up the nerve to ask the leaders to print his essay. They agreed and then published their own essay in response.[1] Davenport's experience shows that, from its earliest days, the American press was willing to challenge authority, an essential ingredient of investigative reporting. It also demonstrates that those in power, at least some of them, accepted the value of letting writers dig for the truth.

The roots of American investigative reporting stretch back to the 1600s, when writers such as Davenport put in practice the emerging Enlightenment theory that people have a right to question their leaders. In the colonial years, the press consisted of pamphlets and broadsides (large sheets printed on only one side) and eventually newspapers, books, and magazines. The men who wrote them—and they were always men at first—did not think of themselves as reporters, much less investigative reporters. They filled their pages with opinions and information gleaned from official pronouncements, other publications, letters from friends, and conversations with neighbors and travelers. Their motivations were mixed: to make money, argue politics, provide a community service, and promote their faith.[2]

From this willingness to challenge people in power, the other ingredients of modern investigative journalism gradually came together over the next two and a half centuries. We will see how reporters began writing in-depth stories rather than brief notices, going to places to observe events directly, interviewing witnesses and participants, using documents as evidence, finding people who would leak them information, and expressing outrage at society's injustices. These developments would make investigative journalism a powerful force by the start of the twentieth century.

The investigative impulse made a bold appearance in America's first newspaper, *Publick Occurrences, Both Forreign and Domestick*. Its publisher, the rebellious Benjamin Harris, had escaped to the colonies after being imprisoned twice in England for criticizing King Charles II and the Church of England. Vowing to expose falsehoods by Massachusetts's leaders and to cure the "Spirit of Lying, which prevails among us," Harris took the daring step of not obtaining government permission for *Publick Occurrences* before printing it in Boston in 1690.[3]

Most of the newspaper's three pages (a fourth was left blank) were filled with what journalists today call "spot news" such as a local fire, a suicide, and the status of a smallpox epidemic. It also contained a juicy rumor about the king of France sleeping with his daughter-in-law (the American press has always loved sensationalism, even then). Harris devoted the most ink, however, to his report about a colonial militia expedition to Canada to confront French forces and their Native American allies. The story began the American tradition of watchdog journalism by uncovering facts that the colonial authorities wanted to keep hidden. It included embarrassing revelations including a lack of canoes to transport the troops, the "barbarous" treatment of prisoners by the colonists' Mohawk allies, and the unexpected absence of other Native Americans who were supposed to assist the campaign but "sent their Excuses."[4]

With this story, Harris embraced, in the words of historian James Aucoin, "the essential qualities of investigative journalism—revelation of public wrongdoing, documentation of evidence, a challenge to established public policy, and an appeal to public opinion for reform."[5] The authorities reacted to *Publick Occurrences* like many other powerbrokers have done: They tried to suppress the press. Only four days after Harris began publishing his newspaper, the colonial governing council forced him to stop.[6]

The publication of the first continuous American newspaper fourteen years later showcased a competing trend that weakened investigative journalism: heavy reliance on the words of authorities. Unlike Harris, *Boston News-Letter* publisher John Campbell bowed to the wishes of the colonial rulers and avoided controversy. Rival pamphleteers, however, did not hesitate to reveal information that embarrassed the government. They offered some of the first exposés about official misconduct by disclosing Governor Joseph Dudley's brawls with two farmers, efforts to increase his own salary, and connections with a man convicted of selling supplies to enemy troops.[7]

James Franklin continued the pamphleteers' aggressiveness when he began publishing his *New-England Courant* newspaper in Boston in 1721. He documented instances when the government's smallpox inoculation program actually induced the disease (even though it ended up being effective) and criticized colonial authorities for failing to protect the coastline from pirates. In response to his crusading, Franklin was tossed in jail and banned from publishing any more issues of the *Courant*. But Franklin's younger brother, the soon-to-be-famous Benjamin, took the *Courant*'s watchdog spirit to Philadelphia, where his *Pennsylvania Gazette* openly challenged the powerful Penn family and other leaders of the colony.[8]

One of the first big showdowns between the watchdog press and government rulers took place in New York City. Merchants and other local leaders who opposed Governor William Cosby helped printer John Peter Zenger launch the *New-York Weekly Journal*. In 1733, the newspaper alleged that Cosby allowed a French boat to gather military intelligence in the city's harbor. In response, the governor's council declared four issues of the *Weekly Journal* to be libelous, ordered copies of the newspaper burned, and threw Zenger in jail. Under the legal theory of the day, any criticism that might cause unrest was considered seditious libel and criminal. But when Zenger's case came to trial, attorney Andrew Hamilton argued that a story could not be libelous if it were true.

He added that the freedom to speak and print the facts about government was necessary to expose "arbitrary Power." The jury agreed, and Zenger was released, creating a valuable precedent for future journalists who dared to reveal government wrongdoing.[9]

Still, watchdog journalism was hardly the norm in colonial times. By the mid-1700s, most colonies had newspapers, but the majority of publishers, struggling to survive, shied away from investigating their rulers. One exception was William Parks, whose *Virginia Gazette* printed a story unmasking a member of the colony's House of Burgesses as a sheep thief. The legislators wanted to punish Parks but relented when he produced court records showing the accusation was true.[10]

As revolution came closer, other printers became as daring as Parks. When more British troops arrived to quash unrest, Boston publishers created the daily *Journal of Occurrences* in 1768 to publicize their city's plight. It reported on threats by British troops against civilians, the unpopularity of a local justice of the peace, and accusations that the British were using tax money to monopolize trade. A year later Boston printers Benjamin Edes and John Gill published the confidential letters of the Massachusetts governor, forcing his recall to England. The journalists who backed the British countered with their own investigations. When some Americans formed an association to pressure merchants to stop importing British goods, the *Boston Chronicle* printed manifests showing that ships owned by patriot leader John Hancock had carried forbidden items. Hancock's allies responded by assaulting *Chronicle* publisher John Mein, forcing him to flee town.[11]

By the end of the colonial era, the aggressive spirit of the American press had taken hold. It grew stronger after independence as Federalist and Republican leaders, struggling bitterly to control the new nation, sponsored newspapers that they wielded as political weapons. Publishers used the freedom of the press guaranteed by the First Amendment to bash their political enemies. These newspapers, known as the partisan press, often relied on innuendo, rumor, and invective but on occasion revealed fresh information that made their opponents squirm. Republican editor Philip Freneau's *National Gazette* implicated Treasury Secretary Alexander Hamilton and other top Federalists in a financial scandal. After a congressional investigation, an assistant treasury secretary was sent to prison for illegally using insider knowledge of bond sales.

Not to be outdone, Benjamin Franklin Bache, the grandson of Benjamin Franklin, launched his own crusade against the Federalists. His Philadelphia *Aurora* used a network of informants to uncover the secret dealings of George Washington's administration. Bache was the first American journalist to thoroughly quote from a leaked government document to expose corruption—in this case questionable Federalist financial activities.[12]

In response to this disclosure, enraged Federalists passed the Alien and Sedition Acts in 1798, making it illegal to "write, print, utter, or publish . . . any false, scandalous and malicious writing . . . against the government of the United States. . . ." The Sedition Acts allowed officials to arrest Bache and other Republican editors but failed to silence the government's opponents, who argued that the press had a right to question leaders' actions. Thomas Jefferson allowed the laws to die when he became president three years later. He suffered the consequences of journalists' renewed freedom in 1802 when Virginia editor James Callender revealed that Jefferson had an affair with his slave Sally Hemings.[13] Such partisan exposés would not fit most modern definitions of investigative reporting because they relied more on leaked information than on original reporting, but they showed a growing willingness by journalists to uncover the secrets of the powerful.

The ability to dig for secrets grew stronger as the number of reporters increased. During colonial times, most newspapers had been family operations owned by printers with one or two employees. After the Revolution, owners hired more people and developed specialized jobs as their businesses grew. Publishers, desperate for firsthand reports of political battles in the newly created Washington, D.C., started hiring regular correspondents for the first time during Jefferson's presidency. As the specialty of reporting developed, publications began gathering news not found elsewhere. The amount of original reporting further multiplied as printers followed the nation's rising population into new territories. The number of newspapers jumped from thirty-five at the end of the Revolution to 234 by 1800 and 1,200 by 1833. The number of magazines soared from five in 1794 to more than a hundred by 1825.[14]

Journalists also began paying more attention to injustice. African Americans, ethnic minorities, women, religious groups, and the burgeoning antislavery movement started their own publications to cover issues ignored by most newspapers. *El Misisipi* in New Orleans became the nation's first Latino newspaper in 1808. In the 1820s, Benjamin Lundy launched the antislavery *Genius of Universal Emancipation,* Elias Boudinot started the *Cherokee Phoenix* in defense of Native American rights, and John B. Russwurm and Samuel E. Cornish published the nation's first black-owned newspaper, *Freedom's Journal.* Although they rarely had enough reporters to conduct in-depth reporting of their own, these newspapers presented information that challenged the established order and nourished a spirit of outrage. *Freedom's Journal,* for example, included many reports detailing the brutality of slavery in the South and attacks against African Americans in the North. The *Genius of Universal Emancipation* ran the first published account in an American newspaper of a lynching. This story described how an Alabama justice of the peace allowed a slave accused of theft to be taken away by a mob and burned to death.[15]

Original reporting gained more ground in the middle third of the century as the partisan press lost some of its influence. The growing number of literate and middle-class Americans demanded more news as farms, villages, and cities became linked in a national economy. Improved printing presses and a greater supply of paper allowed publishers to feed that demand. Meanwhile, the democratic ideals stirred by the presidency of Andrew Jackson encouraged newspapers to pay more attention to the needs of the common man. These economic, technological, political, and demographic changes transformed journalism in the 1830s, encouraging the birth of what became known as the penny press. These newspapers reached a larger audience by being sold on the streets for only one cent a copy (at least at first), five cents less than the price of other papers. They focused their coverage on the concerns of the expanding urban population rather than the business and political elite catered to by previous publications. Penny papers such as Benjamin Day's *New York Sun* and James Gordon Bennett's *New York Herald* grew politically independent in their news gathering because they relied on advertising rather than party subsidies.[16]

The newspapers of the penny press started using a controversial new technique that greatly aided future investigative reporters: the interview. Bennett, a Scottish immigrant with a fondness for gossip, is often credited as the first reporter to interview people. When he investigated the ax murder of prostitute Helen Jewett in

1836, he interviewed the owner of the brothel where Jewett died. He also examined the crime scene and the victim's possessions rather than rely on police statements. Bennett's story raised doubts about the guilt of the man arrested for the murder, who was later acquitted.[17]

The investigative impulse spread as the penny newspapers hustled to attract more readers with exciting exposés. In the 1840s, Margaret Fuller of the *New York Tribune* wrote about conditions for prostitutes and reported from almshouses, Sing Sing prison, and the infamous Blackwell's Island asylum for the mentally ill.[18] Bennett invited the *Herald*'s readers to send evidence of corruption to assist the newspaper's investigations; one tip from a reader helped expose fraud at the local customs office.[19]

This spirit of exposing wrongs was embraced by some magazine publishers. In 1858, Frank Leslie's eponymous weekly featured an investigation of New York City's powerful milk industry. After visiting a Brooklyn dairy, Leslie described in vivid detail the way it fed swill, a waste product from nearby distilleries, to its cows. The swill made the cows produce unhealthy milk, and Leslie provided statistics showing that the childhood death rate in New York was higher than in similar cities as a result. Leslie followed milk deliverers after they left the dangerous dairies, and he outlined their routes for his readers. By the next week, he claimed, all of these routes were canceled, and the dairy he had named was obtaining healthier milk from the countryside.[20]

During the Civil War, investigative reporting weakened as reporters focused on the great battles and bitter political struggles of the era. They often simply reprinted official documents from the Union and Confederate governments and armies, who censored stories and jailed reporters they disliked. The war, however, stimulated newspaper sales to readers hungry for news of the battles.

Once the war ended, new technology helped make investigative journalism more common. The spread of telephones and typewriters improved the speed and accuracy of reporting. The harnessing of electricity, the availability of less-expensive paper, and the invention of rotary presses allowed publishers to print newspapers ten times faster than they did at the start of the century. As the expanding U.S. population followed the railroads westward to new cities and towns, the number of newspapers soared from about 4,000 dailies and weeklies in 1860 to more than 13,000 by 1900.[21]

This growth encouraged publishers to compete fiercely for readers by promoting exciting, enterprising stories. They hired more reporters and launched crusades against public problems to attract readers of different ethnic backgrounds who were immigrating by the millions to towns and cities. In addition to the sensational crime stories that were their bread and butter, they covered the impact of rapid industrialization, wretched housing conditions, and the corruption that saturated postwar governments.[22]

Some of the most startling revelations of corruption appeared in the pages of the *New York Times* in 1870 and 1871 as it uncovered the unscrupulous practices of the Tammany Hall political machine. Under boss William Tweed, Tammany Hall controlled New York City government and stole millions of dollars from municipal coffers. While other newspaper publishers accepted bribes to ignore the improprieties, the *Times* ran stories revealing the Tweed ring's secret account books and hundreds of thousands of dollars in payments to contractors for work that was never done. Much of the money was then kicked back to Tweed and his allies, whom the *Times* called "soulless vampires." In one instance, a Tammany Hall ally was paid $7,500 for a thermometer. The *Times* strengthened investigative reporting standards by including entries from the account books themselves to document the abuses. The *Times* stories led to government investigations of Tammany Hall; Tweed died a few years later in prison.[23]

Not to be outdone by the *Times,* the *New York Sun* published stories in 1872 revealing that financiers of the Crédit Mobilier railroad corporation bribed thirteen congressmen and other officials to avoid a government investigation of fraud. The *Sun* unveiled the complex transactions by tracking down the plotters' secret testimony and correspondence. The first story ran with a less than subtle headline: "The King of Frauds. How the Crédit Mobilier Bought Its Way Through Congress. Colossal Bribery. Congressmen who Have Robbed the People, and who now Support The National Robber. How Some Men Get Fortunes." The stories led to the resignation of two congressmen.[24]

Many journalism history books focus their attention on New York City as the center of crusading journalism in the late 1800s, but its spirit was found throughout the country among a new generation of publishers, editors, and reporters who came of age following the Civil War. For example, *Chicago Evening Daily News* owner and editor Melville Stone liked to do what he called "detective work." He once pursued the president of a failed bank as he fled Chicago to Canada and then to England, France, and Germany, where Stone finally found him and got his confession. Stone's stories prompted a new state law requiring inspections of savings banks.[25]

In the pages of the rival *Chicago Tribune,* Henry Demarest Lloyd used court records, business documents, and interviews to expose the shady practices of William H. Vanderbilt, John D. Rockefeller, and other tycoons. His two-page article "Our Land," published in 1883, described railroad companies profiting from the sale of land the government had given them for free. The *Tribune* enhanced the presentation of his in-depth story by using a new way to show complex information—a full-page map that graphically displayed the extent of the railroads' fraud.[26]

The crusader spirit spread to other cities. In 1881, Edward H. Butler's *Buffalo News* began investigating the discrimination, poverty, and squalor endured by the city's rapidly growing Polish immigrant community. *News* reporters visited the shanties where the immigrants lived and detailed the malnutrition and health threats posed by terrible conditions. The stories struck a chord with the newspaper's readers, and immigrant living conditions improved.[27]

St. Louis Post-Dispatch owner Joseph Pulitzer, a Hungarian immigrant who became America's most powerful publisher, was one of the founders of what became known as "new journalism." Pulitzer and other new journalism proponents sought to attract readers, and thus advertisers, by exposing wrongdoing and championing causes of importance to common people. *Post-Dispatch* reporters unveiled voting fraud, questionable real-estate deals, and government protection of brothels and gambling halls. One series of articles revealed that some of the city's wealthiest citizens and municipal leaders paid no taxes on their property.[28]

The crusading spirit was adopted by William Randolph Hearst, the wealthy young owner of the *San Francisco Examiner,* who boasted that he produced "the journalism that acts." Sometimes this approach led to outrageous publicity stunts, other times to important investigative journalism. Hearst took on San Francisco's businessmen and other leaders, running a series of stories disclosing that the city's private water company was raising its rates while paying stockholders large dividends and allowing its pipes to deteriorate. The *Examiner* also documented how the Southern Pacific Railroad never paid back millions of dollars in government loans while it increased rates for customers.[29]

Hearst took his crusading to New York, where he bought the *Journal* in 1895. Hearst and Pulitzer, who now owned the *New York World,* boosted their newspapers' circulations by inventing what became known as "yellow journalism," named after a popular cartoon character. Yellow journalism was criticized for its lurid sensationalism, but it also attracted readers by crusading on behalf of the working class against government corruption and businesses' monopolies. Reporters at Hearst's *Journal* and *Examiner* investigated crimes the police did not solve, doctors who faked X-rays, labor union bosses who cheated workers, and politicians who protected vice rings. "The new journal of to-day prints the news, too, but it does more," the *Journal* proclaimed. "It does not wait for things to turn up. It turns them up."[30]

Hearst's main rival, Pulitzer, was also trying to turn things up. He found the perfect reporter for this aggressive journalism in Elizabeth Cochrane, a master of undercover reporting who used the pen name Nellie Bly. She began her career in 1885 when she wrote a letter to the *Pittsburgh Dispatch* criticizing its coverage of working women. Editor George Madden was so impressed that he hired Bly to become the first woman on the newspaper's staff. Her first project was an eight-part series describing the difficult lives of the city's female factory workers. Although her investigation was a success, Bly was expected to perform a more traditional job for women: editing the society page. Later that year, however, she persuaded Madden to let her write exposés of prison and factory conditions. Soon she was off reporting on the Mexican government's corruption, but when she returned to Pittsburgh, she once again was told to write reviews and features.

Bly quit and ventured to New York City. Although most editors were reluctant to hire women, Bly talked her way into a tryout at Pulitzer's *World.* She got the attention of the *World*'s editor by proposing an audacious story idea: pretend she was crazy and get sent to Blackwell's Island, an asylum for the mentally ill. To prepare for her undercover investigation, Bly dressed as shabbily as she could and made her way to a temporary shelter for women. There she began muttering to herself, told people she could not remember where she came from, and spent the night staring at a wall. The next day a doctor examined her, declared her insane, and sent her to Blackwell's Island.[31]

Bly spent a week and a half at the asylum, observing its cruelty and wretchedness. According to Bly, she and the other inmates were forced to sit for fourteen hours on a hard bench in a freezing room. If they talked, slumped, or tried to walk, they were told to shut up. Baths consisted of being scrubbed by another inmate and having icy water dumped on them. Patients told her how nurses beat them, pulled their hair, choked them, and submerged them under water if they complained. Some inmates, Bly observed, were perfectly sane but were sent to Blackwell's Island because judges could not understand their foreign accents. When Bly asked for a nightgown, one of the matrons told her, "Well, you don't need to expect any kindness here, for you won't get it."[32]

Even though Bly stopped acting insane once she arrived, three more doctors examined her and said she should continue to be detained. She was only released when a lawyer for the *World* came for her. Five days later, Bly's story, "Ten Days in a Madhouse," stunned the city. A grand jury was convened to study her findings and issued a report demanding reforms. The city responded by spending an additional million dollars on its hospitals, including Blackwell's Island.

Over the next two years, Bly continued her undercover reporting. She posed as a prostitute, a maid, and a factory worker to give the *World*'s readers firsthand accounts of mistreatment. She had herself sent to a jail and a charity hospital to describe their conditions. Once she pretended to be an innocent country girl visiting the city so she could unmask a notorious pimp. Playing the role of a businessman's wife eager to prevent passage of legislation, she revealed the misdeeds of a corrupt lobbyist. The *World*'s illustrator, Walt McDougall, said of Bly, "Nothing was too strenuous nor too perilous for her if it promised results."[33]

Whenever one of Bly's daring stories appeared, more readers bought copies of the *World*. Her success inspired other newspapers to hire reporters, including more women, to engage in similar firsthand reporting of abuses. Winifred Black, whose pen name was Annie Laurie, investigated conditions at a local hospital for Hearst's *San Francisco Examiner* by pretending to be ill and allowing herself to be carried there in a prison van. Because of the sensationalism of their stories, reporters such as Bly and Laurie were derided as "stunt journalists" or "sob sisters" if they were women. But their ability to report extensively on wrongdoing hidden from the general public constituted effective investigative journalism.[34]

Jacob Riis shared Bly's zeal for investigating the terrible conditions so many New Yorkers endured. Riis photographed and wrote about the hundreds of thousands of immigrants crowded in New York's Lower East Side. Working as a reporter for the *New York Tribune,* Riis exposed the terrible conditions in shelters run by the police department, described the miserable tenement housing in immigrant neighborhoods, and showed how nearby towns were dumping sewage into waterways that provided the city with its drinking water. Riis's 1890 book *How the Other Half Lives* documented the evils of New York's slumlords. It was a popular and critical success, influencing the progressive policies of future president Theodore Roosevelt.[35]

One of the bravest reporters of the late 1800s, or of any era, was

Ida B. Wells, who had been born a slave. In the 1890s, she investigated lynchings for the *Memphis Free Speech,* which she edited and co-owned. Carrying a pistol in her purse for protection, she went to the places where the hangings occurred. She reported that all the cases involved white women who accused black men of rape to preserve their reputations after having consensual sex. A mob responded by posting death threats and destroying the newspaper's press and office. Wells, who had traveled to Philadelphia, did not dare return to Memphis. She began writing for another black-owned newspaper, the *New York Age,* where she continued to expose the injustices of lynching.[36]

Wells was one of the few reporters in the 1800s who investigated national concerns. Most investigative reporting focused on local issues and rarely targeted the most powerful people in government. Limited transportation and communication slowed the creation of national news organizations that could tackle the country's biggest problems. The publication of government notices was lucrative for many newspapers, making them less inclined to challenge the officials who provided them with profits. The frequent use of libel lawsuits also put the watchdog press on a leash.[37]

This parochialism was fading by the dawn of the twentieth century when investigative reporting began to flourish in the pages of popular magazines. The federal government's creation of second-class mailing rates lowered the cost of distribution, and the new transcontinental railroads meant magazines could be delivered across the country, making them America's first national medium. Photoengraving enhanced the quality of illustrations, and improved printing presses made publishing easier and less costly. The growth of nationwide businesses wishing to sell their goods to a mass market allowed publishers to rely on advertising for revenue and reduce prices to boost circulation. Demand soared as more people completed high school and wanted to understand the quickly changing ways of the newly industrialized and urbanized country.

Because of these factors, the number of magazines more than quadrupled from 1,200 in 1870 to 5,500 by 1900. As competition intensified, magazine editors tried to lure readers with hard-hitting stories about corruption, abuse of workers, and dangers to consumers. The writers of these stories were indignant at the wrongdoing of greedy businesses and crooked politicians. Between 1903 and 1912, a group of about two dozen investigative reporters produced about 2,000 magazine articles often running in highly promoted series. Their extensive reporting incited public outrage and contributed to the Progressive Era of social and business reforms during the twentieth century's first decade.[38]

Nowhere did this investigative reporting shine brighter than in *McClure's Magazine*. Owner and editor S. S. McClure, whose enthusiasm and energy captivated his reporters, did not shy away from stories with a strong point of view. In contrast to most other publishers, McClure hired full-time writers who were experts in their fields, paid them well, and gave them ample time to complete their work. The result was thorough, accurate, and better-written stories.

McClure sent Lincoln Steffens, known for his keen interviewing skills, to investigate municipal corruption around the country. Typical of Steffens's work was "The Shame of Minneapolis," which revealed that the city's mayor and police were behind its rampant and lucrative vice. Steffens saved his most severe indictment for the typical big businessman, whom he described this way in his 1904 collection, *The Shame of the Cities:* "I found him buying boodlers in St. Louis, defending grafters in Minneapolis, originating corruption in Pittsburg [sic], sharing with bosses in Philadelphia, deploring reform in Chicago, and beating good government with corruption funds in New York."[39] Once he was finished with corrupt cities, Steffens turned his attention to state government and uncovered graft in Illinois, Missouri, New Jersey, Ohio, Rhode Island, and Wisconsin.

The January 1903 issue of *McClure's* showcased the power of investigative reporting. It featured Steffens's "The Shame of Minneapolis," Ray Stannard Baker's report of union bosses abusing laborers in the nation's coal mines, and the third chapter of Ida Tarbell's *The History of the Standard Oil Company,* which detailed John D. Rockefeller's ruthless rise to wealth and power. Tarbell, a tall, independent-minded woman with tremendous research skills and an unquenchable desire to find the truth, was the first reporter to systematically use documents to investigate wrongdoing. Her series became the magazine's most famous and influential exposé. During her reporting, Tarbell read through hundreds of thousands of pages of secret company documents, government reports, legislative testimony, newspaper files, and court records from around the country. She also interviewed Standard Oil executives, government regulators, academic experts, and businessmen who had fought the company. Her methodology—analysis of public documents, direct observations of people and places, interviews of people with personal knowledge of the topic, character-driven narratives, disclosure of information sources to readers—set the standard for future investigative reporters.[40]

Originally planned as a series of three articles, *The History of the Standard Oil Company* proved so popular that it was stretched to twelve installments and turned into a best-selling book. The stories took readers to the country's oil fields to describe the bitter struggles between Rockefeller and the independent producers. Tarbell revealed Standard Oil's use of espionage, threats, illegal rebates, and other bare-knuckled tactics to crush competition and create a monopoly that led to higher prices, lower wages, and the destruction of competitors in a crucial industry. Spurred by Tarbell's reporting, the U.S. Department of Justice filed an antitrust lawsuit against Rockefeller and Standard Oil. The Supreme Court found the company guilty of illegally restraining trade and forced it to dissolve in 1911.[41]

McClure's popularity and investigative zeal continued with Baker's 1905 series, "Railroads on Trial." Using the companies' accounting statements, he revealed how the railroad companies connived to build monopolies through secret rebates and discriminatory rates. After reading Baker's stories, Roosevelt pushed Congress to pass the Hepburn Act, which gave the Interstate Commerce Commission enhanced power to regulate railroads. The new law, however, did not completely stop railroad abuses. Over the next five years, Steffens and other journalists continued to document their predatory practices.[42]

McClure's success with investigative reporting was contagious. Eight other magazines regularly ran exposés, and at least seven more periodically joined the fray.[43] *Everybody's* and *Hampton's* magazines published Charles Edward Russell's "The Tenements of Trinity Church," which revealed how the nation's wealthiest house of worship became Manhattan's biggest slumlord. Russell and two assistants combed through tax records and Trinity's annual reports, visited hundreds of its properties, and interviewed tenants as well as Trinity officials. Russell described in heartbreaking detail the conditions faced by tenants and their "chalk-faced" children. His stories pressured Trinity to replace its slums with model housing and open its financial books to the public. The church responded with a public relations strategy later employed by other institutions challenged by investigative reporters: it emphasized the good work the church did, criticized Russell for overstepping his journalistic limits, and confused the issue by emphasizing that it did not own many of the terrible tenements even though it owned the land on which they were built.[44]

In 1905 and 1906, *Collier's Weekly* published one of the most astonishing investigations of the era, Samuel Hopkins Adams's "The Great American Fraud." As part of his research into the $75 million a year patent medicine industry, Adams used a new reporting technique: laboratory testing. To check the actual content of these "medicines," he arranged for their chemical analysis. The ten-part series disclosed that gullible Americans were swallowing "huge quantities of alcohol, an appalling amount of opiates and narcotics, a wide assortment of varied drugs ranging from powerful and dangerous heart depressants to insidious liver stimulants; and, far in excess of all other ingredients, undiluted fraud."[45]

In 1906, Upton Sinclair's best-selling book *The Jungle* exposed the dangerous, miserable, and unsanitary conditions of Chicago's unregulated meatpacking industry. Although *The Jungle* was a novel, its pages reflected Sinclair's investigative reporting. For seven weeks he had immersed himself in the lives of the meatpackers by dressing like one of them and entering the factories during shift changes. Sinclair described workers dying in plants where rats roamed the floors and corrupt inspectors allowed moldy and tubercular beef to be processed.[46]

That same year William Randolph Hearst, who had recently bought *Cosmopolitan,* decided to boost readership and his own White House ambitions by publishing David Graham Phillips's "The Treason of the Senate." The nine-part series was a sensation, boosting *Cosmopolitan*'s circulation by 50 percent. Phillips, a well-known writer with the handsome looks of a movie star, documented the corruption of nineteen senators who did the bidding of rich industrialists. For example, he wrote, seventy companies paid directors fees to New York Senator Chauncey Depew. Phillips used melodramatic language and included sweeping, forceful conclusions:

> The treason of the Senate! Treason is a strong word, but not too strong, rather too weak, to characterize the situation in which the Senate is the eager, resourceful, indefatigable agent of interests as hostile to the American people as any invading army could be, and vastly more dangerous; interests that manipulate the prosperity produced by all, so that it heaps up riches for the few; interests whose growth and power can only mean the degradation of the people, of the educated into sycophants, or the masses toward serfdom.[47]

Phillips peppered his stories with insults; he called Depew a "buffoon," "spineless sycophant," and "traitor to the people." The political establishment reacted with rage to Phillips's stories, accusing him of offering thin evidence for some of his far-reaching conclusions. His work, however, helped reformers pass the Seventeenth Amendment to the Constitution, which allowed voters to elect senators directly.[48]

At first, Theodore Roosevelt appreciated journalists whose reporting supported his reformist agenda. He met and exchanged letters with Sinclair, Steffens, Baker, and other writers. But soon the president resented the journalists who were claiming credit for progressive reforms and criticizing him as a timid compromiser. Complaining that Hearst was trying to whip up hysteria and build his own political power by running "The Treason of the Senate," Roosevelt gave a speech in 1906 criticizing the negativity of Phillips and other writers. He compared them to the muckraking

character in John Bunyan's *Pilgrim's Progress* who only looks
downward: "There is filth on the floor, and it must be scraped up
with the muck-rake; and there are times and places where this
service is the most needed of all services that can be performed,"
Roosevelt said. "But the man who never does anything else, who
never thinks or speaks or writes save of his feats with the muckrake, speedily becomes, not a help to society, not an incitement
to good, but one of the most potent forces of evil."[49] Roosevelt
meant it as an insult, but some of the investigative journalists of the
era started to wear the "muckraker" label proudly.

Despite his frustration with the muckrakers, Roosevelt pushed
a conservative Congress to pass reforms to improve some of the
dangerous conditions these writers highlighted. In the summer
of 1906, Roosevelt signed the Meat Inspection Act, which ad-
dressed health hazards described by Sinclair. He also approved the
Pure Food and Drug Act, which added protections Adams had
championed. These muckraker-inspired laws forever changed the
country by expanding federal authority over the previously unregulated capitalist economy.

The muckrakers' influence was not confined to Washington.
By the end of the muckraking era, twenty-five states had enacted
workers compensation laws, twenty had approved new pension
laws, and most had passed child labor protections. Municipal governments adopted stronger building codes to reduce the squalor of
tenements and passed new laws to curb corruption. Still, business
interests were able to persuade legislators to leave loopholes in the
laws with vague standards and weak enforcement provisions. The
Meat Inspection Act, for example, did not require the dating of
inspection labels, allowing the packers to sell old cans of meat.[50]

After their attacks against corporate greed and political corruption, the muckrakers turned their attention to poverty, racial

discrimination, and the daily struggles of working women and children. Photographer Lewis Hine posed as a fire inspector and a Bible seller to enter mines and factories to document the cruel conditions faced by child laborers. Edwin Markham's "The Hoe-Man in the Making" exposed the dangerous and bleak conditions suffered by children as young as five years of age working in the textile mills of the South and the factories of the North. Baker's "Following the Color Line" described the segregation, poverty, race riots, and lynch mobs faced by African Americans. And Will Irwin's "The American Newspaper" revealed how publishers and editors muzzled their news coverage to suit the needs of large advertisers. For example, Irwin divulged that San Francisco newspapers suppressed coverage of a bubonic plague outbreak because they feared the news would harm the city's economic interests.[51]

But muckraking began to decline by the end of the century's first decade. Rising printing costs, pressure from advertisers, a growing number of libel lawsuits, and new ownership steered popular magazines away from expensive and controversial stories. *McClure's* and other muckraking magazines lost their investigative edge after being bought by large corporations, and *Everybody's* went into bankruptcy after banks stopped extending them credit. The new laws regulating the worst excesses of big business muffled the popular clamor for reform, and the reading public grew weary of the constant sounding of alarms about the food they ate, the medicines they took, and the businesses they patronized. Tarbell, Steffens, Baker, and other star reporters left *McClure's* and bought their own publication, which they named *American Magazine.* Its stories, they decided, would be more hopeful and less critical than their prior work.[52]

The final curtain fell on the muckraking era with the start of World War I, which diverted attention from problems at home and led to comprehensive restrictions on the press. The military aggressively censored information about the war effort, and new laws allowed the government to prosecute anyone who printed stories deemed critical of the national interest; more than a hundred publications were suppressed as a result. In the tug-of-war between the government and press over control of information, the advantage slid to the government's favor. The popular magazines that once cultivated investigative reporting turned to fiction, romance, self-help, and other less-controversial topics.[53] The muckrakers had given the investigative impulse its greatest expression since American journalism began more than two hundred years earlier, but now it would need to be found elsewhere.

TWO

CHALLENGING AUTHORITY

From all this, it should be apparent that the muckraking or reform tradition is very much alive in American journalism. But there is not nearly enough of it.
　　—Carey McWilliams, "Is Muckraking Coming Back?" 1970

Many accounts of journalism history suggest that investigative reporting evaporated between World War I and the Vietnam War. The era has been called "the quiet period," a time of "decline" and "a kind of 'Dark Ages'" for muckraking.[1] The outraged reporting that *McClure's* spotlighted had disappeared from most newspapers and magazines by the 1920s. So had the "journalism of action" practiced by Hearst's *Journal* and Pulitzer's *World*. They were largely replaced by the kind of detached reporting found in the *New York Times* and its imitators. As a result, many of the largest publications and broadcast outlets were slow to investigate some of the most important stories of the twentieth century: the financial speculation that led to the

1929 stock market crash, the Holocaust, the rise of McCarthyism, and continued discrimination and violence against African Americans.[2]

But muckraking did not disappear during this era. The black press, left-leaning magazines, small newspapers, self-published writers, and a few metropolitan newspapers kept the watchdog spirit alive with extensive and courageous reporting. Reporters around the country exposed the misdeeds of mobsters and crooked politicians.[3] This valiant journalism set the stage for the investigative reporting that flourished in the 1960s and 1970s and led to the uncovering of Watergate.

Journalists who wanted to investigate during this era had to fight against the tide of respected opinion. Some newspaper leaders and educators lumped all muckraking together with the worst sensationalism of yellow journalism and warned against bias by crusading reporters. Walter Lippmann wrote in his influential 1922 book *Public Opinion* that the press should develop an objective method to counter its own subjectivity. Lippmann encouraged the collection of information prepared by government and discouraged the questioning of authority that investigative reporting requires.[4] Textbooks written for the new journalism schools sprouting around the country embraced objectivity and mostly ignored muckraking. The 1947 history textbook *Journalism in the United States* included nary a mention of the great muckrakers Tarbell, Baker, or Steffens.[5]

The growth of the Associated Press and other news services helped spread the objective method. It became cheaper for local newspapers to subscribe to a news service than to invest in their own aggressive reporting. The news services needed to produce stories acceptable to local markets in different parts of the country, so they avoided upsetting readers with controversial stories. Reporter and journalism educator Paul Williams observed that this style conflicted with the approach needed for muckraking: "Its maxims were simple: be fast, be brief, be accurate. Write about the here and now—what happened in the last twenty-four hours and what is likely to happen tomorrow."[6]

One reason muckraking receded, at least on national issues, was the decrease in independent newspapers following World War I. The number of dailies in America fell from a high of 2,461 in 1916 to 1,753 by 1969, a 29 percent decline despite the country's steadily growing population. No longer did cities such as New York and Chicago have more than a dozen daily newspapers vying for readers' attention. Frank Munsey in the East, Ira Clifton Copley in the Midwest, and other publishers began buying and combining multiple newspapers, starting a trend of expanding chain ownership.[7] Americans were even less likely to get original reporting from the growing broadcast industry. Radio stations, which began spreading across the country in the 1920s, were more interested in protecting their commercial interests than in digging for news.[8] When television became popular in the 1950s, it did not sponsor much muckraking either.

Increasingly sophisticated public relations efforts further tamed the investigative spirit. Governments and corporations established press offices, hired public relations experts, and sent out press releases to manipulate and limit independent reporting. It became easy for reporters to meet their daily deadlines by relying on press releases rather than digging for their own news. One study showed that 147 of 255 stories appearing in the *New York Times* one day in 1926 originated with press agents. "What had been the primary basis for competition among journalists—the exclusive, the inside story, the tip, the scoop—was whisked away by press releases and press conferences," journalism scholar Michael Schudson observed. "Newspapers that had once fought 'the interests' now depended on them for handouts."[9]

Investigations, however, continued to appear in some metropolitan newspapers. Criminal activity and corruption were usually the targets. In 1920, the *Boston Post* uncovered the illicit investment "pyramid" swindle operated by Charles Ponzi. A year later the *New York World* unmasked one of the country's most secretive groups, the Knights of the Ku Klux Klan. For two weeks the *World* ran stories by Rowland Thomas highlighting the Klan's violence against blacks, Catholics, Jews, Asians, labor unions, and immigrants. Thomas exposed the Klan's infiltration of local police forces, the Army, and the Navy. He disclosed how Klan leaders profited from membership fees and the sale of KKK regalia.[10]

In 1922, reporter Paul Y. Anderson of the *St. Louis Post-Dispatch* uncovered the Teapot Dome scandal. He revealed that some of President Warren Harding's top aides had taken bribes in return for selling Navy oil reserves at Teapot Dome, Wyoming, to companies at a steep discount. Reporters at the *Wall Street Journal* and the Hearst newspapers also contributed to exposing the Harding administration's corruption. Congressional hearings led to the indictments and convictions of oilman Harry Sinclair and Interior Secretary Albert Fall.

The *Post-Dispatch,* still owned by the Pulitzer family, also unearthed corruption by local and state politicians. In 1947, the newspaper investigated an explosion at the Centralia coal mine in southern Illinois that killed 111 miners. Its reporters discovered that workers and mine inspectors had repeatedly warned about dangerous conditions at the mine, but Illinois Governor Dwight Herbert Green had ignored their complaints while receiving campaign donations from mining companies. Reporter John Bartlow Martin followed with an extensive investigation of the mining disaster, filling nearly an entire issue of *Harper's* magazine. Martin documented that "almost everyone concerned had known for months, even years, that the mine was dangerous." After these revelations, Green lost reelection and mining regulations were strengthened.[11]

Many newspapers, however, resisted running controversial articles during this era. In 1931, reporters Drew Pearson of the *Baltimore Sun* and Robert S. Allen of the *Christian Science Monitor* anonymously published a muckraking book—*Washington Merry-Go-Round*—when their editors refused to print their investigative stories. Even though their newspapers fired Pearson and Allen after their authorship was discovered, the book and its sequel proved so popular that Pearson and Allen launched a syndicated column by the same name. Allen eventually dropped out of the venture, but Pearson carried on the muckraking tradition; he humorously marketed the manure created from his weekend farm as "All Cow, No Bull—Better Than The Column."[12]

Pearson's "no bull" approach was popular, and he became perhaps the best-known journalist in America. His daily "Merry-Go-Round" column ran in 625 newspapers, and 225 stations carried his Sunday night broadcast on the ABC radio network, reaching an estimated sixty million people. While most journalists of the era duly reported the contents of publicity handouts, Pearson insisted what officials hid was more important than what they announced. Pearson's columns could be salacious and nasty, but he and his staff dug for information where no other reporters did, finding informants and documents that proved the corruption and laziness of presidents, congressmen, generals, and corporate chieftains. He infuriated powerful men of all political persuasions. Secretary of State Cordell Hull, a Democrat, labeled him "a teller of monstrous and diabolical falsehoods," and Republican Senator

Joseph McCarthy said he possessed the "diabolically clever voice of international communism."[13]

Pearson's revelations led to the convictions of top members of Louisiana's government in 1939 and the powerful chairman of the U.S. House Armed Services Committee, Andrew Jackson May, in 1947. A year later Pearson and his assistant, Jack Anderson, discovered that J. Parnell Thomas of New Jersey, the ruthless chairman of the House Un-American Activities Committee, had put four women—including his elderly aunt, his secretary's maid, and his daughter-in-law—on the congressional payroll. The women did no government work and sent their paychecks to the congressman's bank account. After Pearson's exposé, Thomas was sentenced to eighteen months in prison.[14]

Pearson was one of the few Washington-based journalists in the 1930s and 1940s who challenged government officials. Franklin Roosevelt's popularity, embrace of economic reforms, and good relationships with reporters weakened their investigative zeal during the dozen years of his presidency. The Roosevelt administration closely reviewed the content of news stories and tried to intimidate journalists whose stories it disliked. Following the start of World War II, his administration tightened secrecy. The press agreed, on the whole, to censor itself, not wanting embarrassing investigations to damage the war effort. This self-censorship by the press and use of intimidation by government continued through the end of World War II, the start of the cold war, the Korean War, and the early days of the Vietnam War.[15] Reporter and columnist Anthony Lewis recalled that when he began his journalism career in 1948, reporting on government in major newspapers resembled stenography. "One did not expect to see stories in the *New York Times* that challenged official truth," Lewis noted.[16]

The official truth that ran in most daily newspapers, major

magazines, and broadcast stations rarely reflected the experiences of African Americans. Until the civil rights movement gained popular attention in the late 1950s, only a few white reporters were willing to investigate racial discrimination. Ray Sprigle of the *Pittsburgh Post-Gazette* was one of them. In 1938, he won the Pulitzer Prize, awarded to the best in American journalism, for revealing that Supreme Court Justice Hugo Black had been a Ku Klux Klan member. A decade later he traveled four thousand miles through the back roads of the South after staining his skin with iodine, walnut juice, and an infusion of mahogany bark so he could pose as a black man. His twenty-one-part series revealed the depths of oppression and humiliation suffered by the region's ten million blacks.[17]

The mainstream press avoided hiring African Americans, who might have provided more aggressive reporting about poverty and discrimination. As late as 1952, only a dozen blacks worked on the reporting staffs of U.S. daily newspapers.[18] One of them, Ted Poston of the *New York Post,* bravely traveled to Tavares, Florida, to cover the trial of three black youths accused of raping a white woman. Poston revealed that a mob had shot a fourth suspect before the trial started. While he covered the trial, local whites jostled Poston, knocked off his glasses, and stomped on them. After an all-white jury sentenced two of the youths to death and a third to life in prison, three cars full of angry whites chased Poston out of town for having the temerity to report on the case. But his stories about the dubious convictions of the three youths led to a federal investigation and encouraged an appeal to the U.S. Supreme Court, which overturned two of the convictions.[19]

Some of the most fearless reporting of the era was conducted by the African American press, which exposed the violence of race riots in cities across the country in 1919, the prevalence of lynching in the South, and the deplorable conditions suffered by many African Americans in the North. At the *Chicago Defender,* Ethel Payne detailed the travails faced by unwed mothers and the troubles with the adoption system for black children.[20] In 1942, Lucile Bluford of the *Kansas City Call* traveled to southeast Missouri to investigate a lynching. Her reporting disclosed that local authorities knew in advance a mob was planning to lynch a local man named Cleo Wright but did nothing to stop his murder.[21]

In 1950, Marvel Cooke joined the staff of the left-leaning *Daily Compass,* making her the first African American woman to report full-time for a white-owned New York daily newspaper. For her first story with the *Compass,* she followed Nellie Bly's tradition of undercover reporting and posed as one of the hundreds of black domestic workers who stood on street corners waiting to be "bought" for a day to clean the homes of white housewives. Her front-page exposé began, "I was a slave" and described in great detail how the laborers were paid half the legal minimum rate, often went unpaid for some of the hours they worked, and were subjected to degrading conditions. Cooke also investigated drug addiction among African American teens and children and wrote a series about the lives of prostitutes and their mistreatment by the women's court, vice squad, and women's prison.[22]

Until the 1960s, most publications did not take the work of female reporters such as Cooke seriously. Few were hired as reporters or editors, and those who did win jobs were usually consigned to special "women's" sections. *Time* and *Newsweek* hired women as researchers but not reporters.[23] A handful of female journalists, however, muckraked for women's magazines. Anna Steese Richardson was an investigative reporter for *McCall's, Delineator,* and *Woman's Home Companion.* Vera Connolly wrote about working women's struggles and problems in juvenile jails and schools for

Good Housekeeping and *Delineator* in the 1920s and 1930s. For a series about terrible conditions endured by Native Americans, Connolly spent a year traveling to far-flung reservations, conducting extensive interviews, and combing through data and government reports. In one story, she described the experiences of Native American children as young as six years of age forced to leave their families and attend distant boarding schools:

> It was a story of frightened, lonely, hungry, exhausted childhood they told. Of children poorly housed in crowded dormitories, with so little protection against disease that infections rage through the schools. Of children cruelly overworked. Of children so underfed that they snatch like famished little animals at plates of bread. Of children struck and thrown into the school "jails" for infringement of minor rules.[24]

The kind of rage at injustice felt by Connolly was also shown by Phillippa Allen, who used the pen name Bernard Allen. In 1935, the small radical magazine *New Masses* published Allen's "Two Thousand Dying on a Job," a story describing a giant tunnel-blasting project in West Virginia that left workers choking on the deadly silica dust filling their work site. Allen used legislative records, court testimony, medical research, and interviews to document one of America's deadliest industrial tragedies. Her reporting prompted congressional hearings and the inclusion of silicosis coverage in the workers' compensation laws of forty-six states.[25]

As *New Masses* demonstrated, some of the boldest investigative reporting was found in the pages of small leftist publications. In the 1930s, the *Dubuque Leader,* an alternative weekly newspaper owned by a cooperative of working-class shareholders, regularly probed the actions of the city's civic and business leaders. Editor Archie Carter ran stories exposing connections between local politicians and the state's slot machine racket and documenting questionable expenses by the county sheriff and local police.[26] The New York newspaper *PM,* which only survived eight years, also regularly published investigative stories. In 1941, *PM* ran Lowell Leake's article "Hitler Gets Millions for War Chest Through Links with American Firms." Leake used financial records, credit reports, and government transcripts to document the complex ties between the Nazi war machine and U.S. companies including Standard Oil, Ford, and DuPont.[27]

The liberal *Nation,* whose circulation rarely rose over 25,000, was another publication that consistently published muckraking stories between 1920 and 1960. After Paul Y. Anderson left the *St. Louis Post-Dispatch* in 1923, the *Nation* printed his continued revelations about the Teapot Dome scandal. In the 1930s, it ran an investigation by Carey McWilliams, later its editor, detailing the horrible conditions endured by California farmworkers and the bare-knuckle tactics of the state's large property owners to control valuable land and water. Matthew Josephson's 1956 series, "The Big Guns," explored the massive spending behind the arms race.[28]

The *Nation,* however, was one of the few publications with a nationwide circulation willing to publish such exposés. *Chicago Tribune* foreign correspondent George Seldes grew so frustrated with the lack of muckraking opportunities in the mainstream press that he turned to book writing. Seldes's books investigated the armaments industry, ties between the Catholic Church and fascist groups, and links between American corporations and the Nazis. In 1940, Seldes launched *In Fact,* a four-page weekly newspaper devoted to stories the major newspapers refused to print. *In Fact* ran investigations of Republican presidential candidate Wendell

Willkie, the fascist White Shirts organization, and the National Association of Manufacturers. Renowned journalist A. J. Liebling called Seldes "a fine little gadfly" who "was about as subtle as a house falling in."[29]

Seldes made his greatest mark with a decade-long series of articles documenting the connection between tobacco and cancer, a topic most newspapers and magazines refused to touch because they profited from cigarette advertising. In the late 1940s, Seldes revealed that Senator Joseph McCarthy had fudged his tax returns and plagiarized from a fascist pamphlet in his speeches. Challenging McCarthy was courageous because the powerful Wisconsin Republican ruined many careers after accusing government officials and other public figures of being Communists. The right wing struck back against Seldes, claiming he was on the payroll of the Soviet Union. The FBI compiled a list of his readers, intimidating many of them into dropping their subscriptions. In 1950, Seldes stopped publishing *In Fact* and returned to writing books. When Seldes died in 1995, fellow journalist I. F. Stone said his friend "was the dean and granddaddy of us investigative reporters."[30]

Like his hero Seldes, I. F. Stone was a rebel. A small man with a big ego, mischievous grin, and ever-present glasses, Stone worked for thirty years in newspapers and magazines. He was blacklisted from writing for mainstream publications during the Red Scare following World War II because he was considered too sympathetic to the Soviet Union. So he started his own newsletter, *I. F. Stone's Weekly*, in 1953. Rather than rely on press briefings and cozy relationships with officials, Stone tracked down documents that no one else bothered to read to find instances of government lies and misconduct.[31]

Stone used this approach to write exposés of the Supreme Court, FBI, CIA, Joseph McCarthy, and U.S. involvement in the

Korean and Vietnam wars. He combed through congressional testimony to find that the FBI wanted to double its budget to hunt
down American Communists while at the same time reporting
that the Communist Party had lost more than half its members.
When the Atomic Energy Commission claimed a 1958 underground nuclear test could not be felt more than two hundred
miles away, Stone found seismologists who gave him a list of nineteen seismic stations that felt the blast as many as 2,300 miles away.
In response to Stone's reporting, the Atomic Energy Commission
admitted it was releasing wrong information.[32]

Stone also dug through historical archives to find contradictions between past and current statements by officials. Stone used
this technique to show that President Lyndon Johnson's administration gave conflicting versions of the 1964 Tonkin Bay incident
that led to the escalation of U.S. forces in Vietnam. By the time
he stopped publishing *I. F. Stone's Weekly* in 1971, its circulation
had grown from 3,500 to more than 70,000. For most of his career, scholar Jack Lule noted, "Stone was a pariah, marginalized
in the profession as a radical outcast."[33] And yet the techniques he
mastered—scrutinizing documents, conducting on-the-scene research, questioning the truthfulness of powerful officials—became
a successful formula for future investigative reporters.

Unlike Stone, most reporters did not challenge McCarthy and
his Communist-hunting allies. Although the evidence offered by
McCarthy was at best flimsy and often false, the journalistic conventions of the day encouraged newspapers and magazines to report whatever public officials said without probing their truthfulness. Fear of being accused of possessing Communist sympathies
no doubt contributed to many reporters' reluctance to question
McCarthyism.

Murrey Marder of the *Washington Post* was one of the few reporters among the capital press corps who dared to investigate the red-baiters. In McCarthy's home state of Wisconsin, the *Madison Capital-Times* revealed that the senator failed to pay taxes on stock income, and the *Milwaukee Journal* exposed McCarthy's lies about being wounded in World War II. In 1949, Edwin Guthman of the *Seattle Times* relentlessly followed a trail of documents to prove a University of Washington philosophy professor, Melvin Rader, was innocent of accusations he had been a Communist. State legislators said Rader had attended a Communist training school, but Guthman proved the professor could not possibly have been there, allowing him to regain his reputation and job.[34]

The most widely seen challenge to McCarthy came from the team of reporter Edward R. Murrow and producer Fred W. Friendly, whose CBS program *See It Now* built the model for television documentaries. Murrow, an elegant man who always seemed to have a cigarette in hand, became the biggest star of television news after boldly broadcasting radio reports from the rooftops of London during World War II as German planes rained bombs on the city. In 1953, he decided *See It Now* should tell the story of Lieutenant Milo Radulovich, whom the Air Force wanted to expel from its reserves. Radulovich was accused of having "close associations" with Communist sympathizers: his father, whose crime was subscribing to a Serbian-language newspaper, and his sister, who had the audacity to walk a picket line. During Radulovich's hearing, the Air Force offered no witnesses and did not allow the lieutenant to see any of the evidence. Despite Pentagon pressure not to broadcast the story, Murrow, Friendly, and reporter Joe Wershba refuted the government accusations. After the story aired, the Air Force cleared Radulovich. The next year, Murrow's team used McCarthy's own speeches and congressional hearings to highlight his cruelty, distortions, and lies. On *See It*

Now, Murrow countered every accusation McCarthy made. The public overwhelmingly supported Murrow's efforts against McCarthy, accelerating the senator's downfall.[35]

The public's response to Murrow demonstrated the growing power of television. Between 1952 and 1957, the number of television stations jumped from 108 to 544. By the end of the decade, American households watched five and a half hours of television on average each day. Television's growth drew advertising money away from newspapers, magazines, and radio stations. The three national networks, dependent on advertisers for revenue and on government regulators for licenses, usually played it safe when it came to investigative reporting, which was difficult to present visually. Their fifteen-minute evening newscasts usually provided only quick news summaries and rarely dug deeply into issues. CBS canceled the show that did the best investigations, Friendly and Murrow's *See It Now,* in 1957 after advertisers shied away from sponsoring its provocative reports.[36]

Investigative reporting, however, was starting to become more common again in the mainstream press. In addition to crime and political corruption, reporters started to dig into broader issues such as education, housing, transportation, science, medicine, and consumer safety. By 1954, investigative reporting was a term regularly used in the pages of *The Quill,* a magazine for professional journalists. In 1955, national awards were given to a CBS Radio report on the black market for babies, a *Cleveland Plain Dealer* investigation of labor racketeering, and a San Francisco *Call Bulletin* exposé of fraud at the Federal Housing Administration.[37] The next year, Fred J. Cook and Gene Gleason of the *New York World-Telegram and Sun* revealed that an ambitious $1.5 billion program to eliminate slums and remake American cities had demolished healthy neighborhoods. They discovered that just two of 375 proposed projects were completed in the program's first seven years.[38]

Civil rights was another issue that reporters began to investigate more deeply. In 1955, William Bradford Huie, an energetic magazine editor, television host, and book writer, arrived in Sumner, Mississippi. An all-white jury had just acquitted two white men, J. W. Milam and Roy Bryant, despite substantial evidence they had brutally murdered Emmett Till, a fourteen-year-old black youth. After other reporters left town, Huie went to the offices of Milam and Bryant's lawyers and spent five hours chatting and drinking bourbon with them. He persuaded them to accept his offer to pay Bryant and Milam $3,150 and the lawyers $1,260, plus a percentage of profits from the story, in return for an hour-by-hour account of Till's murder. Huie's "The Shocking Story of Approved Killing in Mississippi" appeared in *Look* magazine in January 1956. Without naming Bryant and Milam as the story's sources, it described in brutal detail how they kidnapped, beat, tortured, and killed Till and dumped his body in the Tallahatchie River.[39]

In contrast with Huie, most reporters were discouraged from doing investigative work in the South during the early days of the civil rights movement. *Atlanta Constitution* reporter Jack Nelson recalled that in the 1950s, "my managing editor didn't want me to cover civil rights because he was afraid it was going to interfere with my sources, particularly my sources in law enforcement because most of them of course were segregationist."[40] Nelson went on to win a Pulitzer Prize in 1960 for exposing atrocious conditions at a Georgia hospital for the mentally ill, including major surgeries performed by nurses and experimental treatments done without patients' consent. After switching to the *Los Angeles Times,* he probed the 1968 shooting deaths by police of three black students who had been protesting the segregation of a bowling alley near South Carolina State College. More than two dozen others were wounded in the barrage of bullets, but police claimed they fired at the students in self-defense. Nelson bluffed his way into the local hospital, introducing himself as "Nelson, with the Atlanta bureau. I've come to see the medical records." Thinking he was with the FBI, the staff handed him the students' charts, which clearly showed the students had been shot in the back and feet as they ran away from the confrontation or lay on the ground. Despite official denials, Nelson wrote a story proving the students had been massacred.[41]

By the late 1950s, the growing civil rights movement and the stirrings of the counterculture were changing journalism. Ralph Nader launched the modern consumer protection movement in the pages of the *Nation* with his 1959 exposé of the Detroit auto industry, "The Safe Car You Can't Buy." Nader used engineering reports and accident statistics to reveal that big automakers did not take advantage of existing knowledge to make their cars safer. "Doors that fly open on impact, inadequately secured seats, the sharp-edged rear-view mirror, pointed knobs on instrument panels and doors, flying glass, the overhead structure—all illustrate the lethal potential of poor design," Nader wrote. He expanded his reporting in the 1965 book *Unsafe at Any Speed,* which eventually prompted stronger federal safety laws. The book so enraged General Motors that the company hired a private detective to follow Nader in an effort to find ways to discredit him.[42]

In addition to Nader's work, three popular books appearing in the early 1960s proved that muckraking was regaining strength. Michael Harrington's *The Other America* described widespread hunger and poverty in many parts of the country. Jessica Mitford's *The American Way of Death* exposed the dishonesty and greed of the funeral home industry. And Rachel Carson's *Silent Spring* documented the toxic effects of the 600 million pounds of DDT pesticide used each year in the United States. Carson described in devastating detail how pesticides and other man-made chemicals sickened or killed livestock, fish, birds, and vegetation, threatening human health. Chemical companies, farm interests, and food processors responded by denouncing Carson; the president of the Montrose Chemical Corporation called her "a fanatic defender of the balance of nature." Despite these attacks, Carson's work contributed to a ban on DDT in the United States and helped fuel the modern environmental movement and the creation of the Environmental Protection Agency.[43]

In 1964, the Supreme Court gave investigative reporting a big boost with its *New York Times v. Sullivan* decision. The ruling protected the press from losing libel lawsuits to public officials unless they could prove the information in question was false, defamatory, and used with "actual malice." The decision gave reporters breathing room to make honest mistakes and encouraged them to probe beyond official government statements. They no longer had to hold back information out of fear that something might be wrong and lead to a lawsuit. In the decision, Justice William Brennan wrote that "debate on public issues should be uninhibited, robust, and wide-open, and that it may well include vehement, caustic, and sometimes unpleasantly sharp attacks on government and public officials."[44] That kind of aggressiveness became common in the years after *Sullivan*.

Muckrakers also benefited from the federal Freedom of Information Act, first passed in 1966 and strengthened in 1967 and 1974. For more than two decades journalists had fought for the public's right to see government documents. They argued that better access to information would improve the quality of their watchdog reporting. Although the law had nine exemptions and many bureaucrats dawdled when faced with information requests, it helped reporters gain access to previously hidden information.[45]

Despite these changes in the law, journalists were becoming increasingly frustrated with the federal government's attempts to manage the news in the name of national security. Reporters and editors questioned their deference to officials after the Eisenhower administration denied that an American U2 spy plane had been shot down over the Soviet Union; Eisenhower only admitted the truth after the Soviets displayed the captured pilot. Journalists' suspicions rose higher when a Kennedy administration spokesman supported the government's "inherent right to lie" in some situations.[46]

Distrust of government intensified during the Vietnam War. Initially, most veteran newsmen accepted official accounts of the war as they attended Pentagon briefings and took guided tours of Vietnam. By the mid-1960s, however, young reporters such as David Halberstam of the *New York Times,* Morley Safer of CBS, Neil Sheehan of United Press, Richard Critchfield of the *Washington Star,* and Peter Arnett and Malcolm Browne of the Associated Press were questioning the versions of events provided by President Lyndon Johnson's administration. These reporters ventured from official press briefings and into the jungles to see for themselves that the war was not going as well as the generals and politicians insisted. In the war's early years, their editors and news directors tended not to take their reports as seriously as the stories of veteran Washington correspondents who gave the Pentagon interpretation of the war. But as the fighting escalated, more senior reporters went to Vietnam and began challenging Johnson's policies. In late 1966 and early 1967, esteemed *New York Times* correspondent Harrison Salisbury visited North Vietnam. He revealed that American planes were bombing civilians, proving that the Pentagon was lying when it claimed it only hit military targets.[47]

Johnson was enraged by press accounts from Vietnam that strayed from the official view of the war. When Safer reported a story showing American troops lighting civilian huts on fire, Johnson called CBS President Frank Stanton early the next morning and accused his network of having "shat on the American flag." Johnson had Safer's background probed to discover whether he was a Communist; the investigation revealed only that he was a Canadian. Still, the Pentagon pressured the network to remove Safer from Vietnam. CBS refused.[48]

Johnson understood that the importance of television news was growing. In 1963, the networks had expanded their evening news shows from fifteen to thirty minutes. Local stations also were increasing the amount of airtime devoted to news. The tumult of the 1960s—the Vietnam War, the space race, political assassinations, riots in American cities, civil rights marches, and antiwar protests—played to television's ability to portray dramatic and highly visual events. In 1964, a poll found that, for the first time, more people used television than newspapers as their main news source.[49]

One way that television investigated important issues in the 1960s was through documentaries. CBS, NBC, and ABC broadcast 447 documentaries in 1962, more than twice as many as four years earlier. This newfound interest came partly from the networks' desire to remove the stench of the 1950s quiz-show scandals and pressure from the Federal Communications Commission to show more public service programs. New lightweight 16-mm cameras and wireless synchronizing equipment for sound and film made it easier for producers to pursue stories away from broadcast studios and gather eyewitness observations.[50]

Not all of the documentaries were investigative in nature, but the networks did more muckraking than most newspapers or magazines did during this time. In 1960, CBS producer David Lowe and cameraman Marty Barnett spent nine months traveling with migrant farmworkers, filming them as they toiled up and down the East Coast. Edward R. Murrow, his body gaunt and his voice raspy from pneumonia, went to Florida to narrate the resulting documentary, "Harvest of Shame." Murrow did not use the neutral reporting style common in most broadcast news reports of that era. Instead he adopted the muckraking style of a half century earlier, sharing his outrage at the plight of the farmworkers and calling on viewers to advocate for change. After showing scenes of families without adequate roofs over their heads, enough food to eat, or any medical care for their children, Murrow asked his viewers, "Must the two to three million migrants who help feed their fellow Americans work, travel and live under conditions that wrong the dignity of man?"[51]

"Harvest of Shame" was followed by other hard-hitting documentaries. CBS's "Great American Funeral" revealed funeral homes taking advantage of families. NBC's "The Battle of Newburgh" explored whether welfare was leading to the deterioration of American cities. CBS's "Hunger in America" exposed the failure of U.S. agricultural policies to meet the needs of the country's poorest citizens. About nine out of every ten American households watched a television documentary at least once a month during this time. They became rarer after 1968 as the networks tried to avoid pressure from advertisers and escape FCC requirements that they provide equal time to people criticized on the air.[52]

Television's ability to suck advertising dollars away from newspapers and magazines encouraged publishers to run investigative stories that would make them distinct from the competition. In 1964, the Pulitzer board recognized the upswing in muckraking when it added a prize for "local investigative specialized reporting." The first one went to *Philadelphia Bulletin* reporters who exposed police collusion with a local numbers racket.[53] Through the 1960s and early 1970s, Gene Miller of the *Miami Herald* investigated questionable murder convictions; his reporting helped free four people from death row. Clark Mollenhoff of the Des Moines *Register* and *Tribune* uncovered fraud by Jimmy Hoffa's Teamsters Union and graft by Bobby Baker, a top aide of Lyndon Johnson's. By 1970, the Associated Press, *Boston Globe, Chicago Tribune, Life* magazine, *Miami Herald,* and *Newsday* were regularly assigning reporters to do investigative work.[54]

The work of investigative journalists was made easier by improved technology developed during the 1950s and 1960s. Portable recorders helped reporters tape secret meetings and conversations and retain records of their interviews in case their truthfulness was questioned. Photocopy machines allowed journalists to get copies of government documents that they would not otherwise have been able to obtain. And new offset printing made publishing magazines and newspapers easier and cheaper.[55]

The new technology helped small groups of young people start their own alternative magazines and newspapers, which quickly spread across the country. By 1970, there were more than 450 underground American newspapers with an estimated combined circulation of nearly five million. Their pages were filled with irreverence toward authority and disgust with the status quo.[56] They also occasionally scooped the conventional press with stories that probed beneath the surface of daily news. After a 1968 peace march in Chicago, for instance, the underground *Seed* newspaper exposed police brutality ignored by the mainstream press.

The Liberation News Service, which distributed stories to the underground press, was the first to disclose that the U.S. military had created assassination squads in Vietnam. The Liberation News Service also revealed that the military was spraying Vietnam with the cancer-causing defoliant Agent Orange, sickening civilians as well as American troops.[57]

A few new muckraking publications of the 1960s avoided the conformity of the mainstream press while verifying information more carefully than the underground press. The radical California magazine *Ramparts* published articles describing the CIA's funding of the supposedly independent National Student Association. It also disclosed South Vietnamese leader Nguyen Cao Ky's participation in heroin trafficking while on the CIA payroll. Led by investigative reporter Jack Newfield, New York's *Village Voice* regularly featured exposés about scams and injustices. The *San Francisco Bay Guardian* investigated campaign contributions from real-estate developers to local politicians, bad investment policies by San Francisco's treasurer, and sweetheart deals between the city and power companies. The *Texas Observer* ran stories unearthing terrible conditions at state mental hospitals, insurance fraud, pollution by oil companies, and corruption by local politicians. One *Observer* investigation revealed that University of Texas regents had approved spending one million dollars on a new chancellor's mansion while cutting teacher salaries and raising tuition. Weekly alternative newspapers like the *Guardian, Voice,* and *Observer* soon sprouted in most major cities.[58]

By the late 1960s, many Americans were doubting the statements of elected officials. Differences between what President Johnson said about Vietnam and what journalists were reporting widened what people called the "credibility gap." Baby boomers flooded America's universities, where they learned to apply critical thinking to government policies and began protesting the war that was claiming the lives of so many of their peers. The adversarial culture germinating on college campuses was absorbed by some journalists (many more of whom had college degrees than their predecessors). Young government workers became increasingly willing to challenge the wisdom of their bosses and become sources for newspaper stories. Political scientist Samuel Huntington noted that this decline in obedience to authority and surge in citizen participation resembled Andrew Jackson's era when the penny press was born and the Progressive Era when the muckrakers thrived.[59]

This willingness to question authority was embodied by Seymour Hersh, a freelance reporter known for his brains, brashness, and badgering of sources until they gave him the information he wanted. Hersh developed his own sources in government, often calling them at home late at night when they could talk more freely than at their offices. When he had worked for the Associated Press, he unearthed a secret Pentagon biological and chemical weapons program. After the Associated Press found the stories too controversial to use, Hersh quit and published them in the *New Republic* in 1967. The series led to a presidential ban on producing these weapons.

Hersh broke perhaps the best-known investigative story of the 1960s: the slaughter by U.S. troops of more than a hundred civilians in the Vietnam village of My Lai. Hersh began reporting the story after receiving a tip that the Army was secretly court-martialing a lieutenant who was being hidden from the press. Hersh pasted together bits of information from his sources to learn the lieutenant was named William L. Calley Jr. Hersh tracked down Calley's lawyer, who told him the lieutenant was charged with the deaths of 109 civilians. Using a $2,000 grant from the nonprofit Fund for

Investigative Journalism, Hersh crisscrossed the country to search for Calley and the soldiers who had served in his unit. The Army was hiding the lieutenant at Fort Benning, Georgia, before the court-martial, but Hersh found him after a long day of knocking on doors. During a night of drinking and eating with Calley, Hersh gathered an account of what had happened and wrote the story the next day on his plane ride home.[60]

A small syndicate, the Dispatch News Service, sold Hersh's story to three dozen newspapers in the fall of 1969. He followed up with more reporting, steadily gathering details of the massacre. His stories did not gain much attention until CBS broadcast an interview, arranged by Hersh, of another soldier who had participated in the killings. Suddenly My Lai was a front-page story and Hersh a celebrity. He published a book about My Lai, won the Pulitzer Prize for international reporting, and became a frequent guest on television interview shows. Additional stories by Hersh revealed that more than five hundred civilians had been killed at My Lai and nearby hamlets. He disclosed that Army officers up to the rank of general tried to cover up the deaths.[61]

As Hersh demonstrated, reporters were becoming more aggressive and resourceful as the muckraking spirit spread throughout American journalism. No institution or leader was immune from investigative reporting. Richard Nixon was to learn this the hard way after he narrowly won the 1968 presidential election and declared war on the press. He began a battle that would lead to the Watergate burglary, the destruction of his presidency, and a new era in investigative journalism.

THREE

CALLING THE PLUMBERS

We're up against an enemy, a conspiracy. They're using any means. We are going to use any means. Is that clear?
   —Richard Nixon, conversation with Henry Kissinger and
   H. R. "Bob" Haldeman, July 1, 1971

Richard Nixon won the presidency promising to preserve law and order amid turbulent times. During the previous five years, assassins had murdered Martin Luther King Jr., Malcolm X, and John and Robert Kennedy. The war in Vietnam, where more than two hundred U.S. troops were dying each week, brought widespread and sometimes violent protests to college campuses, the 1968 Democratic convention, and the streets of America. The civil rights movement had transformed race relations, while Johnson's Great Society programs created a more activist government. Hippies challenged the dominant culture by wearing their hair long, playing their music loud, and experimenting with drugs. This upheaval sparked a backlash from people who supported the war, despised hippies, and distrusted Johnson's economic and civil rights programs. The United States of America was at war with itself.[1]

Once Nixon became president in January 1969, his aides warned him that domestic discontent was bubbling over. During his inauguration parade, demonstrators threw rocks, bottles, and a stink bomb at the president's motorcade. Dissension over Vietnam had driven Johnson from office, and Nixon said the war "poisoned my own relations with the press throughout my Presidency."[2] This sense of crisis reinforced Nixon's instinct to take risks, operate in secrecy, and centralize power (during his first term he hired the largest White House staff in history up to that time and increased the number of senior aides from twenty-four to fifty-two). It also increased his deep insecurity. An introverted man of shrewd intelligence, he had fought his way to the top after a hardscrabble childhood and believed that others were determined to beat him down. *Time* magazine's Hugh Sidey, who covered the presidency for more than two decades, observed that Nixon "didn't trust anybody."[3] His narrow victory in 1968 only deepened his suspiciousness and his determination to beat his political opponents at all costs. The president surrounded himself with aides who were loyal, tough, and savvy political campaigners but who had little experience running a government.[4]

This mistrust, particularly of journalists, led to the Watergate debacle. Early in his career, Nixon had received strong support from the *Los Angeles Times, Time, Life,* and other publications, but after losing the 1960 presidential election and the 1962 California gubernatorial race, he blamed the press. Resentful by nature, Nixon accused the media of being too liberal and was sure many reporters disliked him. In a press conference after his 1962 defeat, he accused reporters of being "delighted that I lost" and of giving him "the shaft" even though most of the big California newspapers had endorsed him. After his 1968 victory, he told prospective cabinet members and their wives, "Always remember, the men and women of the news media approach this as an adversary relationship. The time will come when they will run lies about you, when the columnists and editorial writers will make you seem to be scoundrels or fools or both and the cartoonists will depict you as ogres."[5] Nixon speechwriter William Safire, who later became a *New York Times* columnist, recalled that the president often told him "the press is the enemy," a vicious, irresponsible force to be hated and beaten.[6]

Nixon had some good reasons for his mistrust. During the 1960s, the Washington press corps had become increasingly sophisticated, and some reporters looked down their noses at Nixon's aggressive campaign style and his attempts to fuel the resentments of the white middle class. During his 1968 campaign, Nixon relied on carefully orchestrated appearances and television commercials to promote his message and shunned spontaneous and potentially embarrassing interactions with the press. His campaign manager and future chief of staff, H. R. "Bob" Haldeman, had been a top executive with the J. Walter Thompson advertising agency. Haldeman was an intensely self-disciplined man known for his crisp crew cut and his ability to inspire both loyalty and fear. He grasped the importance of creating events solely for the purpose of impressing television viewers and shielded Nixon from prying reporters. Once they took office, Nixon, Haldeman, and White House Counsel John Ehrlichman (who later became Nixon's chief domestic adviser) further isolated themselves from the public and the press. Like Johnson at the end of his presidency, Nixon avoided regular press conferences.[7]

Although Nixon proclaimed that he did not worry about journalists, in reality he was obsessed by his press coverage and developed a comprehensive strategy to handle the media. It consisted of appealing directly to the public through televised addresses, attacking journalists to keep them on the defensive, feeding stories to a few reporters he thought would be sympathetic, and instructing his aides to spy on journalists he considered enemies. Nixon directed this strategy, and Haldeman, Ehrlichman, and Special Counsel Charles Colson—who proudly called himself "the chief ass-kicker around the White House"—executed it. They created a special White House office to enhance his television coverage and a communications office to control and improve his public image. While every recent president has hired staff devoted to crafting his public image, Nixon was the first.[8]

Most mornings Nixon read a detailed summary prepared by his staff of each day's news coverage, with notations about which reporters were considered friendly or unfriendly toward him. Nixon would then meet with Haldeman and sometimes Ehrlichman to discuss how to control that day's news. After receiving their orders, Haldeman or Ehrlichman would send memos to the White House communications and press offices on how to improve the president's image and challenge news accounts Nixon disliked.

As he kept reporters away from the president, Press Secretary Ronald Ziegler and his staff gave them a steady stream of position papers and prepared statements. Under Nixon's orders, a new White House press room was built that was bigger and comfier than the old one but also farther away from the West Wing action. When Air Force One was remodeled, the White House instructed that the press section be moved as far away as possible from the president's quarters, but Ziegler also made sure reporters had a well-stocked bar.[9]

The press vacillated in its responses to Nixon's press strategy. Valuing objectivity and wanting to gain access to the new administration, most journalists tried to be fair. But some also realized the Washington press corps had been easily manipulated in the past. Influenced by the discord of the 1960s, these reporters distrusted officials and took an adversarial approach toward the White House. Despite some negative stories, however, Nixon experienced better coverage during the first year of his presidency than any other twentieth-century president except Theodore Roosevelt. Nixon received as much time on television during his first eighteen months as Eisenhower, Kennedy, and Johnson did during their combined sixteen years in the White House. The *New York Times* called one of his early press conferences a "tour de force," and the *New Republic* declared it "dazzling."[10]

Still, Nixon was convinced the press was out to get him. In his memoirs he wrote that he "considered the influential majority of the news media to be my political opposition."[11] He and his staff considered any criticism to be unfair and possibly unpatriotic; they sought quick retribution against reporters who did not give the president what they considered balanced coverage. After Stuart Loory of the *Los Angeles Times* wrote a column about how much Nixon's vacation home in San Clemente, California, cost taxpayers, Nixon demanded that his staff ban Loory from the White House. The White House also ordered the Internal Revenue Service to examine the tax returns of Seymour Hersh and other journalists whose work Nixon disliked.[12]

Nixon's anger toward the press magnified its importance in his mind and eventually in the public's mind. Nixon used the term "the media" because it sounded less favorable than "the press." The media, his administration argued, did not represent the public but instead acted as an independent, powerful, and irresponsible interest group that was more liberal than the American people. His hostility toward the press earned admiration from many of his fellow Republicans who, since the days of Franklin Roosevelt, thought the press had been unfair to them.[13]

Nixon had to contend with an increasingly large Washington press corps. The number of reporters covering the White House had climbed during the twentieth century, and stories about the president increased from 2 or 3 percent of a typical newspaper's coverage in the late 1800s to between 10 and 25 percent by the second half of the twentieth century.[14] The administration proved its ability to manipulate these Washington journalists from the start. Soon after Nixon's inauguration, Attorney General John Mitchell's Justice Department leaked documents to *Life* magazine showing that liberal Supreme Court Justice Abe Fortas had received $20,000 from a foundation backed by an accused stock swindler. The resulting article in *Life* created a firestorm of criticism against Fortas. He resigned, giving Nixon the opportunity to put a Republican judge, Harry Blackmun, on the court.[15]

Despite his own administration's fondness for leaking favorable information, Nixon was obsessed with stopping news leaks that cast him in a bad light. "Leaks can kill you," Johnson warned him before the 1969 inauguration. Although leaks to the press had occurred since George Washington's era, Nixon and his national security adviser, Henry Kissinger, became fixated on them. During his first year as president, Nixon counted forty-five leaks from National Security Council files.[16]

Nixon dreamed of using U.S. military might and his own diplomatic skills to create world peace, and he was furious at anybody who publicized information he thought weakened his ability to conduct foreign policy. He wrote in his memoirs that he "saw the government's ability to function effectively in international affairs being undermined by leaks which I felt were a violation of law as well as of the code of honorable behavior."[17] After *New York Times* reporter William Beecher revealed in May 1969 that the United States was secretly bombing Cambodia, Kissinger and Nixon became convinced that someone on the National Security Council was leaking information. Kissinger—who liked to leak information that suited his own interests to the press—persuaded the FBI to place wiretaps on the phones of five members of his own staff and on a senior assistant to the secretary of defense.[18]

The eavesdropping did not stop there. During the first twenty-five months of the Nixon presidency, the administration wiretapped seven members of Kissinger's staff, two State Department officials, three White House aides, one Pentagon senior assistant, and four journalists. Although Nixon justified the taps as necessary for national security, they had as much to do with politics as they did with U.S. defense. Taps were placed on the phones of aides who left the White House to work on the staff of Democratic presidential contender Edmund Muskie. The administration also ordered taps on the phones of speechwriter William Safire and a White House lawyer who was not involved with national security matters but who had a friendly relationship with the press. Nixon ordered that reports of the taped conversations be sent only to Haldeman, whose duties did not include national security.[19]

But Nixon grew frustrated that the FBI and CIA would not carry out all of the illegal spying he demanded of them. When he asked the CIA to place his brother Donald under surveillance because the president feared his brother might embarrass him, the agency refused. Wanting to collect as much intelligence as possible, whether or not the gathering was legal, Nixon told Ehrlichman in March 1969 to create the White House's own espionage unit. Ehrlichman hired two former New York City police detectives, John Caulfield and Anthony Ulasewicz, to do the secret White House work. Their first major assignment was to spy on columnist

Joseph Kraft, who had criticized Nixon's foreign policy and had been in direct contact with the North Vietnamese. Using phony telephone company credentials, the secret White House unit placed a tap on Kraft's home phone.[20] The creation of the White House's own intelligence unit "had the obvious advantage of taking a difficult job away from a recalcitrant bureaucracy," Nixon adviser Leonard Garment later said. "It also had a characteristic disadvantage. When a function like this is assigned to irregulars, working outside established procedures, the price is a loss of the bureaucracy's expertise, its people, and its developed knowledge of where to draw the lines."[21]

By turning to his own espionage team, Nixon demonstrated that he would not hesitate to exploit the resources of the increasingly powerful executive branch for his own political ends. His administration showed this tendency again when it placed Kraft and other journalists on an "enemies list" that eventually contained more than two hundred people and organizations it considered disloyal to the president, including congressmen, businessmen, labor leaders, actors, and even comedian Bill Cosby and football star Joe Namath. The list included fifty-six members of the media and three entire newspapers: the *Washington Post, New York Times,* and *St. Louis Post-Dispatch.* The purpose of the list, White House Counsel John Dean wrote in a memorandum, was to "use the available Federal machinery to screw our political enemies."[22]

By the fall of 1969, Nixon was annoyed at the way network commentators were analyzing his televised speeches. He believed he should be able to speak to the American people without journalists getting in his way. To intimidate the networks, Nixon and Haldeman launched a campaign of harassment against television journalists and their employers by the Internal Revenue Service, the Justice Department's antitrust division, and the Federal Communications Commission. Nixon also decided to publicly attack them. Although other presidents had complained about their press coverage, Nixon was the first to treat the press like a rival political candidate and launch a public assault on the media, a tactic that future politicians would borrow. To deliver the attacks, he chose Vice President Spiro Agnew, who already had a contentious relationship with the press.[23]

Nixon mostly ignored Agnew after the 1968 election because he doubted the vice president's intelligence, but he knew the former Maryland governor was good at talking tough. Agnew began the assault in Des Moines, Iowa, with a November 13 speech drafted by White House speechwriter Patrick Buchanan and edited by Nixon. The vice president accused the network news shows of being biased, arrogant, and controlled by "a tiny and closed fraternity of privileged men, elected by no one, and enjoying a monopoly sanctioned and licensed by the government." The news shows, he said, often presented "a narrow and distorted picture of America."[24]

The networks responded angrily. CBS President Frank Stanton called the speech an "unprecedented attempt by the Vice President of the United States to intimidate a news medium which depends for its existence upon government licenses."[25] The White House organized letter-writing campaigns by supporters to pressure the broadcasters for more favorable coverage. In the days following the speech, the networks received more than 150,000 letters, telegrams, and telephone calls, two-thirds of them supporting Agnew's attacks.[26]

The next week, Agnew expanded his attacks to the print media with a speech accusing the *New York Times* and *Washington Post* of being monopolies. Agnew's heated words signaled to reporters that things would never be the same at the White House.

It became clear that the administration and its supporters would respond to any press criticism with hostility that could damage journalists' reputations and access to sources. Nixon's aggressiveness and vindictiveness permanently eroded the relationship between the White House and the press corps. It also created a siege mentality that nearly guaranteed the tragedy of Watergate.[27]

At first the intimidation strategy worked. Agnew's speeches portraying Nixon as a victim of "a small and unelected elite"[28] who controlled the media captured the unease many Americans felt about press coverage of antiwar protests, urban unrest, and the rapidly changing youth culture. By the end of 1969, polls showed that the vice president was the third most popular American after Nixon and the Reverend Billy Graham. The next time Nixon gave a televised speech, the network commentators simply summarized it rather than trying to analyze its meaning and accuracy.[29]

Agnew was not the only one attacking the press. Private groups such as the conservative Accuracy in Media had formed to challenge what they saw as media bias. Some political scientists were blaming the increasingly oppositional press for reducing confidence in American leaders and institutions. Business groups complained that aggressive journalists were uninformed about economics and irresponsible in their reporting about the economy. This backlash against journalists, which gained strength during Nixon's first term, has continued ever since.[30]

The White House staff was pleased with the impact of Agnew's speeches and its early efforts to manipulate and intimidate the press. Convinced that a "silent majority" of Americans shared the president's antagonism toward the media, the administration decided to escalate its battle. Executive branch employees were prohibited from talking to the press without permission from the top. Colson was assigned to visit the chiefs of the three networks to pressure them to give the president more favorable coverage. Angry at the *Washington Post* for its White House coverage, Nixon wrote a memo banning his staff from seeing the newspaper's reporters or returning their phone calls for a sixty-day period.[31]

John Dean, the president's ambitious young counsel, noticed this hostility toward the press soon after he joined the White House staff in the summer of 1970. The first task Nixon gave him was to see if the Internal Revenue Service could put pressure on an obscure magazine, *Scanlan's Monthly,* which had published a nasty and untrue article about Agnew. Because the magazine was new, it had no revenue for the IRS to check, so Dean had the IRS investigate its owners. "Thus, within a month of coming to the White House, I had crossed an ethical line," Dean recalled. Haldeman soon asked Dean to help implement the "Huston Plan," a secret and illegal scheme concocted by White House aide Thomas Charles Huston and approved by Nixon. The plan allowed the government's intelligence agencies to spy against left-wing groups by reading their mail, tapping their phones, and burglarizing their homes and offices. Only FBI Director J. Edgar Hoover's concern that the risks of the spying outweighed the possible benefits (and possibly his wish to block competition with the FBI) stopped the plan.[32]

The illegal activities expanded in 1971 as Nixon worried increasingly about his reelection. Unemployment was climbing, and antiwar protests had grown larger. The previous spring, students had shut down college campuses around the country after National Guardsmen shot and killed four students at Kent State University. By the middle of 1971, polls showed Nixon trailing Democratic Senators Edmund Muskie and Edward Kennedy among likely voters. The president had hoped Republicans would take control of Congress in the 1970 midterm elections, but instead they lost more seats. Nixon blamed the defeats on dirty tricks by Democrats and became even more determined to destroy his opponents in the 1972 election. The White House during this time, aide Jeb Magruder remembered, operated in "a state of permanent crisis."[33]

In February 1971, CBS aired a three-part documentary, "The Selling of the Pentagon," which traced the way taxpayer dollars were being used to burnish the military's image through movies, air shows, and parades. The documentary infuriated the White House, which considered it another example of liberal attacks against Nixon. Agnew denounced the program, the Defense Department accused CBS of misrepresenting the facts, and Colson organized a campaign to have the FCC chairman, military officials, and others criticize CBS's reporting techniques. To prove the network's bias, conservative Democrat Harley Staggers of West Virginia scheduled hearings by the Investigations Subcommittee of the House Interstate and Foreign Commerce Committee. The subcommittee subpoenaed all materials related to the making of the documentary, including internal CBS files and unused footage.

Arguing that congressional oversight of its editing decisions would have a chilling effect on free speech, CBS supplied only a transcript and copy of the documentary. The subcommittee wanted to hold CBS President Frank Stanton in contempt of Congress for refusing to hand over all the subpoenaed material. The full House narrowly voted against the contempt citation, allowing Stanton to avoid jail, only after the network mounted an intense lobbying campaign and spent about $3 million in legal fees to defend the documentary. Although CBS succeeded in beating back the subpoena, the congressional investigation and public attacks against the network turned attention away from the subject of the documentary and toward the conduct of its reporters and producers, a result that would become common in future years.[34]

The struggle over "The Selling of the Pentagon" was a prelude to a more epic battle in June 1971. It started when former Pentagon consultant Daniel Ellsberg gave *New York Times* reporter Neil Sheehan a copy of a top-secret study that became known as the Pentagon Papers. This forty-seven-volume report, commissioned by the Defense Department, documented more than two decades of the government's policies in Vietnam. It described the government's many failures and efforts to mislead the public and Congress. The *Times,* which had begun challenging the government more aggressively in the 1960s, decided to publish excerpts from the Pentagon Papers. Even though they did not cover Nixon's years in office, Kissinger (who had been part of the Johnson administration) argued that making them public endangered national security. He persuaded Nixon that the administration should order the *Times* to cease publishing the documents.

When the *Times* refused, the administration obtained a restraining order from a federal district court prohibiting the newspaper from printing any more installments until the government could ensure that their publication did not harm national security. It was the first time since the Alien and Sedition Acts of 1798 that the U.S. government had tried to exercise prior restraint of the press. The *Washington Post,* however, received its own copies of the Pentagon Papers and two days later began printing them. When it too received a restraining order, nineteen other newspapers began printing installments. The case went rapidly to the U.S. Supreme Court. When asked what was the most sensitive secret that would be exposed by publishing the papers, the administration's lawyers pointed to an effort to use Polish diplomats to negotiate with the North Vietnamese. The publicity would undercut U.S.

diplomacy, they claimed. They did not mention that this effort had already been revealed in several publications, including Johnson's memoirs. On June 30, the court ruled 6-3 against the administration and in favor of the newspapers. The press had challenged the Nixon administration and won.[35]

The Pentagon Papers case encouraged reporters to more aggressively expose what happens behind government's closed doors. Ben Bradlee, the executive editor of the *Washington Post,* said the case "convinced us we could do this kind of reporting."[36] It also increased Nixon's certainty that liberals, including the press and most government workers, were out to get him. "We've checked and found that 96 percent of the bureaucracy are against us; they're bastards who are here to screw us," Nixon told his cabinet in the midst of the Pentagon Papers case. He later added that the press "is only interested in news or screwing me."[37]

Following the Supreme Court ruling, the White House lost any remaining restraints on devious and often illegal attacks against anyone the president considered an enemy. Nixon told Haldeman and Kissinger he wanted "a son of a bitch" working for him "who will work his butt off and do it dishonorably." The president ordered his aides to have someone break into the safe of the Brookings Institution, a liberal think tank that he thought was hiding a copy of the Pentagon Papers. "I saw absolutely no reason for that report to be at Brookings, and I said I wanted it back right now—even if it meant having to get it surreptitiously," he wrote in his memoirs.[38]

That summer, Colson pushed a plan to set fire to Brookings to create a diversion for a group of burglars to sneak into the building. Colson's scheme was aborted, but in the weeks following the Pentagon Papers publication, Nixon met several times with his advisers to develop a strategy. "We have got to go after everybody who is a member of this conspiracy," Nixon said to Haldeman and Colson.[39] The president told Colson, "I don't give a damn how it is done, do whatever has to be done to stop these leaks and prevent further unauthorized disclosures. . . . I don't want excuses. I want results. I want it done, whatever the cost."[40]

One plan was to discredit Ellsberg. The administration turned to the secret espionage unit the president had ordered Ehrlichman to form in 1969. "If the FBI was not going to pursue the case, then we would have to do it ourselves," Nixon later wrote.[41] The unit, nicknamed the "Plumbers" because it was created to plug leaks, had an office in the Executive Office Building basement. In addition to investigating leaks, they were told to find incriminating information about Senator Edward Kennedy and create fake documents in an effort to implicate John F. Kennedy in the assassination of Vietnamese leader Ngo Dinh Diem.[42]

The Plumbers wasted little time in breaking the law. Under Ehrlichman's and Colson's instructions, two of the Plumbers—CIA veteran E. Howard Hunt and former FBI agent G. Gordon Liddy—and three men from Miami broke into the office of Ellsberg's psychiatrist in Beverly Hills. They tried to find incriminating information about the man who leaked the Pentagon Papers but found nothing of interest. The burglary was the first of several illegal acts by the Plumbers that ended in failure and eventually harmed the president.[43] Nixon later insisted he had not known about the Plumbers' activities. That was simply untrue. "We had one little operation. It's been aborted out in Los Angeles, which I think is better that you don't know about," Ehrlichman told Nixon soon after the burglary. "But we've got some dirty tricks underway. It may pay off."[44]

Ellsberg was not Nixon's only target. In 1971, the White House asked the FBI to investigate CBS correspondent Daniel Schorr, who had angered the administration with his reporting on contradictions in its education policy and had earned a spot on Nixon's enemies list. Haldeman also directed administration staffers to find out who was leaking secret information to Jack Anderson, a longtime Nixon antagonist who had succeeded Drew Pearson as the author of the "Washington Merry-Go-Round" column. The White House ordered the FBI to wiretap Anderson's phones and the IRS to audit his taxes. It told the Plumbers and CIA agents to follow the columnist and his staff around Washington after they disclosed Nixon's secret support of Pakistan during the 1971 India-Pakistan war. The Plumbers even discussed giving Anderson hallucinogenic drugs but never carried out the plan. The campaign did not stop Anderson, who later revealed a plan by the ITT Corporation to give $400,000 toward the 1972 GOP national convention in return for the Justice Department dropping antitrust lawsuits against the company.[45]

Nixon's antagonism toward the press prompted Ben Bradlee, the *Washington Post*'s executive editor, to say on national television that "the First Amendment is in greater danger than any time I've seen it." CBS anchorman Walter Cronkite told an audience of broadcasters that Nixon's antipress campaign was "a grand conspiracy." The Senate Subcommittee on Constitutional Rights, led by North Carolina Democrat Sam Ervin, held hearings in the fall of 1971 on attacks against the press. "Ervin's witnesses voiced a growing sense among Washington journalists that Nixon was waging an unprecedented war against them," Nixon scholar David Greenberg wrote.[46]

Despite the press's concerns about Nixon, the president's popularity climbed during the winter and spring of 1972. He gradually withdrew troops from Vietnam, oversaw an economy that was beginning to boom, and boldly became the first president to visit

Communist China. But Nixon and his aides still fretted about his reelection; some polls showed him running neck-and-neck with Muskie. The president was not going to leave anything to chance after squandering a huge lead in the polls and barely winning the 1968 election. He had also led Kennedy early in the 1960 campaign and still lost. He and his staff were convinced that the Democrats had tried to sabotage his 1968 campaign and would break the law during the 1972 campaign. Nixon was determined to play a tougher game of political hardball than his opponents.

To ensure that the president would face the weakest possible opponent in November, Haldeman approved a plan to increase spending on political intelligence and subversive tactics to influence the Democratic primaries and nominating process. Spies placed in the campaigns of Muskie, Hubert Humphrey, and Henry "Scoop" Jackson swiped memos, while eavesdropping devices were installed in Senator George McGovern's headquarters. As usual, Nixon insisted on making the major decisions in the campaign. He suggested producing phony polls that would show McGovern, whom he considered the weakest potential opponent, as more popular than other Democrats. The Nixon campaign also paid unpopular groups to endorse the Democrats.[47]

The previous fall, the president's staff had hired a young lawyer named Donald Segretti to organize dirty tricks against other candidates. Using secret funds funneled through Nixon's personal lawyer, Herbert Kalmbach, Segretti paid twenty-eight people to disrupt the campaigns of Democrats in seventeen primaries. As part of his sabotage efforts, they used stationery from Democratic campaign offices to send out letters alleging that one of the candidates was mentally unstable and two of them had engaged in embarrassing sexual liaisons. Their prime target was Muskie, the candidate Nixon feared most. Nixon's aides secretly paid for and organized a write-in campaign to support Kennedy in the crucial New Hampshire primary in order to drain support from Muskie. Voters received middle-of-the-night calls from a fake group called the "Harlem for Muskie Committee." Nixon's aides also hired agents to disrupt the distribution of Muskie's campaign material, picket his rallies, and even slip the pilot of his campaign plane a phony schedule so that the candidate landed in the wrong city.[48]

Nixon and his aides got their wish: McGovern won the Democratic nomination after a volatile primary season that weakened the Democrats' image. It is impossible to know whether McGovern would have won the nomination if Nixon's men had not spied on and sabotaged the other candidates' campaigns. Nixon and his aides referred to Segretti's work as "pranksterism that got out of hand," but in reality it was much more. The illegal campaign activities were an extensive effort to subvert the democratic process.[49] As historian Daniel J. Boorstin noted, the Nixon administration failed "to repress primitive desires—the desire to kill off the enemy, the desire to follow the leader wherever he leads, the refusal to compromise with others, the lack of liberal charity toward your electoral opponent."[50]

The zealotry of the president's team was personified by G. Gordon Liddy, a man who would do just about anything to help Nixon. At the end of 1971, the Committee for the Re-election of the President (known by its friends as CRP and by its enemies as CREEP) hired Liddy away from the White House Plumbers. Liddy, a former prosecutor, liked to show how tough he was; he bragged that he had proven his manliness by biting the head off a rat and holding his hand over a candle until his flesh burned. During his days as a prosecutor, he had once fired a gun into a courtroom ceiling during a trial. Liddy received the title "general counsel" but was actually in charge of the campaign's espionage.[51]

A few weeks after Liddy joined the campaign, he presented Attorney General Mitchell, Presidential Counsel Dean, and Deputy Campaign Director Jeb Stuart Magruder with an extraordinary million-dollar plan. Liddy proposed disrupting the Democratic election effort through kidnapping, eavesdropping, burglaries, muggings, sabotage, and the use of prostitutes for political blackmail. Liddy's scheme, called "Gemstone," even included a scheme to shut off the air conditioning at the Democratic convention in Miami so sweaty delegates and candidates would look bad on television. While Mitchell listened and puffed on his pipe, Liddy bragged that he had hired "professional killers who have accounted between them for twenty-two dead so far." Mitchell responded to the Gemstone presentation by telling Liddy, "Gordon, that's not quite what I had in mind." But the attorney general—the nation's chief law enforcement officer—never squelched the illegal scheme or reported it to law enforcement authorities.

Liddy came back a week later with a $500,000 plan that focused on electronic surveillance and no longer contained the kidnappings, prostitutes, or mugging squads. Mitchell, who would soon resign his position as attorney general and become the campaign's director, did not say at the meeting whether to go ahead with the plan or not. Liddy eventually put a $250,000 version of Gemstone into action. Mitchell, Dean, and Magruder later disagreed about who actually approved the plan.[52]

Liddy quickly formed his espionage and sabotage team. Howard Hunt joined him from the Plumbers. James McCord, a retired FBI and CIA agent who was the campaign's chief of security, was picked for his electronics experience. Hunt brought on board two of the men who had helped him break into the office of Ellsberg's psychiatrist—Bernard Barker and Eugenio Martinez. Two other exiles from Communist Cuba, Virgilio Gonzalez and Frank Sturgis, rounded out the team.[53]

The fanaticism of Liddy's team was matched only by its incompetence. McCord and campaign security guard Alfred Baldwin III unsuccessfully tried two times in May to burglarize McGovern's headquarters. The first time Liddy's crew tried to break into the Democratic National Committee headquarters at the swanky Watergate hotel-office complex, they ended up locked in a banquet hall. Over Memorial Day weekend, McCord, Barker, Sturgis, Gonzalez, and Martinez were able to break into the headquarters. While Barker photographed documents, McCord placed taps on the phones of the deputy director and Democratic National Chairman Lawrence O'Brien's secretary. They also hid a microphone and radio transmitter inside a smoke detector.[54]

Once they left, they realized the wiretap on O'Brien's secretary's phone did not work and that the other phone mostly revealed information about the love lives of campaign workers. Baldwin, who was monitoring the signals from a Howard Johnson Motel across the street, could not pick up useful information. Told that Mitchell and Magruder were disappointed, Liddy and his crew plotted another burglary to fix the tap and photograph more documents. In the early hours of June 17, McCord, Barker, Gonzalez, Martinez, and Sturgis broke into the Democrats' offices at the Watergate one more time. Once again Baldwin watched for police from the Howard Johnson as Liddy and Hunt monitored the operation from a Watergate hotel room. The burglars carried cameras, pen-sized tear gas guns, forty rolls of unexposed film, a walkie-talkie, lock picks, and wiretapping equipment. They were dressed in business suits, wore surgical gloves to avoid leaving fingerprints, and carried nearly $2,300 in their pockets, almost all of it in hundred-dollar bills.

As they worked on placing the new wiretap, security guard Frank Wills called the police after noticing the burglars had placed tape on a basement door. Baldwin did not alert them when the police arrived three minutes later, because the three officers came in an unmarked car and were not wearing uniforms. Searching the building, the officers found the five burglars in the Democratic headquarters and arrested them at 2:30 A.M.[55]

Ever since the Watergate break-in, theories have abounded about why Liddy and his crew targeted the Democratic headquarters. After they were caught, the burglars refused to talk about their motives, identifying themselves simply as "anti-Communists." At first prosecutors suggested Watergate was part of a Hunt scheme to extort money from Democratic officials. In his 1984 book *Secret Agenda,* Jim Hougan argued that the burglary was part of a complex CIA domestic spying operation involving clients of prostitutes in a nearby apartment building. Sex was also the motive offered by Len Colodny and Robert Gettlin in their 1991 book, *Silent Coup.* They theorized that White House Counsel John Dean organized the break-in to steal evidence that his future wife was involved in a prostitution ring. Colodny and Gettlin wrote that Alexander Haig, a Kissinger aide who later became the president's chief of staff, participated in the scheme to hide his role in a military plot to spy on Nixon. Others have suggested the White House was trying to gather evidence of ties between O'Brien and controversial billionaire Howard Hughes, or to find out whether the Democrats had any evidence of Nixon's own dealings with Hughes. Rather than taking responsibility and clearing up the mystery, Nixon's top aides denied involvement as long as they could, and then pointed fingers of blame at each other.

Given Nixon's paranoia and desire to win at any cost, the most likely explanation is that the burglars were simply trying to gather as much information as they could about the Democrats' campaign. Nixon was obsessed with O'Brien, a friend of the hated Kennedy family, and wanted as much dirt on him as possible. The president also wanted to start piecing together his strategy for the fall campaign and was desperate to know whether O'Brien would be backing McGovern or Humphrey as the divided Democrats headed toward their national convention. As historian Stanley Kutler noted, Nixon had an "insatiable desire for more information, more intelligence, about his political foes."[56] His staff knew what the president wanted and were not about to let legal niceties get in the way.

Watergate became the key that unlocked what John Mitchell called "the White House Horrors": domestic spying, political sabotage, and campaign slush funds. At first, however, the burglary seemed routine to Nixon and his aides in the context of their other criminal efforts. They reasoned that other politicians had used shady tactics (although not to the extent of Nixon's reelection effort). But they also realized that if investigators followed the trail of evidence, it would expose all of their illegal and politically embarrassing activities. Their immediate instinct, which no one in the administration questioned, was to hide the campaign's and White House's involvement.[57] They did not count on two young reporters from the *Washington Post* who were determined to find out the truth.

—————◆—————

FOUR

TOPPLING A PRESIDENT

*Many people wondered then—and even now, so many years later—
how the Post dared ride over the constant denials of the President of
the United States, and the Attorney General of the United States, and
the top presidential aides like H. R. Haldeman, John Ehrlichman, and
Charles Colson, and stand by the guns of Woodward, Bernstein, and
Deep Throat. The answer isn't that complicated. Little by little, week
by week, we knew our information was right when we heard it, right
when we checked it once and right when we checked it again. Little by
little we came to realize that the White House information was wrong
as soon as we checked it. That all these statesmen were lying.*
    —Ben Bradlee, *A Good Life: Newspapering and Other Adven-
    tures,* 1995

I gave them a sword, and they stuck it in, and they twisted it with relish.
    —Richard Nixon, 1977

The Watergate burglary was a perfect hometown story for
the *Washington Post.* Under Publisher Katharine Graham and

Executive Editor Ben Bradlee, the *Post* was trying to challenge the *New York Times* as the nation's top newspaper while competing every day for local dominance over the *Washington Star*. The elegant Graham had taken over the newspaper after the suicide of her husband, Philip, and was determined to improve its mediocre reputation. She had picked Bradlee, *Newsweek*'s former Washington bureau chief and a friend of John F. Kennedy, to become the *Post*'s top editor in 1968. The charismatic, strong-willed Bradlee soon made clear to his reporters and editors that he wanted the newspaper to write more exposés and keep a close eye on government. Graham's steadfast support of her newsroom during the Pentagon Papers case made the *Post*'s reporters and editors confident she would stand behind them as long as they pursued the truth. "There was this sense that we don't flinch," reporter Bob Woodward said years later about the *Post* newsroom in the early 1970s.[1]

The *Post*'s newfound aggressiveness showed when Joseph Califano, a lawyer for both the *Post* and the Democratic party, called Managing Editor Howard Simons early in the morning of June 17 with news of the Watergate break-in. "Right from the beginning, we understood that it was a big story," City Editor Barry Sussman said in a 2008 interview.[2] Put in charge of the day's coverage, Sussman started phoning reporters from his bed before he even went into the newsroom, eventually dispatching ten reporters to cover various angles of the crime. Alfred Lewis, a veteran police reporter, was sent to the Watergate complex. Arriving with the acting police chief, Lewis was able to walk past the police lines and up to the sixth-floor Democratic headquarters, where other reporters were not allowed, so he could gather details of the break-in.

That same morning, Sussman called Woodward at home and assigned him to the story. Woodward, twenty-nine years old, had been working at the *Post* for only nine months after graduating from Yale, spending five years as a Navy lieutenant, and reporting for a year at a weekly newspaper in Maryland. Woodward was already a favorite of Bradlee, Sussman, and Metropolitan Editor Harry Rosenfeld. As a rookie reporter with one of the lowest salaries on the staff, Woodward started off covering the police from 6:30 P.M. to 2:00 A.M., a beat most reporters hated. He came in early many afternoons to do extra work, however, and quickly became known for his productivity, hustle, and ingenuity. Showing the instincts of a natural investigative reporter, he wrote stories about health violations at fancy restaurants, drugstores dispensing out-of-date prescriptions, and corruption in an elite police unit. During his first nine months at the newspaper, he had more front-page stories than any of the other sixty reporters on the *Post*'s metropolitan staff. "Woodward was an outstanding reporter," Sussman said. "There's no way he wouldn't be assigned to the story if I could choose someone."[3]

At the arraignment that afternoon of the five arrested men, Woodward received his first hints the break-in was more than a simple burglary. He observed that two lawyers were representing the five men even though none of them had made a telephone call from jail. All of the defendants wore suits or sport coats, not the normal garb for burglars. And sitting in the front row, he heard burglar James McCord whisper to the judge that he was recently retired from the CIA. The *Post* ran three stories in Sunday's newspaper about the bizarre burglary, but the newspaper was scooped by the Associated Press, which discovered that McCord was the security coordinator for the Committee for the Re-election the President (CRP).[4]

Sussman asked only two of the ten reporters who worked on the first day's Watergate coverage—Woodward and Carl Bernstein— to come to the newsroom on Sunday to work on a follow-up story.[5] They wrote their first story together that day, a front-page article detailing McCord's career and job with the Nixon campaign. "We started checking on him [McCord]," Woodward recalled. "He was this kind of uptight, by-the-book guy, and it was pretty obvious that he was not financed by the militant campfire girls, that it [the burglary] probably had been done by somebody connected to Nixon, his campaign, or the White House."[6]

As they worked together, Bernstein and Woodward demonstrated that they shared some traits: they were smart, possessed endless energy and curiosity, and loved newspapers and reporting. Otherwise, they had little in common. Woodward was a Republican who had voted for Nixon in 1968; Bernstein most assuredly had not. While Woodward was clean-shaven, organized, and tidy, Bernstein was a college dropout with long hair and an even longer list of debts. He had a penchant for staying out late at night, constantly bumming cigarettes from his colleagues, and wearing military fatigues in the hippie style.

Bernstein, twenty-eight years old, had worked his way into reporting after starting at age sixteen as a copy boy at the *Washington Star*. A Washington native, he had the advantage of knowing the city better than almost any other *Post* reporter and having many childhood friends who could supply him with information. Bernstein was street smart and a colorful writer but lost focus and missed deadlines if he lacked enthusiasm for a story. He was kicked off the local government beat after an editor found him asleep on the couch of the city hall press room at noon. According to office legend, Bernstein had once rented a car while on an assignment and then forgot about it, costing the *Post* $500.

Because he was unreliable, Bernstein was in danger of losing his job in the summer of 1972. He was in the newsroom when the Watergate story first broke only because an editor had ordered him to work that weekend after he was late with a story. Despite Bernstein's reputation, Sussman thought he was an excellent reporter who did well on big stories and whose flair and intuitions would complement Woodward's dogged reporting style. "Woodward was slow to draw conclusions from facts, preferring simply to report what he had found out on a given day," Sussman wrote in his book *The Great Coverup.* "Bernstein was often eager to make assessments, to underscore what his stories *meant.*"[7]

They both benefited from the work of other *Post* reporters. Woodward worked Monday on a tip from colleague Eugene Bachinski, who had developed great sources after three years of covering the D.C. police. When Bachinski asked a friendly sergeant what he knew about Watergate, the officer invited him to his home for drinks and placed on his kitchen table the evidence the police had seized from the burglars. The items included two address books, one with Howard Hunt's White House and home phone numbers. Woodward tracked Hunt down and learned he was a former CIA agent who had worked in the office of Charles Colson, one of Nixon's closest aides. The next day, a story with Bachinski's and Woodward's bylines appeared linking the burglary to Hunt and mentioning his connection with Colson.[8]

While working on that story, Woodward called an acquaintance, W. Mark Felt, for help. He had met Felt a few years earlier when Woodward was stationed at the Pentagon as a Navy lieutenant. Felt had risen through the ranks to become the number-two man at the FBI, in charge of day-to-day operations. He was bitter that Nixon nominated L. Patrick Gray instead of him as acting FBI director after J. Edgar Hoover died in May 1972. Felt considered Gray "a neophyte not only to the FBI, but to the profession of law enforcement" who was submitting to White House pressure to limit the Watergate investigation. Felt did not easily

volunteer information when Woodward first called about Watergate. Woodward persisted, however, until Felt confirmed Hunt was
a prime suspect in the burglary.[9]

Throughout his Watergate reporting, Woodward continued to
contact Felt periodically for guidance. Because the White House
was determined to stop leaks, Felt wanted to stay anonymous.
He would only meet Woodward late at night in a Rosslyn, Virginia, underground parking garage where no one could see or
hear them. According to Woodward, they concocted an elaborate
scheme to signal each other when one of them wanted a meeting:
Woodward would move a flowerpot on his apartment's balcony,
and Felt would have page twenty of Woodward's home-delivered
New York Times circled and the hands of a clock drawn on it to
signal what time to meet. To this day, Woodward says he does not
know how Felt managed to get access to his *Times.*

Felt never gave Woodward new information. He remained on
what journalists call "deep background," meaning the *Post* could
use the information but not attribute it in any way. "He was scru-
pulous about staying away from specifics in FBI files," Woodward
later wrote. "I suspect he did not consider that he was 'leaking'
information—he was only supposed to confirm what I had and
steer me. But the sum of all the confirmations and guidance added
up to more than a leak. It was a road map."[10]

Felt went through elaborate precautions to conceal he was giving information to Woodward because he feared disrespect from
his FBI colleagues and retribution from the White House. He
"lived in solitary dread, under the constant threat of being sum-
marily fired or even indicted, with no colleagues in whom he
could confide," his attorney John O'Connor wrote in a 2005 *Vanity Fair* article that disclosed Felt's secret. "He was justifiably suspicious that phones had been wiretapped, rooms bugged, and papers

rifled. He was completely isolated, having placed his career and his institution in jeopardy."[11] Nixon and Haldeman, the White House chief of staff, suspected Felt was leaking secrets to the *Post* but did not fire him because they were afraid he would then release even more damaging information.[12]

Because Woodward's source remained on deep background, *Post* Managing Editor Simons dubbed him "Deep Throat" after a popular pornographic movie of the era. Deep Throat's identity may have been the best-kept secret in journalism history. Until Felt's family and attorney revealed the truth in 2005, only six other people knew he was Deep Throat: Woodward, Bernstein, Bradlee, Leonard Downie Jr. (who succeeded Bradlee as executive editor in 1991), Woodward's wife, and a Justice Department lawyer who stumbled upon the truth in 1976 but kept the secret.[13]

Despite the hype that later centered on Deep Throat, his importance remains controversial. Sussman maintains the secret source was useful but not essential to the *Post*'s Watergate coverage. Felt met Woodward infrequently and offered little concrete information. If he had been important, the *Post*'s editors would have demanded to know his name, Sussman insists. (Bradlee only learned it was Felt more than three years after he became Woodward's source.) Although Deep Throat became Woodward and Bernstein's most famous source, he was hardly their only one. The two reporters also got crucial information from former campaign treasurer Hugh Sloan Jr., administration employees, and CRP lawyers, bookkeepers, and secretaries.[14]

But even though Felt did not provide Woodward and Bernstein with new information, he still played a crucial role. He assured the reporters they were on the right track and encouraged them to pursue the Watergate story to the top levels of the White House. His FBI position allowed him access to information the Nixon administration was suppressing. Bernstein noted that Felt met with Woodward less than twelve times during their Watergate coverage but provided the *Post* reporters with the context they needed. "He gave us—and our editors—confidence that what was going into the paper was factually unimpeachable," Bernstein said in 2005.[15]

Bernstein and Woodward needed secret sources because Nixon and his aides began lying immediately about Watergate while destroying and hiding evidence. They pushed the CIA to block the FBI from investigating any crimes beyond the break-in itself, but the CIA eventually refused to get involved. Colson had an assistant destroy pages in the White House directory indicating Hunt worked for him. Nixon, Haldeman, Presidential Counsel Dean, and other aides discussed ways to pay hush money to the seven Watergate defendants. As CRP officials shredded and burned files about their illegal activities, it became clear that any White House or campaign employee who openly divulged information about Watergate would lose his or her job.[16]

Nixon and his staff developed a press strategy of denying any involvement with the Watergate crimes. John Mitchell, the former attorney general who was directing Nixon's reelection campaign, said the five burglars "were not operating either on our behalf or with our consent." Mitchell lied about McCord, claiming the Watergate burglar worked for a private security agency rather than on the campaign's staff. Press Secretary Ronald Ziegler said Watergate was a "third-rate burglary" that had no connection to the White House. Haldeman started a whispering campaign that columnist Jack Anderson had organized the break-in to get information for his columns.[17] In response to the only question about Watergate at a June 22 press conference, Nixon said, "The White House has had no involvement whatever in this particular incident." No reporters asked about Watergate during the next two press conferences on June 29 and July 27. During an August 29 news conference, Nixon lied when he insisted that six investigations, including one by Dean, indicated "that no one in the White House Staff, no one in this Administration, presently employed, was involved in this very bizarre incident."[18]

Dean later said he had never conducted the kind of investigation described by Nixon and was working hard to deflect the other five. "Although the White House press machine conveyed a media image of Olympian disdain for so piddling a matter as the break in, the truth could hardly have been more different," Dean wrote. "The scramble was on. People were worried about fingerprints. High officials were already playing dumb, even to each other, shoveling guilt out of their own offices."[19]

The *Post* covered the Watergate story sporadically during the first few weeks following the break-in. Against his wishes, Bernstein returned to covering Virginia politics, while Woodward took a vacation. For the first six weeks after the burglars were caught, the *Post* was "flailing" for information, Bradlee recalled. "We were picking at the story, knowing it was there but unable to describe what 'it' was, finding what looked like pieces of the puzzle but unable to see where—or even worse if—these pieces fit," he wrote in his memoirs. That changed in the end of July after *New York Times* reporter Walter Rugaber wrote a story revealing that burglar Bernard Barker had called the Nixon campaign at least fifteen times. A second Rugaber story divulged that the $2,300 in hundred-dollar bills found on the burglars came from money that a Mexican lawyer had deposited into Barker's Miami bank account.[20]

Rugaber's stories persuaded *Post* Managing Editor Simons to form a team of reporters to investigate Watergate full-time and to make Sussman their leader. It was a wise choice. The gentle, pipe-smoking Sussman loved the story and had a thorough mind that could remember all of the case's complex facts. "More than any other editor at the *Post,* or Bernstein and Woodward, Sussman became a walking compendium of Watergate knowledge, a reference source to be summoned when even the library failed," Bernstein and Woodward wrote in *All the President's Men.* "On deadline, he would pump these facts into a story in a constant infusion, working up a body of significant information to support what otherwise seemed like the weakest of revelations." Woodward and Bernstein biographer Alicia Shepard said Sussman "became the glue that the *Post* relied on to piece the puzzle together."[21]

Woodward, who was a rising star in his editors' eyes, was an obvious choice for the team. Sussman took a chance and assigned Bernstein to the investigation even though Bradlee and Simons had earlier considered firing the talented yet erratic reporter. Bernstein quickly proved his worth. He began calling his network of Washington sources and was able to follow the Watergate money trail to Florida. On August 1, Bernstein and Woodward reported that a $25,000 check given to Nixon's campaign had ended up in Barker's Miami bank account. This revelation put the *Post* at the forefront of Watergate coverage and forever linked Woodward and Bernstein together.[22]

Bernstein and Woodward's stories prompted the chairman of the House Banking and Currency Committee, Democrat Wright Patman of Texas, to call for hearings to explore the connections between Watergate and Nixon's campaign. The president's inner circle worked furiously to derail the hearings by getting committee members to vote against giving Patman the power to subpoena witnesses. Nixon's aides made backroom deals to give extra support to some of the committee members' reelection campaigns in return for their votes. At Dean's request, Deputy Attorney General Henry Petersen wrote a letter arguing that publicity from the hearings would prevent the Watergate defendants from receiving a fair trial. The White House effort worked. A majority of the committee voted against giving Patman subpoena powers, and the hearings fizzled. Patman's probe, however, encouraged Senator Edward Kennedy to open his own quiet investigation, which found enough evidence to persuade the Senate to hold Watergate hearings the following summer.[23]

While Bernstein and Woodward continued digging for information, the majority of newspapers and television newscasts barely covered Watergate in the summer and fall of 1972. Most ran a few reports right after the burglars were caught and then stopped pursuing the story. CBS reporter Bob Schieffer recalled being on the way to Miami to prepare for the Republican and Democratic conventions when he first read about the Watergate break-in. "I can remember reading this and thinking, 'What could this be about? Why would anybody break into a campaign headquarters?' This is where they keep the yard signs and the things like that," Schieffer said. "I immediately just brushed it off and thought I better get on down to Miami where the real news was going to take place this summer. Little did I know."[24]

Like Schieffer, most national political correspondents were busy that summer writing about the party conventions, the Vietnam War, and the presidential campaign. They were distracted again when Democratic vice presidential candidate Thomas Eagleton withdrew from the race after admitting he had once received electric shock therapy. Reporters tended to follow the campaign in a pack, worried they might miss a big story if they strayed too far from the rest of the press. *Time* magazine's Sandy Smith, a reporter with a strong independent streak, was one of the only other journalists to pursue Watergate that summer and fall besides Woodward and Bernstein.[25]

The daily White House reporters were some of the slowest to pursue the story. Most remained deferential toward the president and used Ziegler's news releases as the basis for many of their stories. When the *Post* scooped them, they often responded with a story emphasizing the administration's denials. On the defensive after Agnew's attacks against the press, they failed to penetrate the veneer of White House public relations.[26] The press "seemed reluctant to take on the power of a President," Dean observed. "I was sitting in an Administration in which a dozen high officials were guilty of criminal violations that I knew of, and I watched the President's lead in the polls climb steadily; roughly twenty points ahead in August and still rising."[27]

Besides Rugaber, the *New York Times* Washington bureau displayed little interest in Watergate. It did not have good sources in the D.C. police department and relied on Henry Kissinger's assurances that Watergate had no connection with senior White House officials. In August, *Times* reporter Robert Smith learned from FBI Director Gray about the dirty tricks of Nixon's reelection campaign and about Mitchell's involvement in the Watergate cover-up. When Smith asked whether Nixon was involved, Gray did not deny it. Before leaving the newspaper the next day to go to law school, Smith told his editor what Gray had said, but the *Times* did not pursue the story. Smith was never sure why Gray leaked the information to him or why the *Times* dropped the ball.[28]

In contrast, Bernstein and Woodward refused to ignore the story. They were young and idealistic and did not care about making the administration angry. Bernstein had always been one to question authority, and Woodward's time in the Navy during the

Vietnam War taught him that governments do not always tell the truth. "Vietnam set the context for government doing big things in secret that weren't going to be explained in press conferences," Woodward later said.[29]

On September 15, a grand jury indicted the five Watergate burglars plus Liddy and Hunt with as many as eight counts each of burglary, conspiracy, and wiretapping. The indictment did not include any charges beyond the burglary itself or mention any larger conspiracy. Richard Kleindienst, who had replaced Mitchell as attorney general, said the grand jury and FBI were finished with their active investigation. Nixon and his aides were delighted because no top White House or campaign aides were named. Dean was able to reassure Nixon that "the press is playing it just as we expect."[30]

Over the next five days, however, Woodward and Bernstein revealed that Nixon's campaign had a special account for espionage activities and that leading Nixon campaign officials had ordered the destruction of financial records following the discovery of the burglary. Next they learned that Mitchell, while still attorney general, and four other people had controlled a secret fund, stashed in a campaign headquarters safe, used to finance spying on the Democrats. When Bernstein called Mitchell late at night for comment, the former attorney general screamed his infamous threat: "Katie Graham's gonna get her tit caught in a big fat wringer if that's published." The *Post* published the story anyway.[31]

Woodward and Bernstein discovered these stories by being exceptionally dogged. Rather than rely on official sources and daily White House press briefings, they made a steady stream of phone calls and went door to door to the homes of lower-echelon workers on Nixon's reelection campaign and asked them what they knew. Gradually they pried information out of people who were reluctant to talk. "It was like selling magazine subscriptions," Bernstein said. "One out of every 30 people will feel sorry for you and buy one."[32] After one hearing, according to a *Time* magazine article, several of the Watergate defendants crowded into a taxi. Bernstein, not wanting to lose a chance for an interview, dove into the taxi as it pulled away and ended up on a defendant's lap.[33]

Sussman noted that Woodward and Bernstein developed ways to get facts "that were unknown to most newspapermen."

> They could often get telephone, hotel, and travel records. Like the superior investigators they had become, they could make sources think they knew much more than they did; they could cajole, bluff, or plead their way to eliciting information. As they amassed information, they often were able to get confirmation or denials, and sometimes a little more, from certain federal investigators.[34]

Gradually Bernstein and Woodward put together small pieces of the complex puzzle until a clearer picture emerged. They were blessed with editors who gave them the time and the backing to pursue the story full-time. Bradlee said the reason for such support was simple: "Their accuracy rate was very high."[35]

An October 10 Bernstein and Woodward story, using information confirmed by Felt, connected Watergate for the first time to the administration's larger scheme of illegal activities. The story began, "FBI agents have established that the Watergate bugging incident stemmed from a massive campaign of political spying and sabotage conducted on behalf of President Nixon's re-election and directed by officials of the White House and the Committee for the Re-election of the President." The spying and sabotage, Bernstein and Woodward reported, was led by Donald Segretti. It included swiping confidential campaign files, planting provoca-

teurs at the Democratic convention, disrupting campaign sched-
ules, assembling files on the private lives of the candidates' families,
and leaking false information to the press. One of the dirty tricks
was a forged letter created by Colson's office. It said Democratic
frontrunner Edmund Muskie laughed when an aide referred to
French Canadians as "Canucks." The concocted slur contributed
to Muskie's disappointing showing in the important primary in
New Hampshire, where many French Canadians lived.[36]

Nixon's aides, realizing the evidence of sabotage and spying
could eventually point to Haldeman, decided to stonewall and told
Segretti to disappear until after the 1972 election. Five days after
their first Segretti story, Bernstein and Woodward reported that
one of his contacts was Nixon's appointments secretary, Dwight
Chapin. The next day they wrote that Herbert Kalmbach, Nixon's
lawyer, had paid Segretti $35,000 from the campaign's secret fund
for spying and espionage activities.[37]

Nixon remained convinced he was a victim of nasty political
opponents and a biased, mean-spirited press. He plotted ways to
spread negative publicity about twenty "vicious" journalists he
disliked in order to "just kill the sons of bitches." He and his aides
held at least five discussions during the summer and fall of 1972 to
plan a counterattack against the *Post*. "The main thing is the Post
is going to have damnable, damnable problems out of this one,"
the president told Haldeman and Dean. ". . . [T]he game has to be
played awfully rough."[38]

Nixon hatched a plan with his designated tough guy, Colson, to
"screw around" with the licenses of television stations owned by
the *Post*. Out of all the stations in the country with licenses up for
renewal that year, only two were challenged, both of them owned
by the *Post*. Members of the groups challenging the licenses had
close ties to the president: the chief Florida fundraiser for Nixon,

a friend of the vice chairman of Democrats for Nixon, the former general counsel of Nixon's campaign, and a close Nixon friend. In the end, the challenges were dismissed, but they hurt the *Post* where it counted—the bottom line. The company spent more than a million dollars in legal fees to keep the licenses, and its stock price fell from $38 per share to $28 in the first two weeks after the challenges and eventually down to about $17.[39]

Katharine Graham wrote that she lay awake many nights during this period worrying about the *Post*'s future.

> Beyond its reputation, the very existence of the *Post* was at stake. I'd lived with White House anger before, but I had never seen anything remotely like the kind of fury and heat I was feeling targeted at us now. . . . The moments of anxiety increased in quantity and intensity. Naturally, we were worried when our stories were denied repeatedly and vehemently. Even we, it seems, underestimated for a long time the capacity of government to hide and distort the truth.[40]

Graham later described the Watergate years at the *Post* as similar to walking on "a high wire over a canyon."[41]

Despite the pressure, Graham and Bradlee never backed down. "There was never a moment when I felt any pressure from my editors or from Kay Graham to slow down," Sussman said.[42] After the *Post* was issued a subpoena to turn over many of its Watergate notes and tapes, Graham took possession of the material and said she would go to jail to protect her reporters' work. Turning over the tapes and notes would expose sources that had been promised confidentiality and cripple the efforts of her reporters to get more information. Bradlee told Bernstein and Woodward that "if the Judge wants to send anyone to jail, he's going to have to send

Mrs. Graham. And, my God, the lady says she'll go! Then the Judge can have that on his conscience. Can't you see the pictures of her limousine pulling up to the Women's Detention Center and out gets our gal, going to jail to uphold the First Amendment?" After spending time and money fighting the subpoenas, they were eventually quashed and Graham avoided jail.[43]

While planning his offensive against the *Post,* Nixon avoided reporters, appearing publicly only at well-orchestrated campaign events and letting his surrogates do the attacking. Ziegler accused Woodward and Bernstein of basing their stories on "hearsay, innuendo, guilt by association." The Republican national chairman, Senator Robert Dole of Kansas, called the Watergate coverage "a barrage of unfounded and unsubstantiated allegations by George McGovern and his partner-in-mud-slinging, *The Washington Post.*" Colson said, "Mr. Bradlee now sees himself as the self-appointed leader of . . . the tiny fringe of arrogant elitists who infect the healthy mainstream of American journalism with their own peculiar view of the world." Clark MacGregor, who succeeded Mitchell as director of the Nixon election campaign, declared, "Using innuendo, third-person hearsay, unsubstantiated charges, anonymous sources and huge scare headlines—the *Post* has maliciously sought to give the appearance of a direct connection between the White House and the Watergate—a charge which the *Post* knows—and half a dozen investigations have found—to be false."[44]

The Nixon team's attacks and denials reinforced the reluctance of most voters—and journalists—to believe a president was capable of the kind of corruption of which Nixon was guilty. "People did not believe, even at the *Post,* what we were writing," Woodward recalled.[45] Out of the more than four hundred journalists covering Washington for the sixteen leading news bureaus, fewer than fifteen investigated Watergate on a regular basis during the fall campaign. Other newspapers carried Watergate stories in 1972, but unlike the *Post*'s coverage, their stories only occasionally appeared on page one and were rarely investigative in nature. Often they featured the White House's denials of wrongdoing. *New York Times* columnist Tom Wicker later observed, "Most of us were dragged kicking and screaming into Watergate."[46]

As a result, Nixon's reputation suffered little damage during that time. Late summer and early fall polls showed that more than three-quarters of Americans had heard of the break-in at the Democratic headquarters, but only 17 percent thought Nixon's campaign or the Republicans were behind it. Only 1 percent thought Nixon was involved. That fall, 71 percent of newspapers endorsed Nixon for reelection, only 5 percent backed McGovern, and the rest remained neutral. Those that backed Nixon downplayed Watergate coverage the most.[47]

Bernstein said the pressure during this time was intense. "Every day the leader of the free world and his spokesman got up and made the conduct of the press, particularly Bradlee, Woodward, and myself, the issue in Watergate, instead of the conduct of the president and his men, and it worked for a very long time," he said.[48] But Sussman found the attacks against the press oddly comforting. He noticed that White House and Republican statements never directly contradicted the information discovered by Bernstein and Woodward. "To me the statements confirmed our stories because they weren't denying anything," Sussman said.[49]

Still, the *Post*'s editors sometimes wondered why other publications were not competing with them for the story. Could they be making a mistake in trusting Woodward and Bernstein so much? "The assertions we had given air to—that sabotage was basic reelection strategy, formulated in the White House—were as serious as any that had been placed at the door of a sitting President of the United States," Sussman noted.[50] Some reporters at other publications were wondering if they were making their own mistake by not covering Watergate more thoroughly. Philip Meyer, a Washington correspondent for the Knight chain at the time, said he felt paralyzed because he did not know where to begin reporting the stories that Woodward and Bernstein were finding. "It took guts for the *Post* to be out on a limb like that for so long," Meyer said.[51]

Graham felt somewhat reassured that Bradlee and the other editors were enforcing strict rules on how to report the Watergate story:

> First, every bit of information attributed to an unnamed source had to be supported by at least one other, independent source. Particularly at the start of Watergate, we had to rely heavily on confidential sources, but at every step we double-checked every bit of material before printing it; where possible, we had three or even more sources for each story. Second, we ran nothing that was reported by any other newspaper, television, radio station, or other media outlet unless it was independently verified and confirmed by our own reporters. Third, every word of every story was read by at least one of the senior editors before it went into print, with a top editor vetting each story before it ran. As any journalist knows, these are rigorous tests. . . . There were many times when we delayed publishing something until the 'tests' had been met. There were times when something just didn't seem to hold up and, accordingly, was not published, and there were a number of instances where we withheld something not sufficiently confirmable that turned out later to be true.[52]

Graham and Bradlee staked their newspaper's reputation on the accuracy of Bernstein and Woodward's Watergate reporting. Bradlee said he would have quit if the *Post* had gotten the story wrong.[53]

On October 25, Bernstein and Woodward did get part of a story wrong. They reported that Haldeman was one of five people who approved payments—including the ones for the Watergate burglary—from CRP's secret fund for spying and sabotage. This part of the story was correct. But Bernstein and Woodward made a big mistake: they mistakenly wrote that former campaign treasurer Hugh Sloan had testified about Haldeman's role before the grand jury investigating Watergate. Sloan's lawyer denied this, and the *Post* had to retract part of the story. Under a barrage of criticism, Woodward and Bernstein contemplated resigning from their jobs. In his morning White House press briefing, Ziegler spent thirty minutes denouncing the *Post,* calling the Haldeman story a "blatant effort at character assassination" and accusing the newspaper of practicing "shoddy and shabby" journalism. As reporters from around the country called Bradlee demanding a comment, and his demoralized staff tried to figure out what went wrong, he issued a simple statement: "We stand by our story." The next night, Felt told Woodward the mistake would strengthen Haldeman and set back the investigation. "You've got people feeling sorry for Haldeman," he said. "I didn't think that was possible."[54]

Although shaken, Woodward and Bernstein continued to investigate, skipping sleep, meals, and showers along the way. "If you think this was glamorous, it was not," Woodward recalled. "It was smelly."[55] Graham said the *Post* was "lucky that both Woodward and Bernstein were young and single and therefore willing and able to work sixteen- and eighteen-hour days, seven days a week for months on end, at least with fewer repercussions than married men might have had."[56] Bradlee said Woodward and Bernstein's greatest asset was how "spectacularly hard" they worked. "They would ask fifty people the same question, or they would ask one person the same question fifty times, if they had reason to believe some information was being withheld," he said.[57]

In the fall of 1972, a Watergate story was running on the *Post*'s front page nearly every other day. The networks and a handful of other publications were also paying more attention as the presidential election drew closer. Jack Nelson and Ron Ostrow of the *Los Angeles Times* became the first reporters to provide a Watergate conspirator's firsthand account. After interviewing Alfred Baldwin, Nelson and Ostrow wrote on October 5 that he had given eavesdropping logs to the CRP less than two weeks before the Watergate arrests. Their Washington bureau chief, John Lawrence, went to jail for two days rather than give U.S. District Court Chief Judge John Sirica tapes of the Baldwin interview. On October 24, the *Los Angeles Times*'s Robert Jackson disclosed that Segretti had recruited people to infiltrate the campaigns of Democratic candidates Edmund Muskie and Hubert Humphrey. The *New York Times* reported that Segretti had made at least twenty-eight calls to the White House, Hunt's house and office, and Chapin's home.[58]

Most evenings at least one network news show carried a Watergate story. The average segment, however, lasted only seventy-five seconds and featured little investigative reporting. Most of the broadcast stories relied on official sources and framed the scandal in terms of campaign politics. As CBS reporter Daniel Schorr explained, "Watergate, in the early days before the 1972 election, was a classic example of a story in search of pictures." Schorr, however, was able to break the important news that Hunt and Liddy were not only listed in the burglars' address books but also were near the scene of the burglary to monitor its progress.[59]

The network coverage intensified eleven days before the election when the *CBS Evening News* ran a Watergate report filling nearly fifteen of the broadcast's twenty-two minutes. CBS relied heavily on the reporting the *Post* had already done, but having the story introduced by anchorman Walter Cronkite (considered by many the most trusted man in America) gave it legitimacy outside of Washington and helped make Watergate a household word. Bernstein recalled thirty-five years later that "once CBS put that story on the air, it meant we weren't out there alone, and it had been a fairly lonely place in terms of the great journalistic institutions until then."[60]

Cronkite finished the story by telling his audience a second part of the Watergate report would run the following Monday. Nixon's aides quickly complained about the story running so close to the election, and Colson warned CBS Chairman William Paley that the network could expect retribution from the administration following the president's near-certain reelection. Paley ordered the news division to delay the second Watergate segment by a day so it could be cut in half.[61]

Despite the CBS broadcasts, Nixon easily won the November election, capturing more votes than any presidential candidate in history up to that time. He carried 61 percent of the total votes and forty-nine out of fifty states. As Nixon and his aides predicted when they worked to influence the Democratic primaries, voters saw McGovern as weak and too liberal.[62] After the election, Nixon was ready for revenge. He told his aides to push the Internal Revenue Service to investigate the tax returns of Katharine Graham, *Post* lawyer Edward Bennett Williams, and other individuals and groups he considered enemies. He decreed that members of the administration should not return the phone calls of the *Post*'s reporters and even banned the newspaper's society writer from covering White House parties.[63]

While Nixon sought vengeance, the *Post*'s Watergate coverage stalled for nearly two months following Nixon's landslide victory. Bernstein and Woodward kept digging for new information, but they could not find anything substantial. Feeling desperate, they visited the homes of Watergate grand jurors and tried to get them to talk about the case in violation of court rules. Bernstein and Woodward failed, and Judge Sirica was furious when he learned about it. Their one big story during this dry spell came on December 22 when they revealed for the first time the existence of the White House Plumbers.[64]

In early 1973, the *New York Times* improved its Watergate coverage by assigning the story to Seymour Hersh, whom the newspaper had hired after his My Lai massacre exposés. Suddenly, Bernstein and Woodward had a talented and tenacious competitor. One week after the trial of the original seven Watergate defendants started in January, Hersh wrote an article revealing that at least four of them were receiving up to $1,000 a month in hush money. The defendants denied they were being paid to stay quiet, and the story temporarily disappeared. The sixteen-day trial of the Watergate burglars ended on January 30 with Hunt, Liddy, and the five burglars either pleading guilty or being found guilty. None of the men admitted that anyone besides them was involved. But even though the cover-up had worked so far, Judge Sirica was suspicious. A former Golden Gloves boxer known as "Maximum John" due to his fondness for giving out long sentences, Sirica let the defendants know he did not think he was getting the full truth from them.[65]

Then L. Patrick Gray changed everything. As he sought Senate confirmation in late February and early March to become the permanent FBI director, Gray testified he regularly shared files from the FBI's investigation of Watergate with the White House and allowed Dean to observe FBI interviews of presidential aides. Gray also shared documents showing that Kalmbach, the president's personal lawyer, funneled money to Segretti to disrupt the Democratic primaries. Gray added that the FBI possessed evidence the president's campaign committee had destroyed documents after the burglary arrests. The acting FBI director himself had even burned evidence from Hunt's White House safe at the direction of Dean and Ehrlichman, the *New York Daily News* reported. Gray's testimony corroborated the accuracy of many of the *Post*'s stories that the White House had been denying. After his bruising testimony, Gray announced his resignation on April 27.[66]

While Gray created fireworks, a letter from Watergate burglar James McCord further damaged Nixon. Facing a long prison term, McCord wrote to Sirica in March disclosing that the White House and Nixon campaign had engaged in a high-level cover-up. He said White House officials pressured the seven defendants to plead guilty and keep quiet about the involvement of top administration and campaign officials in planning Watergate. The *Los Angeles Times* disclosed a few days later that McCord named Dean and Magruder as two of the top Nixon aides who knew about the Watergate burglary in advance. In his diary, Nixon called McCord's letter a "bombshell."[67]

Thanks to McCord and Gray, Watergate started dominating the headlines and the evening newscasts. Suddenly stories were flowing from all directions. Reporters regularly filled the hallways of the U.S. District Courthouse to see if any White House aides were testifying before the grand jury. The *Providence Journal-Bulletin*'s

Jack White wrote about Nixon's surprisingly small income tax payments. The *Santa Ana Register*'s John Blackburn revealed that Nixon secretly used campaign funds to pay for his Western White House in California and renovated it using taxpayer dollars.[68]

Bernstein and Woodward continued to pursue the story. They disclosed that Nixon campaign funds were used to pay McCord $3,000 a month and the four other burglars $1,000 a month to remain silent. They also reported that Colson knew about the Watergate bugging plans in early 1972.[69] One of the biggest stories of all was dug up by James Polk, who described in the *Washington Star* how financier Robert Vesco had made a secret $250,000 contribution to Nixon's campaign. Attorney General Mitchell then arranged a meeting between Vesco's lawyer and the chairman of the Securities and Exchange Commission, which was investigating the financier's shady stock deals.[70] The White House could no longer control the coverage. On April 17, Ziegler said his previous denials of White House involvement in Watergate were "inoperative."[71]

The power of Watergate to wound the president became clear on April 30, when he announced the resignations of his two most-trusted aides: Haldeman and Ehrlichman. In his heart, he knew his presidency was nearing its end. "I cut off one arm, then cut off the other," Nixon later said to describe how painful this move was for him.[72] He also announced that Attorney General Kleindienst had resigned and Dean had been fired. The next day, Ziegler publicly apologized to the *Post* and specifically Bernstein and Woodward for his past attacks on them. Against Nixon's wishes, the new attorney general, Elliot Richardson, appointed Archibald Cox, a Harvard Law School professor and former solicitor general in the Kennedy administration, to be the special prosecutor in charge of investigating Watergate.[73]

By this time, Hersh was competing with Bernstein and Woodward for the best Watergate scoops. On May 1, he wrote that investigators had found evidence indicating Haldeman, Ehrlichman, Mitchell, Dean, Magruder, and CRP Deputy Director Frederick LaRue had tried to obstruct justice by covering up the administration's and campaign's links to the crime. The next day, Hersh revealed that Haldeman had approved "espionage and sabotage efforts" against the Democratic presidential contenders. On May 15, Hersh disclosed that Nixon had approved wiretapping the phones of more than a dozen of his aides as far back as 1969 to find out who had leaked information about U.S. bombing strikes against Cambodia. And five days later, Hersh wrote that the "White House established a secret intelligence unit in 1970 to collect and evaluate information about radical and antiwar groups. . . ."[74] Hersh said he and other journalists were able to collect much of their information from the president's own appointees.

> Reporters were in frequent contact with members of Nixon's Cabinet and with high-level investigative and intelligence officials. Some of the men who met with the President, and advised him, provided scathing details about his demeanor and his often ill-advised outbursts. . . . Many people in government were outraged by the sheer bulk and gravity of the corrupt activities they witnessed in the White House. Reporters were their allies and confidants.[75]

Television coverage of Watergate was also accelerating, bringing the story of White House misconduct into living rooms throughout the country. In the first twenty-eight weeks of 1973, the networks ran twice as many stories about Watergate and devoted more than six times as many hours to the scandal than they did in 1972. Between mid April and mid May, more than half of the weekday network newscasts began with the Watergate story, although they still featured little investigative reporting. As people decided that Watergate was more than a typical political prank, Nixon's popularity in the polls started to decline from the 68 percent approval rating he received in January, the highest of his entire time in office. By April, the president's approval rating had plummeted to 40 percent, and by mid May only 9 percent of the public thought he was being "frank and honest" about the case. Many Republicans and independents joined Democrats in thinking Watergate was a serious problem.[76]

Television played an even more prominent role when the Senate Select Committee on Presidential Campaign Activities began its Watergate hearings on May 17, 1973. Senate Republicans had agreed with Democrats to create the bipartisan, seven-member committee chaired by Sam Ervin, the North Carolina Democrat. Before the hearings began, Ervin called Woodward into his office and asked the reporter for ideas on how the committee should pursue its investigation. Woodward shared his conviction that Watergate was part of "a massive Haldeman under-cover operation." Ervin assured him the committee would be unafraid to subpoena the chief of staff and other Nixon aides.[77]

All thirty-seven days of the committee's hearings were televised live, sometimes by all three national networks at once, and then replayed on public television in the evenings. On some days the hearings attracted more viewers than competing soap operas and game shows. White House and campaign officials—Haldeman, Ehrlichman, Mitchell, Colson, Dean, Liddy, Hunt, and others—testified about political espionage, illegal hush money, and the president's enemies list. As the hearings continued, it became clear that many of Nixon's top aides not only tried to cover up

Watergate but also planned other crimes such as the break-in at the office of Ellsberg's psychiatrist. This ugly view of the administration's inner workings cast substantial doubt on Nixon's insistence he had previously known nothing about the Watergate break-in, cover-up, or other illegal activities.[78]

The White House counterattacked. Charges were denied, witnesses' motives questioned, and the media accused of unfairness. Nixon's own fury at the press had grown steadily throughout the year as he sought to portray himself as a victim. In May he spoke of "grossly misleading" news accounts. In August he said journalists were trying to exploit Watergate to keep him from doing his job as president. That same month, Nixon angrily shoved Ziegler toward a group of reporters who were covering him on a trip to New Orleans. Agnew meanwhile accused the press of using "character assassination," "double hearsay," and "undisclosed source rumor" that resembled "McCarthyistic techniques" in its Watergate coverage.[79]

The critics of the press had some good reasons to complain. Television viewers regularly saw reporters surrounding Watergate figures for interviews and staking out people's homes. As more journalists covered Watergate and tried to come up with original stories, more mistakes were made. The Associated Press incorrectly reported that Ehrlichman was at a key meeting, CBS wrongly implicated a Maryland bank in money laundering, and ABC had to apologize for falsely incriminating a Nixon aide. Even Democratic Senators Mike Mansfield of Montana and William Proxmire of Wisconsin criticized the press. While acknowledging that journalists had done a "tremendous" job covering Watergate, Proxmire said "a reckless momentum of reporting innuendo and rumor" was unfairly destroying the president.[80]

It was Nixon's own words, however, that ultimately destroyed his presidency. White House aide Alexander Butterfield told the Watergate committee in July 1973 that the president had secretly taped conversations for two years. Judge Sirica, Special Prosecutor Cox, and the Senate Watergate Committee demanded copies of the tapes so they could hear in Nixon's own words whether he was telling the truth or not about his knowledge of criminal activities. The president resisted, noting that Kennedy and Johnson had also taped conversations. He argued that releasing the tapes would violate executive privilege and threaten the independence of the executive branch of government. A long court battle ensued while many of his previous supporters stopped backing him.[81]

On October 1, Cox subpoenaed more tapes. Nixon offered to provide transcripts prepared by the White House in return for a ban on further subpoenas, but the special prosecutor refused. An enraged Nixon ordered Attorney General Richardson to fire Cox on October 20, but Richardson resigned rather than carry out the president's orders. Deputy Attorney General William Ruckelshaus also refused to dismiss Cox and resigned (although Nixon's new chief of staff, Alexander Haig, insisted he was fired). Finally Solicitor General Robert Bork agreed to fire Cox. The White House announced the special prosecutor's office had been abolished and the FBI had sealed off its offices. Sirica later observed that Nixon's use of force looked "as if some colonels in a Latin American country had staged a coup."[82]

Cox's firing and the departures of Richardson and Ruckelshaus became known as the "Saturday Night Massacre." Many of the day's events were televised, and the public reacted with outrage, flooding the White House and congressional offices with an unprecedented number of telegrams and phone calls, most of them protesting Nixon's actions. Within five days, eighty-four different congressmen introduced bills and resolutions calling for

Congress, at the very least, to investigate the possibility of impeaching Nixon. Bowing to public pressure, Nixon agreed to give some of the tapes to Sirica and to name a new special prosecutor, Leon Jaworski, to replace Cox.[83]

By then Nixon had lost one of his most vocal supporters. Earlier in the year, a Maryland builder testified before a grand jury that he had given payoffs to Agnew in return for his help in getting government contracts. The payoffs had lasted more than a decade, from the time Agnew was a local official through the years he was vice president. Facing charges of extortion, bribery, and tax evasion, Agnew resigned on October 10. He avoided prison by pleading no contest to one count of failing to report income to the Internal Revenue Service. He agreed to pay a fine and accepted three years probation. Nixon named House Republican leader Gerald Ford of Michigan, well liked in Washington but little known around the country, to replace Agnew as vice president. The Senate and House confirmed Ford in early December.[84]

Nixon knew he was in a battle for his political life and that the key to survival was winning public opinion. He understood that a successful strategy depended on how he appeared in the media, especially television. In a tense press conference six days after the Saturday Night Massacre, Nixon attacked the "outrageous, vicious, distorted reporting" about Watergate. The president avoided meeting with White House reporters for the next four months, but their daily briefings with Ziegler grew increasingly contentious as they lost their fear of offending Nixon.[85]

The resurgence of aggressive reporting made some journalists proud. The *New York Times*'s Tom Wicker said that "for the first time in my experience, the press has suddenly become what it has touted itself to be all these years—an adversary." But many Republicans thought the media's conduct was disgraceful. The conservative *National Review* magazine described the White House press corps during the height of Watergate coverage as "sweating, jumping and shouting, hair matted, eyes glazed—wondering about *Mr. Nixon's* emotional stability."[86]

On November 20, White House lawyers made an astonishing disclosure: eighteen and a half minutes had mysteriously been erased from the tape of a discussion between Nixon and Haldeman three days after the Watergate arrests. Haldeman's notes from the meeting showed they had talked about Watergate. Electronics experts later found that the tape had been erased manually at least five times, making unlikely the original White House explanation that Nixon's secretary, Rose Mary Woods, had accidentally deleted the conversation while transcribing it. Jaworski and Sirica continued to press for the subpoenaed tapes' release, but Nixon refused, setting up a constitutional showdown.[87]

Congress and the courts were ready. On February 6, 1974, the House voted 410 to 4 to begin an impeachment investigation of Nixon. On March 1, a grand jury handed down indictments against former top Nixon aides including Haldeman, Ehrlichman, Mitchell, and Colson, charging them with conspiracy to cover up the break-in. Under pressure from the Senate, House, Sirica, and Jaworski, Nixon finally released edited transcripts of some of the tapes on April 30. They were shocking. The transcripts revealed an often vengeful, petty, and deceitful president who spouted obscenities and ethnic slurs. They contained numerous notations of "expletive deleted" to replace the president's many profanities. Senate Republican leader Hugh Scott, who had often backed Nixon, called his conversations "deplorable, disgusting, shabby, immoral." Newspapers printed long sections of the transcripts, which were also published as paperback books that sold three million copies within a week. For the first time, the private words of a president, shrouded in secrecy throughout American history, were fair game for the probing of reporters and discussion by the public.[88]

Nine days after the release of the tape transcripts, the House Judiciary Committee began impeachment hearings. Although the tapes offered embarrassment after embarrassment for Nixon, he continued to blame the press, claiming reporters would have barely covered Watergate if he had been a liberal.[89] On July 24, the Supreme Court ruled unanimously that the president must turn over sixty-four tapes of White House conversations that he had refused to give Jaworski. Between July 27 and July 30, the House Judiciary Committee passed three articles of impeachment against Nixon: obstruction of justice, failing to uphold laws and engaging in conduct "violating the constitutional rights of citizens," and disobeying the Judiciary Committee's subpoenas. The second article mentioned the actions of the Plumbers, the use of the FBI and other federal agencies to spy on his opponents, and efforts to have the Internal Revenue Service act against his enemies.[90]

Complying with the Supreme Court ruling, the White House finally released transcripts of tapes containing the smoking gun that proved Nixon's guilt: six days after the Watergate burglars were arrested, Nixon had ordered a cover-up of the crime and then continued to instruct his staff to withhold and hide information from investigators. After these revelations, most of Nixon's Republican supporters abandoned him. Facing almost certain impeachment by the full House, the president resigned on August 9, 1974.

In a 1977 television interview, Nixon told David Frost that his motive for the cover-up was to protect his aides from vicious partisan attacks after the discovery of the Watergate burglary. He failed to protect them, however. More than two dozen White House and campaign officials would eventually be convicted and sentenced for Watergate-related crimes. Haldeman, Ehrlichman, Mitchell, Colson, Dean, Magruder, Kalmbach, Hunt, Liddy, Se-gretti, and the five Watergate burglars all spent time in prison. "I made so many bad judgments," Nixon told Frost, although he continued to insist he had committed no crimes. "I screwed up terribly on what was a little thing and became a big thing."[91]

Although Nixon insisted Watergate began as a minor matter, investigative journalists proved it was not. Many reporters contributed to the coverage, but no one else put together the pieces of the puzzle like Bernstein and Woodward in those difficult early days of the investigation. Their stories strongly influenced the people who took the actions that eventually led to Nixon's resignation and the prosecution of his top aides.

Some Bernstein and Woodward critics maintain they simply reported what the FBI and prosecutors had already learned. The reporters' work was insignificant, the argument goes, because the FBI, Sirica, the grand jury, prosecutors, and congressional committees applied the pressure that destroyed the cover-up.[92] Woodward and Bernstein "were interviewing the same people we had interviewed but subsequent to our interviews and often after the interviewee had testified before the grand jury," FBI official R. E. Long wrote in a 1975 memo.[93]

The *Post* reporters and their bosses agreed they should not get all the credit for exposing Watergate. Soon after Nixon resigned, Graham wrote Bernstein and Woodward a letter reminding them that they did not do it on their own: "I concede all the blessings we must all concede—incredible amounts of luck, sources willing &

even finally a few eager to talk & help. I concede the role of the courts, grand juries & congressional committees. We didn't bring him down."[94]

But it is doubtful that others would have brought Nixon down without Woodward and Bernstein's work. From the start, FBI Director Gray, Attorney General Kleindienst, and Assistant Attorney General Petersen bowed to White House pressure to limit the scope of the investigation to the Watergate burglary itself and not to probe the broader illegal activities of the Nixon administration and campaign. Kleindienst was the first law enforcement official to learn Nixon's aides might have had a connection with the bugging, but he did not disclose it.[95]

The FBI and Justice Department allowed Dean, the president's counsel, to closely monitor their investigation, and Gray passed confidential FBI reports to him. With this information in hand, Dean coached witnesses before they testified to the grand jury or were interviewed by the FBI. Whenever prosecutors questioned anyone from CRP, Petersen allowed a campaign lawyer to watch the interview and thus potentially intimidate witnesses. Gray let Dean or his assistant attend FBI interviews with White House staffers. The FBI gave information about campaign sabotage to the Justice Department but was told not to investigate the matter further.[96] As Bernstein noted,

> The prosecutors and the FBI interviewed the same people we did, but always in their offices, always in the presence of administration attorneys, never at home, never at night, never away from jobs and intimidation and pressures. Not surprisingly, the FBI and the Justice Department came up with conclusions that were the opposite of our own, choosing not to triangulate key pieces of information,

because they had made what the acting FBI director of the day, L. Patrick Gray III, called "a presumption of regularity" about the men around the president of the United States.[97]

As a result, chief prosecutor Earl Silbert made no attempt during the initial Watergate trial to show who was behind the actions of Liddy, Hunt, and the five Watergate burglars. Silbert failed to connect Watergate with Segretti's dirty tricks and other illegal campaign activities. Dean boasted to Nixon that Silbert's boss, Petersen, had made sure the investigation was kept narrow and that the Justice Department had let the White House know the details of its probe.[98] After the trial in the spring of 1973, Petersen met regularly with Nixon, sometimes as often as twice a day, to brief him about the investigation and to let him know what his aides and former aides were saying to the grand jury. When Petersen told the president that prosecutors had learned about Liddy and Hunt's break-in of the office of Ellsberg's psychiatrist, Nixon told Petersen to stop investigating that case because it involved national security. Nixon boasted to Haldeman and Ehrlichman that he had the assistant attorney general "on a short leash."

For these reasons, the full extent of the White House's criminal conspiracy probably never would have been exposed without the *Post*'s efforts. "The FBI did a fine job under the circumstances," Mark Felt wrote in his memoir, "but there is no doubt that much of the White House involvement in the break-in and the subsequent cover-up would never have been brought to light without the help of the press." Sirica said reading the *Post*'s investigations made him realize he was not hearing the full truth in his courtroom, and Senator Ervin was reading Bernstein and Woodward's stories as he prepared for the Watergate hearings.[99]

Bernstein, Woodward, and other investigative reporters were lauded as heroes after Watergate, but Nixon's approach toward the press—hiding information, shading the truth, staging events, and vilifying reporters—would triumph in the future. Nixon's obsession with secrecy and controlling his public image backfired on him. Journalists' success covering Watergate eventually backfired on the press.

FIVE

BASKING IN GLORY

The glamour of Watergate coverage—something all journalists must now live with—is bound to be both a benefit and a burden for the profession.
 —David Anderson and Peter Benjaminson, *Investigative Reporting,* 1976

By the time Richard Nixon resigned in August 1974, the American press was more powerful than it had ever been. The presidency was weakened and the press was, in the eyes of many, an almost co-equal branch of government. Journalists were trusted and admired more than the president or Congress and nearly as much as the Supreme Court and military.[1] "My own sense of it is that the real winner in these events is the press," historian Robert McCaughey said at a symposium five weeks after Nixon's resignation. "It has become, however unofficial, the most assertive branch of the government."[2] Victor Lasky, a conservative critic of Watergate coverage, observed that the press "had never before felt so powerful."[3] Political scientist Samuel Huntington noted that the press played "a leading role in bringing about what no other single institution, group, combination of institutions and groups had done previously in American history: Forcing out of office a President who had been elected less than two years before by an overwhelming popular majority."[4]

No part of the journalism world enjoyed more post-Watergate glory than investigative reporting. Woodward and Bernstein became marquee names, organizations were created to promote muckraking, books were published to teach journalists how to do investigative journalism, magazines and television shows specialized in it, and the growing use of computers improved the depth and quality of stories. But investigative reporters' success created a backlash that has hurt the press ever since. By the end of the decade, the public was starting to question journalists' constant pursuit of scandal, use of deception, and reliance on anonymous sources.

In the months after Watergate, investigative reporters benefited directly from one change: new legislation. Congress strengthened the Freedom of Information Act in 1974 to force federal agencies to respond to information requests within ten days. Congress and every state also passed open meeting laws by the mid-1970s, requiring elected officials to hold their deliberations in public and making information more accessible than ever before. And in 1978, Congress passed a law protecting whistle-blowers who exposed fraud and abuse at federal agencies from being fired, making it easier for reporters to get information.[5]

By the mid-1970s, newspapers and local television stations in large, medium, and small markets had launched their own investigative units. Watchdog journalism was so prominent that *Time* magazine called 1973 the "Year of the Muckrakers." One Pulitzer Prize winner that year, William Sherman of the *New York Daily*

News, revealed that doctors were abusing the Medicaid program. A Pulitzer also went to a *Newsday* team that traced the supply of heroin from the poppy fields of Turkey to homes in New York. Jack White of the *Providence Journal-Bulletin* earned a prize for detailing Nixon's minuscule tax payments, and Arthur Petacque and Hugh Hough of the *Chicago Sun-Times* won for finding new evidence in an unsolved murder case.[6]

The two journalists earning the most prizes and enjoying the most glory were Woodward and Bernstein. By the spring of 1973, they had already won four major journalism awards. In May, the *Post* won the biggest journalism prize of all: the Pulitzer Gold Medal for Distinguished Meritorious Public Service. The Pulitzer announcement noted that the *Post* "mobilized its total resources for a major investigation, spearheaded by two first-rate investigative reporters, Carl Bernstein and Robert Woodward." At first Woodward and Bernstein were furious they had not won individual Pulitzers, but Bradlee assured them people in the future would remember them as the winners.[7]

By the time the *Post* won its Pulitzer, Woodward and Bernstein had already signed a contract to write a book about their experiences investigating Watergate. Simon & Schuster published that book, *All the President's Men,* in June 1974 as pressure built against Nixon to resign. It earned enthusiastic reviews, quickly climbing to number one on the best-seller lists. Woodward and Bernstein sold the paperback rights to *All the President's Men* for $1 million before the hardback even appeared. The book presented Bernstein and Woodward as daring sleuths investigating a dastardly crime and living exciting lives. Reviewers at the *Denver Post* called it "one of the greatest detective stories ever told," while the *New York Times* described it as a "fast-moving mystery" and a "whodunit." *People* magazine referred to Bernstein and Woodward as Batman and Robin. Columnist Jimmy Breslin said they were "the two that saved the country."[8]

The book's success created a legend that Woodward and Bernstein single-handedly brought down a president, and other young journalists wanted to imitate them. Investigative reporter Robert Greene recalled appearing on a panel in 1976 before a group of six hundred college students. When one panelist asked how many of the students wanted to become investigative reporters, more than half raised their hands. David Kaplan, who became a successful investigative reporter, heard about Woodward and Bernstein's Watergate exploits while he was in college. "When I saw two young guys from the *Washington Post* take down the most powerful man in the world, I thought, 'This is it. This is how we can change things,'" he said.[9]

Kaplan was not alone. The number of students seeking journalism degrees had doubled between 1967 and 1972 and continued to grow through the mid-1970s as baby boomers came of age. Inspired by the success of Woodward and Bernstein and television's dramatic reports of the Vietnam War and other news, many took classes in investigative journalism. Whereas a previous generation of journalism textbooks barely mentioned investigative reporting, whole books began to be devoted to the subject. Within a five-year span, two how-to books called *Investigative Reporting* and a third titled *Investigative Reporting and Editing* were published.[10]

Investigative reporting's glamour shone even brighter after Hollywood star Robert Redford persuaded Bernstein and Woodward to sell him the movie rights to *All the President's Men*. Redford decided to portray Woodward and hired Academy Award nominee Dustin Hoffman to star as Bernstein, Jason Robards to play Bradlee, and Hal Holbrook to take on the role of Deep Throat. After the movie premiered in April 1976, it became a critical and popular success, earning eight Academy Award nominations and winning four Oscars. Nearly 34 million tickets were sold, second that year only to *Rocky.* Howard Simons, Harry Rosenfeld, and Barry Sussman, who played crucial roles as editors of Bernstein and Woodward's stories, were either barely mentioned in the movie or left out altogether, creating hard feelings and a distorted picture in the public's mind of how events unfolded.[11]

Thanks to *All the President's Men,* learning the identity of Deep Throat became a national guessing game. Woodward, Bernstein, and Bradlee vowed they would not reveal his name until he died or released Woodward from his promise of confidentiality. (Felt's lawyer published a story in 2005 saying his client admitted to being Deep Throat, and Woodward, Bernstein, and Bradlee confirmed its accuracy.) Some journalists criticized the mystique surrounding Deep Throat. In his book *Investigative Reporting,* Clark Mollenhoff wrote that too many young journalists were trying to equal Bernstein and Woodward's glory by finding their own secret and often unreliable sources. Experienced reporters realize that some sources take advantage of their confidentiality by peddling "malicious misinformation," Mollenhoff noted.[12]

The use of confidential sources had a long history, especially in Washington, but after Watergate it became more popular. A 1978 survey of Washington reporters found that 28 percent of their interviews were conducted off the record or on background, meaning the interviewees' identities were kept secret.[13] Bernstein and Woodward argued that they could not have uncovered the truth about Watergate without using anonymous sources. "In fact, in our first 100 stories, there is not a single named source who revealed anything of substance about the undercover activities of the Nixon White House," Bernstein said.[14] Leonard Downie Jr., the *Post*'s executive editor after Bradlee, said that by keeping their vow,

Bernstein and Woodward helped future reporters assure nervous sources that their identities would be protected. "Deep Throat is a very good example to be able to cite because everybody knows about it," Downie said.[15]

Like *All the President's Men,* Woodward and Bernstein's next book, *The Final Days,* relied on confidential sources. It used a fly-on-the-wall approach, common in fiction, to narrate scenes as if the authors were in the room at the time. Bernstein and Woodward said they conducted 394 interviews for their description of Nixon's last months in office. Because the interviews were on background, meaning the sources' names remained secret, no information in the book was attributed to specific people. "With this guarantee, those we talked to were willing to give us information we would never otherwise have been able to obtain," Woodward and Bernstein wrote in the book's foreword.[16]

Some reviewers praised *The Final Days* for its thorough and vivid account of Nixon's downfall. Others attacked it. The use of unnamed sources to reconstruct scenes led many critics to question the book's accuracy. They wondered how Woodward and Bernstein could possibly know what Nixon and other people were thinking and feeling when it was unclear whether the reporters actually interviewed them. With the protection of anonymity, sources could embellish or even make up what happened. Reviewers also criticized the authors for engaging in salacious gossip when they depicted the president as a depressed, sexually frustrated man who in one scene knelt on the carpet of the Lincoln Bedroom sobbing and praying with Henry Kissinger.[17] Richard Reeves's review in the *New York Times* was especially damning:

> How do Woodward and Bernstein know what happened in there? Nixon, they say, refused to talk to them. So, for almost two pages of

dialogue, thoughts and facial expressions, readers are dependent on what has to be Kissinger's version or, in Woodward and Bernstein's words from the foreword: "In a few instances, there were meetings between two participants where we were unable to obtain a direct account from either; in those cases, we interviewed people the participants talked to immediately afterward."

The "reconstructed" prayer scene is dramatic and I, personally, don't doubt its general accuracy. But the writers are unnecessarily raising questions about their own credibility with their direct quotations, their "you are there" style.

. . . I am uncomfortable with the two reporters' "extraordinary trust in the accuracy and candor" of unnamed people who are assuredly as self-serving as the rest of us.[18]

The criticism did not stop Bernstein and Woodward from becoming perhaps the most famous reporters in American history. In April 1976, *The Final Days* was the best-selling hardback book in the country, *All the President's Men* topped the paperback bestseller lists, the movie version of *All the President's Men* was number one at the box office, and an issue of *Newsweek* featuring excerpts of *The Final Days* became the fastest-selling issue in the magazine's history. They gave speeches around the country, attracting large crowds and earning up to $7,500 per lecture. To top it off, Woodward and Bernstein had received $1.5 million for the paperback rights to *The Final Days,* a record amount at the time.

Woodward and Bernstein were suddenly wealthy, making nearly $2 million a year before taxes. Their way of handling fame and fortune, however, differed. Woodward worked as hard as ever, while Bernstein became a regular at nightclubs, earning frequent mentions in gossip columns. "Carl had money in his pocket for the first time in his life, and he spent it as fast as he got it, and reveled in everything about fame," Bradlee observed. "Bob bought a house, and socked every spare dime into investments. Carl loved the midnight glitter. Bob loved the midnight oil."[19]

As they won fame and fortune, Bernstein and Woodward's relationship became strained, and they stopped working together (they eventually reconciled but no longer collaborated). Bernstein spent a dozen years writing a book about his parents and served a brief and unhappy stint as the Washington bureau chief for ABC News. Woodward cowrote his next book, *The Brethren,* with Scott Armstrong, a childhood friend who had worked as an investigator on the Senate Watergate committee. The book described how the highly secretive Supreme Court arrived at some of its most controversial decisions. *The Brethren* received a similar reaction as *The Final Days.* It jumped to the top of the best-seller list when it was published in 1979, but its reviews were mixed, with some critics once again objecting to the multiple anonymous sources, omniscient narration, and re-created scenes with no direct attribution.[20]

Woodward and Bernstein's fame infuriated some conservatives who argued that the real Watergate plotters were liberal journalists and congressmen who conspired to whip up a political storm over minor misdeeds. In his book *It Didn't Start with Watergate,* Victor Lasky wrote that other presidential administrations had committed crimes and that the media's hostility toward Nixon blew Watergate "up into hysterical proportions."[21] Historian Paul Johnson went further, calling the Watergate investigations "the first media Putsch in history, as ruthless and anti-democratic as any military coup by bemedaled generals with their sashes and sabers."[22]

When Gerald Ford became president after Nixon's resignation, he tried to heal the wounds opened by Watergate. He enjoyed a friendly rapport with journalists, who extolled his honesty and earnestness and appreciated that he held more news conferences than Nixon. To create a friendlier atmosphere at these news conferences, Ford had his staff move the reporters' chairs closer to his podium and made other efforts to create a more amicable setting. Many journalists worried about the damage to their reputation and to the country if they aggressively challenged Ford. After the turmoil and divisiveness of Watergate, the public had little appetite for attacks on yet another president.[23]

The honeymoon ended, however, when Ford pardoned Nixon a month after his resignation for all crimes he "committed or may have committed." The new president said it was time to restore tranquility and start focusing on the issues that affected the country's security and economy.[24] But the pardon angered those who thought Nixon should have stood trial and rekindled mistrust between the press and government. A new generation of journalists no longer assumed what presidents and other government officials told them was true, making Ford and the presidents who followed him more vulnerable to scrutiny than their predecessors.

They also faced greater cynicism. Nixon wrote in his memoirs that the "American myth that Presidents are always presidential, that they sit in the Oval Office talking in lofty and quotable phrases, will probably never die—and probably never should, because it reflects an important aspect of the American character."[25] But it did die; the Watergate coverage crushed that myth forever by giving the public a glimpse, for the first time, of what really happens behind White House doors. It was not a pretty sight. By 1975, nearly 70 percent of people in a national survey agreed that "over the last ten years, this country's leaders have consistently lied to the people."[26]

The presidents who followed Nixon continued much of his strategy toward the press: appeal directly to the public through television, keep as much information as possible secret, and use the White House communications office to carefully stage presidential appearances. But the strategy did not protect Ford or his successor, Jimmy Carter. One study found that the tone of White House television coverage in the years following Watergate was significantly more negative than in the years before 1972.[27] Between 1901 and 1972, only two incumbent presidents lost reelection bids: William Howard Taft after a three-way race in 1912 and Herbert Hoover in 1932 after he presided over the start of the Great Depression. In the eighteen years following Nixon's resignation, three incumbents lost their reelection bids: Ford, Carter, and George H. W. Bush.[28]

When Carter became president in 1977, he promised a new openness with the press. His press secretary, Jody Powell, said he wanted to "return the relations between the press and government to a more even keel" after they got out of kilter following Watergate and Vietnam.[29] But Carter soon backtracked after growing frustrated with leaks and negative stories. Aloof and self-righteous, he did not have a warm rapport with most reporters. He evaded them whenever he could, rescinded a decision to conduct open sessions with his cabinet, and held fewer news conferences than promised (although more than Nixon). Journalists responded by pouncing on his administration, eager to show they could be as tough on a Democrat as they had been with Nixon.[30]

The most damaging accusations against the Carter administration targeted his budget director and close confidante, Bert Lance. The *New York Times,* Associated Press, *Time,* and *Washington Post* reported in 1977 that Lance engaged in questionable practices at the Georgia bank he managed. *New York Times* columnist William Safire, a former Nixon speechwriter, named the affair "Lancegate" and wrote a string of columns comparing Carter's handling of it to Nixon's handling of Watergate. Safire used Watergate terms such as "cover-up," "smoking gun," and "stonewalling" to describe the scandal. Although a Senate committee found no serious problems with his conduct, Lance resigned in September. He was later indicted but never convicted of any crimes. Safire's Lancegate columns garnered him a Pulitzer Prize.[31]

Soon the press attached the suffix "-gate" to every scandal reporters could find. Charges of criminal activity at Carter's warehouse business were called "Peanutgate." The discovery that Carter's brother, Billy, had made business deals with Libyan dictator Muammar al-Qaddafi became known as "Billygate." A scandal involving a lobbyist's gifts to congressmen on behalf of the South Korean government was dubbed "Koreagate." *New York Times* columnist Anthony Lewis argued that conservatives liked attaching the "-gate" suffix to any hint of scandal in order to minimize the seriousness of Nixon's crimes against the Constitution. "To call anything and everything Watergate is to trivialize a profound event," Lewis wrote.[32]

The sheer size and technological power of the modern media allowed the new scandals to be amplified faster, louder, and wider than ever before. After the performance of the Johnson White House during Vietnam and the Nixon administration during Watergate, reporters assumed that government officials were lying if they denied wrongdoing. With each new scandal, reporters tried to prove a broader conspiracy and a government cover-up, but they failed. The zeal for finding White House dirt escalated with reports that the owner of a New York nightclub had seen Carter's chief of staff, Hamilton Jordan, snorting cocaine. The story was in the news for months until a prosecutor determined the accusations were false. Although the Jordan investigation and others missed their mark, the constant drumbeat of scandal eroded

Carter's credibility and contributed to his 1980 loss to Ronald Reagan.[33]

As White House and congressional misdeeds captured headlines, critics and even some journalists said investigative reporters were going too far. Columnist Joseph Kraft wrote that journalists were unnecessarily hounding public officials, weakening government institutions, and potentially hurting the reputation of the press itself. "The more august the person, the hotter the chase," Kraft wrote. "The more secret the agency, the more undiscriminating the attack."[34] The president of the Associated Press, Wes Gallagher, warned that an investigative reporting binge was causing some readers to see the press as "a multi-voiced shrew nitpicking through the debris of government decisions for scandals but not solutions."[35]

The ethics of the press were starting to receive the same scrutiny as the ethics of public officials. In her 1978 book *Lying,* Sissela Bok scolded not only Nixon but also Woodward and Bernstein for being devious.

> In pursuing their investigation, the two journalists came to tell more than one lie; a whole fabric of deception arose. Persons being interviewed were falsely told that others had already given certain bits of information or had said something about them. One of the reporters tried to impersonate [political dirty trickster] Donald Segretti on the telephone. The other lied to Deep Throat in order to extract corroboration of a fact which this witness would have feared to reveal in other ways.[36]

Such chicanery was common practice for investigative reporters. In Chicago, where competition for stories among newspapers and television stations was fierce, undercover reporting was a tradition that stretched back to Upton Sinclair's visits to the city's slaughterhouses. For a 1975 story, *Chicago Tribune* reporter Bill Gaines posed as a janitor and started working at a hospital he had heard was committing Medicaid fraud and mistreating patients. At one point he was told to put down his mop and go into an operating room, where he was the only person watching over a six-year-old girl under anesthesia while the surgeon, anesthesiologist, and nurses went elsewhere.[37]

In 1977, the *Chicago Sun-Times* went into the undercover business by opening the Mirage, a tavern on the city's North Side. Reporters Pamela Zekman and Zay Smith and investigator William Recktenwald of the Better Government Association, an independent watchdog organization, posed as the Mirage's owners and bartenders. They were soon joined by a *60 Minutes* crew that had learned about the investigation. As photographers and cameramen hid in a loft snapping photographs and shooting broadcast footage, they saw a stream of city and state inspectors visit the bar and demand bribes to ignore health and safety violations. The resulting twenty-five-part series and *60 Minutes* segment unveiled Chicago's rampant corruption, leading to new inspection procedures, code revisions, and indictments of a third of the city's electrical inspectors. The series became a Pulitzer Prize finalist, but it did not win after some judges objected to its use of deception and hidden cameras.[38]

While the Mirage and other undercover investigations were being criticized, a new kind of reporting was transforming journalism. The rapid development of computers allowed reporters to analyze massive amounts of data, giving them the ability to reveal trends they would never have discovered before. Philip Meyer is often credited as the first journalist to use a computer for investigative purposes. As a young newspaper reporter, he became intrigued with the potential for social science research methods to help reporters verify information. After he learned computer programming, his editors at the Knight chain sent him to help *Detroit Free Press* reporters who in 1967 were covering eight days of riots that killed forty-three people. Meyer worked with University of Michigan professors to develop a scientific survey to study the causes of the riots. Using a mainframe computer to analyze the results, they proved the falsehood of popular assumptions that high school dropouts and newcomers from the South were the most likely to riot. The story earned the *Free Press* team a Pulitzer Prize.[39]

The following year Clarence Jones of the *Miami Herald* became the first reporter to use computers for an extensive analysis of government records. Jones hired law students to help him analyze 3,000 local criminal cases. They entered the records onto computer cards, and the *Herald*'s information systems manager created a program to read the data. Within minutes, the *Herald*'s computer produced information showing that most people arrested for major crimes never went to prison and that youths accounted for a third of the county's arrests.[40] In 1972, David Burnham of the *New York Times* tackled an even larger project, using computers to analyze arrest statistics from each of New York's police precincts. His two-part series revealed wide differences among the precincts in crime rates and the ability of police to make arrests.[41]

Meyer spread the use of computer-assisted reporting and social science research methods with the publication of his landmark 1973 book, *Precision Journalism*. Meyer wrote that precision journalism "means treating journalism as if it were a science, adopting scientific method, scientific objectivity, and scientific ideals to the entire process of mass communication." This approach, Meyer suggested, allowed journalists to use hard numbers and rigorous analysis to uncover the truth rather than rely on the conflicting statements of their human sources. By building a stronger knowledge base, Meyer said, journalists could gain the skill and confidence to avoid the domination of powerful politicians and their spin doctors.[42]

Two journalists who took advantage of this knowledge were Donald Barlett and James Steele, the most enduring and successful investigative reporting team in history. They are an unlikely pair. Barlett is a quiet, stocky Army veteran without a college degree; Steele is an outgoing, lanky college graduate. What they share are intense curiosity, talent, persistence, and outrage at injustice. They began working together in 1971 at the *Philadelphia Inquirer*, whose bad reputation had expanded after its chief investigative reporter was convicted of taking bribes. Barlett and Steele's first project detailed how speculators sold substandard homes to low-income people. They combed through handwritten city and county records in a dusty file room and quickly spotted a pattern of foreclosures and repossessions of property bought with Federal Housing Administration loans. The residents, who were promised newly renovated houses, often abandoned the decaying homes, leaving taxpayers with the bill and neighborhoods with blighted property. As a result of their reporting, nearly two dozen people were convicted.[43]

Two years later, Barlett and Steele published a startling series that demonstrated how politics and racial bias skewed justice in Philadelphia's court system. They had spent the previous summer and fall in an alcove of Philadelphia's city hall sifting through warrants, arrest sheets, testimony, psychiatric evaluations, probation reports, and bail applications. After going through about five hundred documents by hand, they decided they would be better off using a computer. They turned to Meyer, who was then

the Knight chain's D.C. bureau chief. From this pile of documents, they took the cases of 1,034 criminal defendants and coded
forty-two pieces of information about each case onto IBM cards.
Meyer wrote a program to answer the questions Barlett and Steele
wanted to ask and found a U.S. Navy computer they could use
between midnight and 4:00 A.M. They ended up with a foot-high
pile of computer paper revealing that judges with tough reputations were actually the most lenient, that District Attorney Arlen
Specter made more plea bargain deals than he admitted, and that
some of the mildest sentences were given to baby killers. Barlett
and Steele bolstered their findings of unequal and sloppy justice
through courtroom visits and interviews with judges, lawyers,
defendants, and victims.[44]

The series was nominated for a Pulitzer Prize but did not win.
One of the judges, Barlett and Steele heard years later, vowed that
no journalist who used computers would win a Pulitzer as long
as he was on the board. But reporters from around the country
called Barlett and Steele to find out about the project, and the use
of computers spread. Their work represented a big break from
the old style of investigative reporting. Instead of relying on secret
tips to develop stories focused primarily on individual wrongdoing, they engaged in a thorough analysis of public documents to
discover what was systemically wrong with institutions that affect
people's lives.[45]

Barlett and Steele used the same thorough approach to reveal
how oil company manipulations contributed to the 1970s energy
crisis. They followed with a Pulitzer-winning investigation documenting the Internal Revenue Service's tendency to go after low-
income taxpayers rather than corporations and wealthy people.
With the help of editors Gene Roberts and Steve Lovelady, they
wrote book-length investigations tackling waste and fraud in U.S.

foreign aid, the chaos of U.S. nuclear energy policy, and the threat posed by nuclear waste. Despite their success and respect among journalists, Barlett and Steele avoided the spotlight and never became household names like Woodward and Bernstein. As their colleagues used to joke, their idea of a good time was hanging out at the copying machine.[46]

Barlett and Steele turned their attention next to biography and wrote *Empire: The Life, Legend and Madness of Howard Hughes.* To research the 1979 book, they searched through a quarter-million pages of personal letters, business memoranda, government contracts, income tax returns, and other documents scattered in more than fifty cities. They were following the example of Robert Caro, a former newspaper reporter who transformed the craft of biography with the 1974 publication of *The Power Broker: Robert Moses and the Fall of New York,* a 1,280-page epic about New York City's master planner. In his biography of Moses and later books about Lyndon Johnson, Caro employed investigative techniques— combing through previously hidden documents, conducting hundreds of interviews—to reveal aspects of his subjects' careers and personal lives they had kept hidden from the public. Biographies written by investigative reporters would soon become common.[47]

Barlett and Steele were two of the stars in Leonard Downie's 1976 book *The New Muckrakers,* which profiled the era's top investigative journalists. Downie called Woodward and Bernstein "The Stardust Twins," the chapter on Seymour Hersh was titled "Scoop Artist," and columnist Jack Anderson's "Washington Merry-Go-Round" team was nicknamed "Muckrakers Inc."[48] Downie's book was just one example of the veneration of investigative reporters in the 1970s. John Behrens's *The Typewriter Guerillas* was another. It profiled twenty top muckrakers, offering chapters such as "Sy Hersh: The Hottest Property in Washington."[49]

Hersh had continued his torrid pace following Watergate. Soon after Nixon's resignation, he reported in the *New York Times* that the CIA had helped coup plotters destabilize Chile, leading to the overthrow and murder of its democratically elected president, Salvador Allende. In late 1974, Hersh revealed that the CIA had conducted a massive domestic spying operation in the 1960s, violating its own charter and U.S. law by keeping files on ten thousand Americans, including antiwar protestors and other dissidents. The rest of the press, still hesitant to break its deference to the intelligence community on matters of national security, was slow to aggressively pursue Hersh's CIA revelations. Hersh, after all, was not just questioning the actions of one president; his stories challenged the institutions of American national security. CBS, *Newsweek, Time,* and the *Washington Post,* among others, accused Hersh of exaggerating and misinterpreting CIA actions. But government investigations later confirmed what he reported, and Congress passed new laws to control U.S. intelligence operations.[50]

Daniel Schorr of CBS followed Hersh's CIA revelations with a story describing the spy agency's violations of U.S. law by becoming involved in assassination attempts against foreign leaders, including Cuba's Fidel Castro. The Hersh and Schorr stories led to presidential and congressional investigations that unearthed more of the CIA's illegal actions, including the planning of murders and overthrows of eight foreign leaders during the Eisenhower, Kennedy, Johnson, and Nixon administrations.[51]

Schorr, however, became trapped in one of the first post–Watergate backlashes against the press. In 1976, he received a leaked copy of a congressional committee's secret report on U.S. intelligence agencies' misdeeds overseas. When CBS refused to publish the text of the report, Schorr arranged for it to be published in the *Village Voice.* In response, CBS took him off the air, and the U.S. House threatened him with jail time unless he revealed who gave him the secret information. Schorr refused. The House backed down, although he was eventually forced to resign from CBS because of the controversy.[52]

Like Schorr and Hersh, Jack Anderson—whose column was syndicated to a thousand newspapers with a combined circulation of up to 70 million people—aggressively probed the inner workings of the American spy agencies. Anderson and his staff of five reporters uncovered an FBI program that spied on people who criticized the government and a failed CIA mission to raise a sunken Soviet atomic submarine. But Anderson sometimes went too far. He falsely accused Democratic vice presidential nominee Thomas Eagleton of having a half dozen drunken driving arrests and inaccurately claimed that Ford's vice presidential nominee, Nelson Rockefeller, was involved in dirty tricks during the 1972 Democratic convention.[53]

Anderson, Downie, and about a dozen other top journalists met in February 1975 to form an organization to help investigative reporters share information, concerns, and advice. They named themselves Investigative Reporters and Editors (IRE). Until then muckrakers often worked in isolation and had little opportunity to learn from journalists in other cities.[54] "Loners by nature, often resented by their own staffs because of their odd hours and independence from such mundane newspaper jobs as preparing obituaries and covering routine press conferences, the investigative reporter more often than not found himself alone on a limb," Michael Wendland of the *Detroit News* explained.[55]

One of IRE's first members was Don Bolles of the *Arizona Republic,* known for his stories uncovering Mafia infiltration of local businesses, billion-dollar land fraud swindles, and corruption in the state's highway patrol. When a local hoodlum named John

Adamson said he had some hot tips on the land fraud connections of local politicians, Bolles agreed to meet him in a downtown Phoenix hotel on June 2, 1976. After Adamson failed to show up, Bolles returned to his car. When he turned the key, six sticks of dynamite exploded beneath him. Eleven days later he died from his injuries.[56]

Adamson was arrested and eventually convicted along with two other men in connection with the murder. Bolles's killing was widely viewed as a warning to other reporters not to probe too deeply into organized crime. Journalists across the country were outraged that one of their own could be murdered in broad daylight in the downtown of a large American city. When about two hundred and fifty journalists gathered in Indianapolis a week after Bolles's death for IRE's first convention, they decided they needed to act. IRE's board voted to form a team to continue his investigations into Arizona's culture of organized crime, fraud, and corruption. They called it the Arizona Project. "We were going to finish Don's work, to find out why a reporter could be assassinated and to ultimately buy an insurance policy for other reporters," recalled Myrta Pulliam, an IRE founder and an Arizona Project member.[57]

The idea of reporters from competing newspapers working together was unprecedented, and the Arizona Project needed a strong leader if it was going to succeed. IRE chose Robert Greene of *Newsday*. He was known as much for his confident and outlandish personality as he was for his talent and tenaciousness, according to his colleague Anthony Marro.

> The stories were legendary and many—Greene pounding on a wall so hard during an argument with editors that he sent pictures crashing off the wall of the publisher's office next door . . . Greene

protesting a ban against reporters flying first class by measuring the
size of a coach seat and the size of his behind, and then announc-
ing to his bosses that he would continue to fly in the front of the
plane ... Greene refusing to take a late-night question from the
news desk until assured he would be paid one hour's overtime,
and then saying, 'I know nothing about it,' and hanging up the
phone ... Greene falling asleep at his desk with a cigarette in his
hand and setting his own pants on fire ... Greene running his car
into a light pole off the parkway and—when the utility company
insisted on payment—measuring the distance from the pole to the
highway and determining that the utility had illegally placed the
pole too close to the road. ... [58]

Greene's investigative team at *Newsday* had already won Pulitzer
Prizes for tracing the trail of heroin into the United States and for
exposing corrupt zoning practices on Long Island.

Nearly forty reporters, writers, and researchers from newspapers, broadcast outlets, and other media organizations around the
country participated in the Arizona Project. Eight office workers
and thirteen local journalism professors and students joined them.
Some newspapers gave reporters time off to go to Arizona, while
other team members used their vacation days or even quit their
jobs. Calling themselves the "Desert Rats," they set up shop in
a Phoenix hotel with Greene's suite serving as headquarters. It
"resembled a War Room," according to Wendland, "with maps,
graphs, reports, and law enforcement documents marked 'confidential' scattered everywhere. The index card boxes and files
were filled to overflowing. Telephones rang incessantly even late
at night, and reporters hustled in and out of the room." [59]

Not every editor, however, backed the project. Abe Rosenthal,
executive editor of the *New York Times,* denounced it, arguing that

the cooperation of reporters from different newspapers weakened the competitive spirit of American journalism. The *Post*'s Ben Bradlee said local reporters, not outsiders, should handle any investigations. As the project continued, the number of participating journalists shrank as some headed back to their jobs and the IRE board and team members squabbled over who owned the rights to publish the investigation's findings. The internal bickering and outside criticism scared away potential IRE members and donors. The organization nearly went bankrupt.[60]

Despite the turmoil, members of the Arizona Project released a devastating exposé of Arizona crime and corruption. The final project's twenty-three main stories detailed the close ties of some prominent Arizona politicians, businessmen, bankers, lawyers, and judges to organized crime, land fraud, prostitution, gambling, and narcotics. The series named U.S. senator and former Republican presidential candidate Barry Goldwater, his brother, and the state's Republican Party chairman as three leaders with ties to organized crime. Some newspapers, including the *Arizona Republic*, refused to run the series, saying they did not have the time to check all the facts or that the stories rehashed previously known information. But the series won several awards, and the American Society of Journalists and Authors called it "the finest hour in American journalism." It eventually prompted more spending on narcotics enforcement and tougher land fraud laws in Arizona.[61]

After the stories ran in newspapers around the country in 1977 and were featured on network newscasts, six people sued IRE. Although the organization did not have to pay damages to any of them, the cases tied up its time and energy for the next four years. The Arizona Project, however, raised IRE's stature. Its membership reached a thousand by the end of the 1970s as it began holding regional workshops around the country. IRE also set up a legal defense fund for its members, handed out annual awards for the best investigative work, and started publishing its own books on investigative journalism. In less than half a decade, IRE had created the kind of organizational support investigative reporters had never before enjoyed. Its annual conventions became opportunities for reporters to train each other. Deborah Nelson, who went on to win a Pulitzer Prize, said fellow IRE members taught her how to conduct stronger interviews and to better use the Freedom of Information Act to pry information from reluctant officials. No matter what topics reporters covered, they could turn to someone at IRE for advice.[62]

While IRE focused on training, two veterans of the Arizona Project—Lowell Bergman and Dan Noyes—decided to form an organization to produce original investigative work. Along with David Weir, they launched the Center for Investigative Reporting (CIR) in 1977, using Bergman's Berkeley, California, garage as its first office. Although it struggled to raise money, the Center's reporters managed to write stories for magazines and newspapers revealing that nuclear storage sites were being built on earthquake fault lines, the U.S. military was transporting nuclear bombs across American cities, and former U.S. servicemen were dying from the effects of atomic testing. In 1980, Noyes worked with ABC's *20/20* on a story detailing how the fundraising branch of the International Year of the Child was engaged in gunrunning and drug smuggling. A year later the Center's Doug Foster produced a story with *60 Minutes* on the dangerous side effects of the prescription drug Selacryn.[63]

The Center's writers often published their stories in a new muckraking magazine called *Mother Jones.* Based out of a small office above a McDonald's restaurant in San Francisco, *Mother Jones* focused on environmental dangers, the growing power of multinational corporations, and the struggles of blacks, women, and farmworkers for equal rights. A year after its 1976 start, the magazine's Mark Dowie documented the Ford Motor Company's decision to avoid spending eleven dollars per car to fix a flaw in its fuel tank designs. The glitch caused Ford Pintos to burst into flames after low-speed collisions, killing at least five hundred people. At first the company denounced Dowie's story, but after a public outcry it recalled more than a million Pintos. Another *Mother Jones* story disclosed that corporate executives knew Dalkon Shield intrauterine devices could cause lethal infections but continued to sell them.[64]

In 1979, *Mother Jones* ran a series of stories by Dowie and other reporters revealing that American companies were selling dangerous pesticides, drugs, and other products banned in the United States to poor countries with weaker regulations. One of the stories by Weir, Terry Jacobs, and Mark Schapiro traced the flow of hazardous pesticides from U.S. corporations to third world countries and then into foods and drinks consumed by Americans. The article won a National Magazine award and led to congressional legislation, tighter EPA regulations, and new standards by poor countries to protect themselves from dangerous pesticides. President Ronald Reagan's administration, angered by *Mother Jones*'s attacks on corporations, borrowed a tactic from the Nixon White House: it had the Internal Revenue Service investigate the magazine. The IRS tried to take away its tax-exempt status, even though the publication never made money, but backed down after fellow journalists protested.[65]

In addition to *Mother Jones,* national print magazines such as the *Nation, Atlantic, New Yorker, Harper's, Newsweek, Playboy, Time, U.S. News & World Report, Vanity Fair,* and *Washington Monthly* were running increasing numbers of investigative stories. So were city and state magazines such as *New York, Washingtonian, Texas Monthly,* and *Philadelphia,* as well as magazines specializing in coverage of industries and professions. *Modern Medicine* probed the poor treatment Vietnam veterans received at military hospitals. *Overdrive,* a magazine for independent truckers, uncovered fraudulent loans made by the Teamsters Union pension fund to organized crime figures. A new libertarian magazine, *Reason,* published exposés of government waste and fraud.[66] Not since the heyday of *McClure's* in the early 1900s were magazines doing so much muckraking.

The emerging gay press was also running investigative stories. The *Philadelphia Gay News* used internal departmental memos to show how the Pennsylvania state police engaged in a systematic campaign to entrap gay men. The *Seattle Gay News* exposed the harassment of gay prisoners in the local county jail. The *Advocate* magazine revealed that the FBI hired an informant in a failed attempt to dig up damaging information about gay journalists and Democratic politicians such as Edward Kennedy, George McGovern, and Hubert Humphrey. The *Advocate's* Randy Shilts described how the country's major health institutions were neglecting cases of venereal disease among gay men, leading to a public health crisis. In his book *And the Band Played On,* Shilts later chronicled the U.S. government's failure to respond quickly enough to the AIDS epidemic.[67]

While investigative reporting flourished in print during the late 1970s, the muckrakers getting the most attention appeared on the CBS show *60 Minutes.* CBS launched the show in 1968 with a different format than traditional news documentaries. Instead of focusing on one subject for an hour, *60 Minutes* included three or more stories in each show that combined the serious topics of documentaries with the fast pacing of entertainment shows. Ed Bradley, Mike Wallace, Dan Rather, Morley Safer, Diane Sawyer, and other *60 Minutes* correspondents did not remain in the background of their stories like most reporters. Instead they were presented as heroic characters in a drama venturing to perilous foreign lands or asking tough questions of villainous corporate chiefs and corrupt politicians. Rather could be seen trudging through the mountains of Afghanistan, Safer driving through the streets of war-torn Belfast, and Wallace sitting face-to-face with America's arch enemy, the Ayatollah Khomeini.[68]

Sometimes the *60 Minutes* reporters appeared on screen for nearly half the length of each story, more than the people they were covering. Executive Producer Don Hewitt boasted that his reporters had more star power than the heroes of *All the President's Men*. "*60 Minutes* is the adventures of five reporters, more fascinating to the American public being themselves than Robert Redford and Dustin Hoffman were playing Woodward and Bernstein," he said.[69]

The *60 Minutes* investigations explored a wide range of topics: land fraud in Arizona, U.S. biological warfare experiments on unsuspecting Americans, potentially fatal pollution at a Virginia chemical plant, deception in the food franchising industry, and the framing of a black New Jersey political candidate on kidnapping charges, among others.[70] Reporter Harry Reasoner said viewers often turned to the show for help. "Now, when people have a problem, something strange or suspicious going on in their community, instead of writing their congressman, they write to Mike Wallace and demand he fix it," Reasoner said.[71]

The show struggled at first, bouncing between different nights of the week until it settled into a Sunday evening slot in 1975. The next year, *60 Minutes* cracked the list of twenty most-watched shows and soon was regularly among the top ten, often topping the ratings of all the shows in prime time. Each *60 Minutes* episode reached a larger audience than any other news form in journalism's history and earned big profits for CBS—$2 billion by the time Hewitt retired in 2004. Dan Rather observed that the show "had become the proverbial cash cow—and a Holstein of a cash cow."[72]

The commercial success of *60 Minutes* encouraged CBS and the other networks to replace their documentaries with more newsmagazines, which were cheaper to make than dramas or comedies. Imitators including *Primetime Live, 20/20,* and *PM Magazine* soon filled the airwaves. After the weakening of federal regulations requiring broadcast stations to serve the public interest, the purpose of television investigations shifted toward making money. Because of the demand to fill a weekly schedule, television newsmagazine producers usually had less time to work on their stories than documentary makers of the 1960s did.[73]

Newsmagazines were not the only shows featuring investigative reporters; they also were becoming frequent characters on television dramas. Programs about reporters were common in television's early days, but from 1964 to 1974, no television dramas were based in newsrooms. In the four years after Nixon's resignation, however, five shows about fictional reporters debuted. Thanks to *All the President's Men,* the lives of investigative reporters suddenly seemed thrilling and glamorous. Three of the shows—*Gibbsville, The Andros Targets,* and *Kingston: Confidential*—overly sensationalized the lives of journalists and flopped in the ratings. Another new show, *Kolchak: The Night Stalker,* took the excitement of investigative reporting to an extreme with its portrayal of a reporter who discovered vampires, werewolves, and other bizarre creatures lurking in Chicago.

The most successful of the new shows, in the eyes of the public and critics, was *Lou Grant.* From 1977 to 1982, it followed the adventures of a city editor and his aggressive team of reporters and photographers at the fictional *Los Angeles Tribune*. The show depicted Grant's reporters writing exposés on gritty topics such as street gangs, battered wives, nuclear power plant safety, prescription drug scams, and abuse at state mental hospitals. During its five seasons, *Lou Grant* won thirteen Emmy awards and was praised by journalists for its realistic newsroom portrayals.[74]

By the start of the 1980s, however, the glamour of investigative reporting was starting to fade in popular culture. The 1981 movie *Absence of Malice* depicted eager young reporter Megan Carter (played by Hollywood star Sally Field) writing damaging stories about a warehouse owner (portrayed by Paul Newman, who was nominated for an Academy Award for his role). Her stories end up being untrue. As a result of the wayward investigation, the girlfriend of the Newman character commits suicide. Rather than showcasing reporters as heroes who use aggressive tactics to expose wrongdoing, *Absence of Malice* presented journalism from the point of view of a victim wronged by a reporter and her callous editors. A publicity line from the movie summed up the feeling that some investigative reporters were going too far: "Suppose you picked up this morning's newspaper and your life was a front page headline . . . And everything they said was accurate . . . But none of it was true."[75]

Unfortunately, the problem of untrue stories was not confined to the movies. In 1980, Janet Cooke, a young *Washington Post* reporter, wrote a front-page story, "Jimmy's World," about an eight-year-old heroin addict. Cooke's compelling story, which included scenes of the lover of Jimmy's mother injecting the boy with heroin, won a Pulitzer Prize for feature writing. Like Bernstein and Woodward's Watergate stories, "Jimmy's World" relied on anonymous sources. Like *The Final Days,* it re-created scenes.

The *Post* editors, including Bradlee and Woodward (recently promoted to assistant managing editor) did not require Cooke to give
them Jimmy's actual name or provide any evidence that he was
real. It turns out he was not.

The day after Cooke received her Pulitzer, the *Toledo Blade*
noted discrepancies in her résumé. After questioning from *Post*
editors, Cooke finally admitted Jimmy did not exist. For the first
time in Pulitzer history, a newspaper had to return its prize because of a discredited story. Bradlee wrote in his memoir that the
Cooke snafu was "a cross that journalism, especially *The Washington Post,* and especially Benjamin C. Bradlee, will bear forever."[76]
Woodward blamed himself for not alerting the police after seeing
Cooke's description of the child addict. Doing so would have
been the moral thing to do, he said, and would have exposed
Cooke's lies before they were printed in the paper. "I made a giant
mistake by not asking the questions that should have been asked,"
Woodward said in a 2009 interview. "I wish I'd said, 'OK, it's a
hell of a story, but let's save the kid, then we can run the story.'"[77]

The Cooke fiasco fed a growing mistrust of the press planted
by Nixon and Agnew a decade earlier. According to surveys, many
people saw the press as a big institution, like government, that
was out of touch with ordinary Americans. Washington reporters
started to be seen as part of the same "inside the beltway" crowd
as congressmen and White House officials. The public was also
suffering from scandal fatigue. In a few short years, the press had
unearthed a startling amount of official misconduct: Johnson lying
about Vietnam, Nixon covering up Watergate, the FBI and CIA
illegally spying on American citizens, the government conducting
medical experiments on prisoners without their knowledge, to
name a few. But some young reporters seeking the glory of Woodward and Bernstein tried to make investigative mountains out of

factual molehills, observed Rosemary Armao, a top editor at several newspapers. "Minor offenses and casual comments," she said, "were turned into major exposés and given exaggerated length and display; nearly all institutions and individuals were presumed to be corrupt or flawed, and they could be described as such on the strength of anonymous sources."[78]

By the start of the 1980s, the balance of power between the press and government was starting to shift back toward the executive branch. The public was ready for a strong president as energy costs skyrocketed, unemployment and inflation soared, Iranian militants held fifty-two Americans hostage, and President Carter warned that the country was suffering from "a crisis of confidence."[79] After his 1980 election, Ronald Reagan would reassert the power of the presidency and effectively manipulate the press in ways first tried by Nixon. Investigative reporters, meanwhile, confronted new challenges. Their post–Watergate glory had faded.

SIX

GETTING DEFENSIVE

A canyon of disbelief and distrust has developed between the public and the news media.
—Bruce Sanford, *Don't Shoot the Messenger,* 1999

In the 1980s and 1990s, powerful economic, legal, and social forces hampered investigative reporting. At the same time, the political landscape shifted, putting journalists on the defensive. After the troubled administrations of Nixon, Ford, and Carter, the presidency regained much of the strength it lost during Watergate. Three of the next four presidents were popular enough to win reelection: Ronald Reagan, Bill Clinton, and George W. Bush.

Part of Reagan's popularity stemmed from his administration's adept use of the press. The mastermind of Reagan's media strategy, Deputy Chief of Staff Michael Deaver, came from a public relations background. Deaver, Reagan, Chief of Staff James Baker, and Communications Director David Gergen did not have the anger of the Nixon administration toward the media or the aloofness of Jimmy Carter and his team. The amiable Reagan was especially skillful at giving speeches and gaining positive coverage through friendly relations with individual journalists. Maynard Parker, *Newsweek*'s editor at the time, told writer Mark Hertsgaard that most reporters covering Reagan "genuinely like the man and find it difficult to be as tough as they might like."[1]

Reagan's aides made sure to feed reporters enough information to meet their need to produce a daily story. "You give them the line of the day, you give them press briefings, you give them facts, access to people who will speak on the record," explained Leslie Janka, a Reagan press officer. "You do that long enough, they're going to stop bringing their own stories, and stop being investigative reporters of any kind, even modestly so." Janka called it "manipulation by inundation."[2] Jody Powell, Carter's press secretary, gave the Reagan team a tip of the hat: "They've been able to get reporters on the things they want them on and away from the things they don't want them on."[3]

The Reagan administration made clear it was determined to restore the power of the presidency vis-à-vis the press and put a lid on information it wanted to keep hidden. It interpreted the Freedom of Information Act as narrowly as possible and reversed Carter's policy of making more government documents available to the media and public. Under an executive order signed by Reagan, government officials could classify documents "top secret" without considering "the public's interest in access to government information." The administration also imposed tight press restrictions during real events that might make the president look bad. When U.S. forces invaded the tiny nation of Grenada, for example, Reagan ordered a complete press blackout of the fighting. Reporters grumbled, but the White House succeeded in avoiding coverage of any civilian casualties.

Deaver, who was like a surrogate son to the president, and other advisers understood how to stage events that put Reagan—a professional actor—in a positive light for television cameras. They went around the Washington press corps by using advertisements, weekly radio addresses, and a new White House News Service that sent Reagan's versions of events directly to small newspapers and radio stations. To avoid being asked difficult questions, Reagan held fewer news conferences than any president since Calvin Coolidge. Whenever he walked from the White House to his helicopter, his aides ordered the pilot to turn the engine on early to drown out any pesky questions while the president smiled and waved. In contrast with the complaints of Nixon and his staff, Reagan's aides were usually pleased with the coverage journalists gave him through most of his two terms. Until the Iran-Contra scandal plagued the end of his second term, Deaver said, "Ronald Reagan enjoyed the most generous treatment by the press of any President in the postwar era."[4]

The Reagan White House, of course, could not control the press completely. Investigative reporters still hunted for scandals and found plenty to write about. In 1981, the United Press International reported that Richard Allen, Reagan's national security adviser, had taken a $1,000 bribe from Japanese journalists to arrange an interview with Reagan's wife, Nancy. The press pursued the story until Allen resigned on the same day the White House counsel's office concluded he had committed no crimes.[5]

The coverage of the Allen affair and other scandals did not seem to hurt Reagan. The president and his staff were so effective at keeping critical information from marring his popularity that he was called "The Teflon President." Like the Nixon administration, the Reagan White House often publicly blamed the press for unfair coverage; the strategy worked for Reagan even if it did not in the end for Nixon. The press, aware of Reagan's popularity and accusations that it was too liberal, backed off from the aggressiveness it showed other recent presidents. Reporters ended up giving Reagan gentler treatment than any president since Kennedy.[6]

The effectiveness of the White House press strategy helps explain why journalists were slow to investigate a government outrage that may have exceeded Watergate in its seriousness: the Iran-Contra scandal. Reporters had sniffed around the edges of the story before the scandal erupted, but most were thrown off the trail by administration assurances that nothing fishy was happening. A few months after Reagan began his second term, the *New York Times* and *Washington Post* revealed that National Security Council staffer Lieutenant Colonel Oliver North was providing military advice to the Contras, a rebel group fighting the leftist Nicaraguan government. The major media, however, failed to pursue evidence that the administration was encouraging an elaborate private network to arm the Contras. In 1985 and 1986, John Wallach, foreign editor for Hearst Newspapers, reported that the administration was conducting secret negotiations with the terrorist-supporting Iranian government, but other newspapers did not pick up the story. In the spring and summer of 1986, Jack Anderson and his colleague Dale Van Atta wrote that the Reagan administration was cutting secret deals to send weapons to the Iranians; the rest of the press did not pursue this angle either. Reporters were not reading each other's work, and as a result the dots were not being connected.[7]

A Lebanese magazine, *al Shiraa,* finally connected the dots in November 1986. It disclosed that Reagan administration officials had arranged the sale of antitank and antiaircraft missiles to Iran in return for the release of seven U.S. hostages held by pro-Iranian terrorists in Lebanon. The money from the Iranians was then used

to fund the Contra battle to overthrow the Nicaraguan government. As political scientist Larry Sabato noted, the scheme "vio-
lated American law and policy all around: Arms sales to Iran were
prohibited, the U.S. government had long forbidden ransom of
any sort for hostages, and it was illegal to fund the Contras above
the limits set by Congress."[8]

The Iran–Contra scandal bore resemblances to Watergate. Both
the Nixon and Reagan administrations created secret operating
units to carry out their policies, developed new theories of executive power to justify violating legislative and judicial rules, and
used adventurers with shadowy pasts rather than regular government professionals to do special tasks. They also both lied to the
public, the media, and Congress about their covert activities.[9] By
early December 1986, more than half of the people surveyed in
a national poll thought the Iran–Contra crisis was at least as serious as Watergate. Reagan's approval rating dropped 21 percentage
points after the link between selling arms to the Iranians and funding the Contras was made public.[10]

In contrast with Nixon's handling of Watergate, the Reagan
White House limited harm to itself by responding quickly to the
allegations. Oliver North and Admiral John Poindexter, two of the
aides most involved in the arms sales, left the administration. Attorney General Edwin Meese was the first to reveal that proceeds
from the missile sales were used to fund the Contras, thus shaping
the story before the press learned about it. Learning from Nixon's
mistakes, Reagan and his aides continued to build cordial relations
with individual journalists while accusing the press as a whole of
hurting U.S. interests by aggressively pursuing the story. "What is
driving me up the wall is that this wasn't a failure until the press
got a tip from that rag in Beirut and began to play it up," Reagan
said in an interview five weeks after the arms sales were revealed.

"This thing boils down to a great irresponsibility on the part of the press."[11]

As Congress held hearings and some critics suggested impeachment, Reagan appointed a three-man commission headed by former Senator John Tower to investigate the scandal. The Tower Commission blamed North, Poindexter, CIA Director William Casey, and National Security Adviser Robert McFarlane for running a clandestine foreign and military policy. The commission also faulted Reagan for being disengaged but absolved him of having prior knowledge of the illegal deals. With no smoking gun to prove Reagan's knowledge of crimes like Nixon's tapes did, the president avoided impeachment.

Iran-Contra stories saturated the news for several months, but in contrast with the work of Woodward, Bernstein, and other Watergate reporters, the U.S. press unearthed little that was new. Instead of pursuing their own investigations, many reporters focused their stories on the more easily covered question of who was winning the public relations battle between the White House and its critics. The Reagan administration cleverly framed the impeachment debate around the question of whether the president knew about the diversion of funds to the Contras, which was never proven. Reagan's poll numbers slowly recovered, reaching a 63 percent approval rating by the end of his second term, the same as before the Iran-Contra deal became public. "The government's obfuscation was far superior than during Watergate," noted Barry Sussman, who after his days as a *Post* editor went on to run the Nieman Watchdog Journalism Project at Harvard University.[12]

The obfuscation continued when Vice President George H. W. Bush ran for president in 1988. Few journalists probed his connections with Iran-Contra. When CBS anchorman Dan Rather interviewed Bush, the vice president aggressively deflected

Rather's questions about the topic. Subsequent press coverage of the interview emphasized the confrontation between the two rather than Bush's evasive answers. By the time Oliver North's trial started in February 1989, most reporters were treating Iran-Contra as a courtroom drama rather than a constitutional crisis. The trial revealed that administration officials, with Reagan and Bush's knowledge and approval, used money Congress had appropriated for other purposes to secretly support the Contras despite a congressional ban, a potentially impeachable offense. The press covered this startling revelation for a day but then mostly dropped it as the trial moved on to other matters.

After North's trial and Bush's interview with Rather, most reporters—with the exception of the *Washington Post*'s David Hoffman—did not investigate the scandal further. Journalists were overwhelmed by the information's complexity, frustrated by the public's fleeting interest in the scandal, intimidated by the administration's allegations of bias, and stymied by the inability of congressional committees to follow the trail of evidence. As a result, Reagan and Bush escaped without major damage to their reputations. "The fervor with which serious journalists pursued Watergate was missing," observed Scott Armstrong, who had been a Senate Watergate committee investigator. "[T]he press seemed to share, rather than challenge, Congress's willingness to pass the buck."[13]

Reporters' ability to probe government policies was blunted by increasingly sophisticated public relations campaigns. After Iraq invaded Kuwait in 1990, for instance, a group called Citizens for a Free Kuwait spent more than $12 million to hire the largest public relations company in the world, Hill & Knowlton, and a dozen other PR firms. Together they conducted a campaign to sway American public opinion in favor of sending U.S. forces to fight

Iraq. Hill & Knowlton arranged a highly publicized appearance by a sobbing fifteen-year-old girl who told a phony story about Iraqi troops killing premature babies by stealing their incubators. It hid the fact that she was the daughter of Kuwait's ambassador to the United States and may not have been in Kuwait at the time she said the atrocities occurred. Hill & Knowlton also produced a film about the alleged murder of the babies, published a book titled *The Rape of Kuwait,* and created video news releases that ran on news shows around the country. The fake story ended up being repeated frequently by journalists, President Bush, and congressmen. It was one of the reasons the Senate voted to authorize a war against Iraq.[14]

Even though the press did not fully scrutinize the case for the Gulf War, reporters investigated other aspects of Bush's administration. After Bush nominated John Tower as his secretary of defense, journalists began checking allegations that Tower was a heavy drinker and womanizer who played a questionable role in the awarding of Pentagon contracts. The Senate rejected Tower's nomination because of the stories. After Bush lost his 1992 reelection battle to Democrat Bill Clinton, the *Washington Post* investigated whether officials in Bush's State Department had improperly gone through Clinton's passport file. Bush complained bitterly about the press coverage of what was dubbed "Passportgate." "The damn *Post* is hostile to a core—nasty to the core," he wrote in his diary.[15] Bush griped in a letter to Woodward that too many journalists were trying to emulate his and other journalists' work during Watergate. "I think Watergate and the Vietnam War are the two things that moved Beltway journalism into this aggressive, intrusive, 'take no prisoners' kind of reporting that I can now say I find offensive," Bush wrote.[16]

The kind of reporting Bush found offensive was growing. In

her book *Scandal,* Suzanne Garment counted more than four hundred candidates for federal office and senior government officials accused by the press of wrongdoing in the fifteen years following Watergate. These scandals drained public officials' time and energy, created low government morale, damaged the legitimacy of national leaders, and diverted attention away from other more important issues, Garment said.[17]

While many reporters searched for the next controversy, they missed important stories such as the growth of terrorism networks around the world and the financial wrongdoing that led to the multibillion-dollar collapse of the savings and loan industry. Reporter Paul Rodriguez of the *Washington Times* was one of the few to investigate misdeeds by the Democratic controlled Congress. During the savings and loan disaster, Rodriguez described how five senators, known as the "Keating Five," had intervened with regulators on behalf of a big campaign contributor with ties to savings and loan banks. Rodriguez also helped uncover embezzlement in the House of Representatives post office, excessive banking overdrafts by House members, and irregularities in Speaker of the House Jim Wright's finances.[18]

The public agreed with Bush that the relationship between politicians and the press had grown too destructive. Since Watergate, trust in both the government and the media had plummeted. Whereas three-quarters of people surveyed in 1972 said they had either a great deal or fair amount of confidence in government to solve problems, by 1993 only 42 percent did.[19] Public confidence in the press suffered the steepest decline of any U.S. institution. A poll conducted in 1995 found that half of the five hundred adults surveyed said they had a "very negative" or "somewhat negative" impression of the news media. Survey respondents said news organizations were biased, tried to cover up their mistakes, did not care about people, and got in the way of solving problems. Media companies were viewed as greedy, faceless corporations rather than watchdogs of democracy. In a survey conducted at the end of the century, nearly three out of four people said the press was too sensationalistic.[20]

The rampant use of anonymous sources whose identities were cloaked with phrases such as "a high White House official" deepened the public's mistrust. Readers were left to wonder if these anonymous sources had hidden agendas, did not really know what they were talking about, or maybe did not even exist. Reporters' constant quests for scoops on the latest controversy also increased the public's cynicism. "It saps people's confidence in politics and public officials, and it erodes both the standing and the standards of journalism," the *Washington Post*'s David Broder wrote in a 1994 column. "If the assumption is that nothing is on the level, nothing is what it seems, then citizenship becomes a game for fools and there is no point in trying to stay informed."[21]

The steady stream of exposés in the press left many people thinking that perhaps it was impossible to end corruption and abuse. Time after time, investigative reporters revealed wrongdoing, leaving readers and viewers with the hope that villains would be defeated and conditions improved, only to learn of some new outrage in the next story.[22] In his book *Bowling Alone,* Robert Putnam documented the downward spiral in public trust and civic engagement since the mid-1960s. The number of people voting dropped by about a quarter, and the portion of the population taking part in civic or political groups declined 40 percent. Participation in election campaigns and public meetings also fell.[23]

Why such cynicism about public institutions? Throughout the 1980s and 1990s, Donald Barlett and James Steele investigated in the pages of the *Philadelphia Inquirer* some of the reasons. In 1989, they won their second Pulitzer for "The Great Tax Giveaway," which documented how the Tax Reform Act of 1986 was filled with loopholes for politically connected businesses and wealthy people without actually naming them. Barlett and Steele went through the 925-page bill line by line to find hundreds of mysterious tax breaks worth billions of dollars for the fortunate few. With the aid of the *Philadelphia Inquirer*'s librarians, they identified these people and businesses by searching through news archives and public documents. For example, one tax break applied only to widows in Tarrant County, Texas, whose spouse died on October 28, 1983, with an estate not exceeding $12.5 million. Barlett and Steele found the one lucky woman who could save an estimated four million dollars from this line in the law; she told them that Speaker of the House Jim Wright had given her the break. The next time congressmen met to revise the tax code, they avoided giving any more special breaks, calling it "The Philadelphia Rule" because they worried about additional Barlett and Steele scrutiny.[24]

In 1996, Barlett and Steele once again explored the reasons for widespread discontent with their monumental "America: Who Stole the Dream?" After interviewing hundreds of people around the country and reviewing 100,000 pages of documents, they concluded that three decades worth of government policies were denying millions of people any hope of a middle-class lifestyle. Using divorce records, they found the example of an industrialist in New Jersey who paid more for the care of his family dog than he paid for the pension of a worker he had fired.[25]

Barlett and Steele were not the only investigative reporters to flourish at the *Inquirer* in the 1970s and 1980s. Editor Eugene Roberts, a soft-spoken man who could command attention with a few well-chosen words, had a simple philosophy: "Every reporter should be a digging reporter."[26] The award-winning stories under his reign included Tim Weiner's probe of a secret Pentagon budget, John Woestendiecks's investigation of a wrongful murder conviction, Arthur Howe's revelations of IRS deficiencies, and Bill Marimow's discovery of abuse by the Philadelphia Police Department's canine unit. Key to the *Inquirer's* success was that Roberts, former editor John McMullan, and owner John Knight never caved in to companies and government officials who complained about investigative stories. Corporate officials would fly to Philadelphia to pressure the *Inquirer* to back away from its investigations, but Knight and the editors never did.[27]

In the meantime, Barlett and Steele's investigation of Philadelphia courts and Philip Meyer's work on the Detroit riots encouraged more reporters to use computers to keep track of information and analyze data. In 1985, Elliot Jaspin persuaded his bosses at the *Providence Journal* to let him use the newspaper's mainframe computer to match lists of the state's 1,367 school bus drivers with records of criminal convictions and traffic violations. Jaspin and reporter Maria Johnson discovered that some of the bus drivers had criminal records for drug dealing and at least a quarter had committed traffic violations in the prior three years. Some drivers had as many as twenty tickets.[28]

For another investigation, Jaspin analyzed a computer tape containing 30,000 records from a state agency that was supposed to sell tax-free bonds to help people with low and moderate incomes buy homes. He found that the agency had created a secret pool to give home loans at reduced rates to "special" people including the daughter of a former governor, the son of a former state treasurer, and several employees of the agency. Jaspin's reporting led to twenty-five indictments, the conviction of the agency's director, and the program's complete overhaul. Computer-assisted reporting made the project possible; Jaspin calculated it would have taken him seventy-three weeks to review the agency's records by hand.[29]

In 1989, Jaspin moved to the University of Missouri to start what eventually became the National Institute of Computer-Assisted Reporting, or NICAR. During this era, most journalists—some of them technophobes, many of them crunched for time—hesitated to learn the new technology. But governments were starting to store a treasure trove of data on computer tapes, and the spread of desktop computers made it easier to use spreadsheets and other software to analyze that information. Training also helped. During an eighteen-month span in the mid-1990s, about five thousand journalists attended seminars hosted by NICAR and its sister organization IRE. "They took the fear and anxiety away," Meyer observed. "They kept sharing examples and making people want to do it."[30]

Bill Dedman of the *Atlanta Journal-Constitution* produced one of the most powerful computer-assisted investigations. In 1988, he sifted through massive amounts of data to expose how Atlanta banks regularly favored whites over blacks when making mortgage loans. Dedman's story won a Pulitzer and had an immediate impact: Atlanta banks agreed to lend $65 million at below-prime interest rates in black neighborhoods, and Congress strengthened laws banning discrimination when making loans.[31]

The value of computer-assisted reporting proved itself again after Hurricane Andrew devastated more than 80,000 Florida homes in 1992. To find out why some homes were damaged and others were not, Stephen Doig of the *Miami Herald* merged databases of property records with damage reports from the storm. Doig described what happened next:

When I ran the numbers, I found the first smoking gun of my career. There was no pattern to be seen when I compared storm damage to such variables as home value, type of construction, location or distance from the shore. But there was a strong, counter-intuitive pattern connected to the year of construction: The newer the home, the more likely to be destroyed. We went on to uncover the reasons for this in other datasets we gathered, including millions of records of often-hasty building inspections and millions of dollars in campaign contributions to politicians who had approved weakened building codes at the urging of the construction industry.[32]

The *Herald* team concluded that homes built since 1979 were three times more likely to collapse during the storm than those built earlier.[33]

Successful investigations like Doig's, training by NICAR and IRE, the growing availability of powerful computers, and the creation of electronic versions of government records led to a surge of computer-assisted reporting. By 1996, computers had played a major role in the reporting of Pulitzer winners six years in a row. At first only newspaper chains, broadcast networks, and large publications could afford computer-assisted reporting on a regular basis. Gaining access to mainframe computers, hiring specialists, buying large databases, and providing training were expensive. Sarah Cohen, a *Tampa Tribune* reporter in the early 1990s, used to borrow the computer of a university professor while he played golf so she could analyze census data. But soon nearly all reporters had computers at their desks, and the spread of the World Wide Web allowed them to explore public records with the click of a mouse instead of searching through dusty file rooms. Computer-assisted reporting became part of daily newsgathering rather than the domain of elite investigative units working on huge projects.[34]

But as IRE Executive Director John Ullmann conducted training sessions around the country, he noticed something troubling: newspaper managers were putting less emphasis on hard-hitting investigative stories. Instead they were requiring shorter stories, fluffier topics, and bigger photos and graphics.[35] Mounting economic pressures, a growing emphasis on celebrity news and sensationalism, and a rising number of expensive lawsuits were crippling the watchdog press.

The *Washington Post* had faced one of those costly lawsuits in 1980 when Mobil Oil Corp's president, William Tavoulareas, sued the newspaper, Bradlee, Woodward, and two *Post* reporters for $50 million. Tavoulareas said he was libeled by a *Post* story that alleged he had used his corporation's assets to improperly help his son become a partner in a shipping company. Although the story was extensively reported, it contained small errors, and the jury and a three-judge U.S. Court of Appeals panel ruled against the newspaper. The panel criticized Woodward, who had edited the story, suggesting the mistakes happened because he was out to enhance his reputation as a high-impact investigator. Eight years later, the full appeals court finally ruled in Woodward and the *Post*'s favor. The *Post* ended up spending $1 million, which was not reimbursed by its insurance company, and countless hours of staff time to defend itself.[36]

The Tavoulareas case was not the only legal attack against investigative reporters. Despite the 1964 *Sullivan* ruling that theoretically made it more difficult to prove libel allegations, the number of lawsuits filed against news organizations actually increased in the next two decades. By the mid-1980s, *60 Minutes* alone had been sued more than 150 times. Before 1980, only one libel award had been settled for more than a million dollars. By the mid-1980s, two dozen cases had topped a million dollars. Nearly two-thirds of investigative reporters surveyed in 1983 agreed that "stories are not being covered that ought to be covered, because of recent libel judgments." By the 1990s, journalists were being sued not just for libel but also harassment, fraud, trespass, conspiracy, and even wrongful death.[37] The lawsuits often shifted public scrutiny away from the big businesses and powerful people who were the targets of investigative stories and toward the news-gathering techniques of reporters.

In 1982, retired General William Westmoreland sued Mike Wallace and CBS for $120 million after they reported in a documentary that Westmoreland had ordered his subordinates to lie to Congress, President Johnson, and the American public during the Vietnam War. An internal CBS review concluded that the documentary was unfair and did not meet the network's standards. The general withdrew the lawsuit after CBS agreed to pay his legal bills and issued a statement saying it did not mean to suggest he was dishonorable. A year after the Westmoreland story, Israeli General Ariel Sharon sued *Time* magazine for reporting he had encouraged a massacre of more than five hundred Palestinian women and children in Lebanese refugee camps. After a jury ruled *Time* had libeled Sharon because it could not document all the accusations against him, Sharon declared victory and did not pursue damages against the magazine.[38]

By 1984, plaintiffs were winning 83 percent of libel cases decided by juries, who tended to sympathize more with people who said journalists wounded their reputations rather than with media companies. Although about 70 percent of the libel rulings were reversed on appeal, the cases were expensive to defend; the Westmoreland case, for example cost CBS $10 million in legal expenses.

The lawsuits led to rising libel insurance costs, lost staff time, and damage to journalists' prestige. Large media companies could absorb the cost, but many small publications could not. Interviews with editors and media lawyers in the mid-1980s found many instances when publications decided not to run stories because they feared lawsuits.[39]

The fear of legal action increased after NBC's *Dateline* reported in 1992 that General Motors pickup trucks with external gas tanks were dangerous. To make the story more visually dramatic, the producers created a fiery test crash using a GM truck rigged with hidden explosives attached to its gas tank. General Motors sued NBC for libel and launched a publicity blitz attacking *Dateline* for rigging the explosion. The lawsuit turned public attention away from the trucks' safety and toward *Dateline*'s reporting tactics. NBC backed down even though the fuel tank design had contributed to as many as three hundred deaths, and GM documents showed the company had been concerned about the truck's design for many years. NBC issued an on-air apology, accepted its news president's resignation, fired three producers, and paid GM an estimated $2 million settlement.[40]

The lawsuits kept coming. The same year as the General Motors story, two producers from the ABC newsmagazine *Primetime Live* took jobs at Food Lion grocery stores after using fake names and concealing their ABC affiliation on their applications. The producers put hidden cameras in their hats and taped Food Lion workers selling cheese gnawed by rats, washing old fish in bleach to make them stink less, and repackaging expired meat in barbecue sauce to make it smell better. Food Lion sued ABC and its Capital Cities owners for trespass, conspiracy, breach of fiduciary duties, and fraud because the producers used phony résumés. Upset with the producers' deceptive techniques, the jury ruled against ABC and awarded Food Lion $5.5 million. Although an appeals court eventually reduced the penalty to two dollars, the jury's verdict sent a chill through the journalism world.[41]

The amount of money involved in the legal attacks escalated in 1994 when Philip Morris and R. J. Reynolds sued ABC for more than $10 billion in libel damages over a *Day One* investigation. The show had exposed tobacco makers manipulating nicotine levels to keep smokers addicted to their products. ABC defended itself for a year but eventually agreed to a settlement to make the case go away as the network neared a merger with Walt Disney Company. Although it had substantial evidence to support its accusations against the tobacco industry, ABC aired a prime-time apology and reimbursed the companies about $15 million in legal fees. ABC also canceled a documentary detailing Reagan administration pressure on Asian countries to open their markets to U.S. tobacco products.[42]

CBS bowed to similar pressure in 1995 when it canceled a *60 Minutes* segment produced by Lowell Bergman. The segment featured an interview with a Brown & Williamson whistle-blower who said he had evidence proving the tobacco company had concealed that cigarettes are addictive and harmful. The network's attorneys feared that Brown & Williamson would sue it for persuading the man to divulge internal company practices. The interview was finally broadcast by *60 Minutes* after the *Wall Street Journal* published a story about the whistle-blower's accusations; the story became the basis for the 1999 movie *The Insider.*[43]

Like CBS, the Gannett chain blinked when faced with a legal attack against the muckraking of one of its newspapers, the *Cincinnati Enquirer.* In 1998, the *Enquirer* ran an extensive investigation of Chiquita Brands International's economic, political, environmental, and legal troubles. Gannett had its own troubles, however, when it was discovered that one of its reporters had broken into the banana company's voice mail system hundreds of times. Gannett paid Chiquita $14 million, and the *Enquirer* published a front-page apology. Even though the facts in the stories were never proven inaccurate, the illegal activities doomed the project. The size of the payout sent a sobering message to investigative reporters and their editors. "Aggressive business interests and celebrities of every stripe are using their wealth and a new arsenal of legal tactics to attack enterprise reporting," media lawyer Bruce Sanford warned. "Media companies, with some reason, are caving. They know that they will not find the receptive audiences they once experienced in court."[44]

In addition to lawsuits, corporations found other ways to block muckraking. They hired their own investigators to spy on journalists, publicly questioned reporters' techniques, and preempted damaging stories with their own versions of events. When Bill Moyers was finishing a 1993 documentary for the PBS show *Frontline* about the impact of chemicals in food, the pesticide industry mounted a public relations blitz to discredit the broadcast before it aired. "Television reviewers and editorial page editors were flooded in advance with pro-industry propaganda," Moyers recalled. "There was a whispering campaign. A *Washington Post* columnist took a dig at the broadcast on the morning of the day it aired—without even having seen it—and later confessed to me that the dirt had been supplied by a top lobbyist for the chemical industry."[45]

The press faced other pressures that weakened muckraking. More readers were migrating to the suburbs and getting news from television and eventually the Internet, sapping the big-city newspapers that had published the most investigative work. From the 1980s to the 1990s, the number of cities with competing daily newspapers dropped from thirty-five to a dozen. Newspapers such as the *Cleveland Plain Dealer* disbanded investigative teams, created in the wake of Watergate, because they were too costly.[46] The number of investigative stories at three newspapers known for their watchdog journalism—the *Philadelphia Inquirer, Chicago Tribune,* and *St. Louis Post-Dispatch*—declined from sixty-nine during a three-month span in 1980 to twenty during the same three months in 1995.[47]

In 1983, Ben Bagdikian warned in his book *The Media Monopoly* that a few large corporations were constricting the flow of news in America. With each successive edition of *The Media Monopoly,* his warnings about the increasing concentration of power in journalism grew grimmer. By the time the fifth edition was published in 1997, Bagdikian wrote,

> In the last five years, a small number of the country's largest industrial corporations has acquired more public communications power—including ownership of the news—than any private businesses have ever before possessed in world history. . . .
>
> Perhaps the most troubling power of the new cartel is its control of the main body of news and public affairs information. The reporting of news has always been a commercial enterprise and this has always created conflicts of interest. But the behavior of the new corporate controllers of public information has produced a higher level of manipulation of news to pursue the owners' other financial and political goals. In the process, there has been a parallel shrinkage of any sense of obligation to serve the noncommercial information needs of public citizenship.[48]

In 1984, Bagdikian wrote that fifty corporations controlled the media. That number had shrunk to ten by the time he published the 1997 edition of his book. In 2004, he wrote, it was down to five: Time Warner, Walt Disney, Viacom, Rupert Murdoch's News Corporation, and the German company Bertelsmann.[49] The number of daily newspapers owned by chains more than doubled between 1960 and 1986 to 1,158, while the number of independent dailies fell from 1,203 to 499. Sometimes the chains improved the content of formerly independent newspapers. The large companies had greater human and capital resources, could offer more diverse information and opinions, and were less dependent on a few advertisers whom local owners might feel pressured to please.[50]

But the increasing concentration of ownership raised the risk of greater homogenization of news. Media company stocks were traded more often on Wall Street, placing control in the hands of large institutions such as pension funds, insurance companies, and mutual funds with more interest in quarterly profits than good journalism. Even as competition from other media increased, stockholders demanded fatter profits. Sometimes those profit rates were as high as 40 to 50 percent for local television news departments. Newspapers could earn profits between 20 and 30 percent, much higher than most industries received.[51]

Nowhere did the push for higher earnings have a heavier impact on investigative reporting than at the *Philadelphia Inquirer.* When Gene Roberts became the *Inquirer's* editor in 1972, owner John Knight gave him the resources to emphasize investigative stories and hire more reporters. The newspaper won a remarkable seventeen Pulitzer Prizes in eighteen years while its circulation jumped nearly 20 percent. Roberts was, in the words of former *Chicago Tribune* Editor James Squires, "far and away the most widely respected newspaper editor in the business." But after Knight merged with the Ridder chain to become Knight Ridder, corporate headquarters pressured Roberts to cut costs and boost profits. His emphasis on hard-hitting, expensive investigative reporting conflicted with the chain's "market-driven, customer-service brand of corporate journalism," Squires said.[52]

Roberts finally quit in 1990. His successors were forced to freeze hiring and cut the amount of space devoted to news as shareholders demanded higher earnings. In 1998, a Merrill Lynch stock analyst encouraged investors to buy Knight Ridder stock because its newspapers were no longer focused on "producing Pulitzer Prizes instead of profits." Unfortunately, the *Inquirer* was attracting fewer readers along with fewer prizes. The *Inquirer* won only one Pulitzer in the decade after Roberts left, and its daily circulation dropped from 520,000 to 365,000 in eleven years.[53] A similar story occurred at the *Journal* and *Constitution* in Atlanta, where executives at the newspapers' owner, Cox Communications, pressured Editor Bill Kovach to leave in 1988 despite his staff earning Pulitzer Prizes two years in a row.[54] Similar cutbacks occurred in publications across the country, and readers noticed the difference.

After Roberts quit, Barlett and Steele left the *Inquirer* to work for *Time*. Among their investigations for the magazine was a May 2000 cover story unmasking the inequities of a pending bankruptcy reform bill being pushed through Congress; the bill died soon after Barlett and Steele's story appeared. The story included their usual thorough analysis of documents, powerful interviews, and outrage at how average Americans were getting the short end of the government and corporate stick. Despite winning two National Magazine Awards, Barlett and Steele lost their jobs at *Time* in 2006 when it decided to cut costs. *Vanity Fair* hired them a few months later.[55]

As Barlett and Steele learned, the magazine market was changing. Some of the largest national publications such as *Life, Look,* and the *Saturday Evening Post* had become extinct, while *Time*'s and *Newsweek*'s readership stagnated. Americans still read magazines, but they were gravitating toward niche publications focusing on health tips, hobbies, business advice, and other specialized interests rather than general news. In response, the major news weeklies cut back the amount of space they devoted to hard news and investigations while increasing their coverage of entertainment and other features.[56]

Television news was also changing. By 1986, the three big networks had been absorbed by large corporations: NBC by General Electric, CBS by Loews Corporation and eventually Westinghouse, and ABC by Capital Cities Communications and later Disney. The previous owners had been willing to let the news divisions operate at low profit margins in return for providing prestige. The new owners demanded that news operations earn more money and slash costs in order to maximize stockholder returns. They closed foreign news bureaus and cut reporting staffs. CBS News alone eliminated nearly 400 jobs between 1985 and 1987. Prime-time documentaries disappeared after the elimination of regulations requiring the networks to provide public-service programs. News divisions meanwhile avoided assigning reporters to investigate the activities of their corporate owners. ABC was loudly criticized when one of its newsmagazines backed away from a story that shed negative light on its corporate sister Disney World. An NBC *Today Show* segment on consumer boycotts failed to mention that one of the nation's largest boycotts was against NBC's owner, General Electric.[57]

The Cable News Network, better known as CNN, was born in 1980 and soon challenged the three broadcast networks with news reports from around the world. While it excelled at providing live coverage of breaking events, CNN rarely offered original investigative reporting. CNN was followed into the cable news market by Fox News and MSNBC, which did not offer much muckraking either. The growth of these cable channels and the Internet created a twenty-four-hour news cycle. Instead of preparing stories for one appearance on the nightly news or in the morning newspaper, journalists now needed to update their reports throughout the day. This constant need to fill airtime made it tougher for reporters to devote the attention needed to probe into issues that had not been covered before. It also allowed the targets of investigations to start spinning their side of the story immediately. "If we had cable television during Watergate, Nixon would have been on Larry King within a week," Sussman said, referring to the cable television talk show host.[58]

The pace of mergers accelerated after Congress passed the 1996 Telecommunications Act. Media companies lobbied intensely for the law and gave four million dollars in congressional campaign contributions in the years leading to the bill's passage. The act changed sixty-two years of communications law by allowing single companies to own more than one radio station in the same metropolitan area, to own television and cable systems in the same market, and to reach up to 35 percent of American television watchers. Clear Channel, for example, took advantage of the new law to gobble up radio stations until it owned 1,200 by 2001. This growing concentration of power in the hands of a few media firms, which tend to be politically conservative, led the press to pay little attention to the country's growing disparity of wealth, the struggles of America's poorest families, or government largesse to large corporations.[59]

A lack of newsroom diversity further narrowed what reporters covered. Because of their high status within the newsroom, investigative reporting jobs were usually given to men, who continued to dominate management. A review of investigative projects from the 1960s to 1990s found that reporting on women, minorities, and gays and lesbians was often repetitive, with many of the stories focusing on the same half-dozen subjects, often emphasizing the sensational rather than the complex.[60] When Deborah Nelson, an award-winning investigative reporter, first started as a journalist in the 1970s, a top editor tried to make her the newspaper's fashion editor even though she "didn't know the difference between silk and polyester."[61]

The hunt for additional readers and viewers led media companies to create more content aimed at young adults, who are the people least interested in watchdog news but most desired by advertisers. Network, cable, and local newscasts grew more sensationalistic and more obsessed with celebrity coverage as they competed for viewers between the ages of eighteen and thirty-four. A turning point came in 1994 when actor and former football star O. J. Simpson was charged with murdering his ex-wife and her friend. The coverage saturated the airwaves from the day CNN televised police chasing Simpson's white sports utility vehicle down a Los Angeles freeway until his acquittal. The Simpson story left less time on newscasts for coverage of government, business, and other weightier subjects; it received more television time than the 1991 Gulf War did. Similar nonstop coverage occurred again when Princess Diana died in a 1997 car crash.[62]

While news shows pumped up their celebrity coverage, more journalists became celebrities themselves like Woodward and Bernstein had after Watergate. Cable talk shows such as *Crossfire* and *The McLaughlin Group,* where journalists argued over the issues of the day, turned previously obscure reporters into household names. News anchors and other well-known journalists became wealthy as they gained fame. By the 1980s, CBS anchorman Dan Rather enjoyed a contract worth $36 million over ten years. In 1998, CNN signed talk show host Larry King to a $7 million deal while cutting seventy out of three hundred positions—nearly a quarter of the staff—at its *Headline News.* By 2001, Peter Jennings of ABC News was said to earn more than $10 million annually.[63]

In the 1980s and 1990s, the most extensive investigative stories on television continued to air on the prime-time magazines. From *60 Minutes,* viewers learned about the deadly trade in fake medicine around the world and one hundred portable nuclear bombs missing from Russian facilities. ABC's *Primetime Live* exposed the high-pressure moneymaking tactics of three prominent televangelists and uncovered a black market in human parts taken from executed Chinese prisoners. In 1992, *Dateline NBC* traveled to Bangladesh, where reporters found children working in sweatshop factories to make clothes that ended up on the shelves of Wal-Mart stores despite the giant retailer's "Made in the U.S.A." advertising campaign.[64]

But the drive for more viewers led the prime-time magazines to feature quicker pacing and flashier graphics and less investigative reporting. *NBC Reports* accelerated this trend in 1987 with the airing of *Scared Sexless* and *Connie Chung: Life in the Fat Lane,* which both gained high ratings. By the late 1990s, CBS, NBC, ABC, and CNN were televising eleven newsmagazines each week, but three-quarters of their content was devoted to crime, celebrity entertainment, lifestyles and behavior, and other kinds of "people" stories. Only 8 percent of the stories focused on politics, national security, education, the military, economics, foreign affairs, or social welfare issues. The PBS show *Frontline,* launched in 1983, was one of the few that consistently aired long-form documentaries. Among the topics it investigated were chemical pollution in drinking water, mortgage-lending discrimination, the rise and fall of Columbian drug kingpin Pablo Escobar, and the shipping of toxic wastes to third world countries.[65]

Local television stations, meanwhile, cut back on their investigative stories. By 2001, nearly half of U.S. commercial television stations were owned by twenty-five chains, which were less likely than independent stations to air hard news stories. A 2002 survey of 103 television newsrooms found that only a quarter had full-time investigative units and less than one out of every 150 stories featured original, station-initiated investigations.[66]

Instead of spending money on producing their own watchdog projects, many stations bought less-expensive prepackaged stories sold by consultants. These packages contained ready-made scripts and videos the local stations could use to create stories they promoted as their own. Rather than trying to hold businesses, governments, and other powerful institutions accountable, these prepackaged reports often focused on consumer and safety tips.[67] Some stations defied the trend and did their own muckraking. KHOU in Houston revealed that Ford Explorer sport utility vehicles with Firestone tires were involved in dozens of fatal accidents. WXYZ in Detroit discovered that Michigan's government had forcibly sterilized thousands of people in institutions for the mentally retarded. Salt Lake City's KTVX unearthed evidence of corruption in the bidding for the 2002 Winter Olympics.[68]

Most of the media, however, were moving away from watchdog stories. The number of stories about government dropped 38 percent, and coverage of international affairs fell 25 percent in the three major networks' newscasts, the *New York Times* and *Los Angeles Times* front pages, and the covers of *Time* and *Newsweek* between 1977 and 1997. Meanwhile, the amount of stories about entertainment and celebrities tripled. Even when covering government, reporters focused more on investigating the personal lives of politicians. Democrat Gary Hart's presidential candidacy was derailed in 1987 after *Miami Herald* reporters staked out his townhouse and reported he had spent the night with a woman other than his wife.[69]

Gossip and sensationalism reached its zenith during Bill Clinton's presidency. Reporters, especially at the *New York Times* and *Wall Street Journal,* devoted significant time and space to investigating whether the president and his wife, Hillary, committed any crimes in the land deals known as Whitewater. No crimes were ever proven, but a special prosecutor was appointed to investigate the charges, and Clinton spent much of his first term defending himself against Whitewater accusations. The Clintons became embroiled in additional scandals over the firings of White House travel office employees and the suicide of their close aide and friend Vince Foster. As Bob Woodward wrote in his book *Shadow,* "Washington was ablaze with speculation and doubt about the basic integrity of the Clintons and their White House."[70]

That speculation grew more intense in January 1998 when independent journalist Matt Drudge put on his tabloid-style Web site a report that the president was having an affair with White House intern Monica Lewinsky. *Newsweek* originally had delayed publishing the information for lack of confirmation, but once Drudge put it on the Web, mainstream journalists jumped all over the story. They investigated the sordid details of Clinton's relationships with Lewinsky and other women with the same zeal as their coverage of the Simpson trial. The scandal, dubbed "Zippergate," was not confined to the evening news shows, newspapers, and newsmagazines; it spread to talk radio, cable entertainment shows, and celebrity magazines. Misinformation about the Lewinsky scandal flooded the news as the growing popularity of the Internet drove news organizations to post stories twenty-four hours a day to beat their competition. Speculation, unverified allegations, and opinion were mixed together with reporting. The *Wall Street Journal* and *Dallas Morning News* both had to withdraw stories on their Web sites reporting that other people had witnessed encounters between Clinton and Lewinsky. The stories ended up being untrue, although they continued to be discussed on television talk shows.[71]

The use of anonymous sources, common during Watergate, proliferated during the Lewinsky scandal. One study found that less than 20 percent of the sources mentioned in stories about the scandal were clearly identified. Instead of conducting their own investigations, many reporters relied on leaks from the White House and Special Prosecutor Kenneth Starr's office, both of which tried to shape coverage. The press also exposed extramarital affairs by some of the Republicans who were working to impeach Clinton. Clinton became only the second U.S. president to be impeached by the House of Representatives, although the Senate did not convict him. His presidency continued to enjoy favorable poll ratings despite the saturated coverage of his sex life.[72]

During his first term, Clinton had reached out for foreign policy advice from a former president who had his own problems with the press: Richard Nixon. Following his resignation, Nixon spent much of his energy trying to rehabilitate his image. He presented himself through books and speeches as a wise elder statesman steeped in the nuances of government and foreign policy. He also maintained his penchant for secrecy. He fought tenaciously to restrict access to information about his presidency, including White House papers and tapes. He took his case all the way to the Supreme Court, where he lost. Even then, he argued that many of his documents should not be released for national security reasons. Since his death in 1994 at age 81, the gradual release of more tapes has shed light on his triumphs as well as the depth of his Watergate involvement.[73]

The next president to take office after Clinton, George W. Bush, used many of Nixon's arguments—executive privilege and the protection of national security—to make access to information stricter than it had ever been. The result was a government steeped in secrecy and a colossal failure by the press.

SEVEN

MUZZLING THE WATCHDOG

The Bush White House operates a media apparatus far more sophisticated in fighting and discrediting the press and political opponents than the little shop directed by Haldeman and Ehrlichman and Colson and Ziegler.
—Carl Bernstein, 2005

The best of investigative reporting is as good today as it ever was, there just is not as much of it as in the 70s or 80s.
—Gene Roberts, 2007

In December 2000, investigative reporter Greg Palast waded into one of the most contentious political events in American history. As backers of Democrat Al Gore and Republican George W. Bush fought over who should win Florida's electoral votes and thus the presidency, Palast documented how thousands of African Americans had been prevented from voting in the state. Florida Governor Jeb Bush (George W.'s brother) and Secretary of State Katherine Harris, also a leading Bush supporter, had denied them the vote because they were "felons," although the state later admitted that many of them were not criminals. Their votes could have allowed Gore to win.

Palast's story ran in two British newspapers and on BBC television. The Internet magazine *Salon* ran one story by Palast, but no U.S. newspapers or television news programs investigated the missing votes. Not until months later, after the Supreme Court issued a ruling that in effect allowed Bush to win, and after the U.S. Civil Rights Commission produced a report agreeing with Palast's findings, did the American press cover the story of the missing votes. Investigative reporting in America, Palast concluded, was dying. Many reporters, editors, producers, and media owners were timid, and those with courage lacked resources. Too many journalists, he said, did not pursue stories until politicians or other officials made allegations or began their own investigations.[1]

Against this backdrop, George W. Bush became president in 2001. Like most other recent presidents, Bush was committed to strengthening the executive branch and controlling government information. He and his vice president, Dick Cheney, wanted to reverse the decline in presidential power since Watergate and to conduct as much of their work as possible in secret.[2] They pursued a media strategy similar to Nixon's: limit reporters' access to the president, avoid answering serious questions at news conferences, speak directly to the American people via television, and retaliate against reporters whose work the administration disliked. But whereas Nixon felt threatened by the press, Bush and Cheney expressed pure contempt. When a reporter asked Bush how he knew what the public was thinking if he avoided reading newspapers and watching television news, the president responded, "You're assuming that you represent the public. I don't accept that."[3]

Murrey Marder, a former *Washington Post* reporter and founder of the Nieman Foundation's Watchdog Project, noted that no previous president was as determined as Bush to discredit the role of journalists in a democracy. "It soon became clear that Bush's response was no fleeting barb," Marder wrote. "It clearly reflected a determination to obliterate the long-held assumption that in the United States a free press is a recognized watchdog agent for holding public officials accountable for their policies and actions and for demanding transparency of public records."[4]

Bush and Cheney's contempt reflected the attitude many Americans held about the press in the first decade of the twenty-first century. The public's already shaky trust in journalists' integrity had plummeted as *New Republic* Associate Editor Stephen Glass, reporters Jayson Blair of the *New York Times* and Jack Kelley of *USA Today*, and *Boston Globe* columnist Patricia Smith were caught fabricating information. Some readers wondered whether they could trust any story no matter how thoroughly it seemed to be reported. The percentage of the public who believed news organizations were immoral jumped from 13 to 38 percent between 1985 and 1999. Those who thought stories were often inaccurate climbed from 34 percent to 58 percent in the same period.[5] When the movie *The Hunting Party* was released in 2007, a publicity poster proclaimed that its two main characters, both of them journalists, were "Liars—Cheats—Playboys—Thieves."[6]

Lack of trust was not the only problem investigative reporters faced. Newspaper readership was dropping, and interest in hard news was falling, especially among young people. A survey taken in 2000 found that only 45 percent of Americans said they enjoyed keeping up with the news. Newspapers were devoting more of their front pages to feature stories rather than costlier investigative and international reporting. Media owners cut their reporting staffs during the economic downturn of the early 1990s and did it again when advertising revenues began declining at the end of 2000.[7]

The remaining reporters complained they received little assistance, training, or travel money to help with investigative work, and the daily pressure to produce stories on deadline allowed little time to embark on long-term projects. Some of the newspapers and magazines that had sponsored the most investigative journalism—the *Washington Post, Los Angeles Times, Atlanta Journal-Constitution, Baltimore Sun, Boston Globe, Chicago Tribune, Dallas Morning News, Minneapolis Star-Tribune, Newsday, Philadelphia Inquirer, Time, U.S. News & World Report*—got rid of reporters during the decade as stockholders demanded expenses be cut to improve profits. The number of entries submitted to the Investigative Reporters and Editors annual awards competition plunged from 1,387 at the start of the decade to 357 by 2007.[8]

Media companies often used the label "investigative" loosely. Reports on consumer complaints, lifestyle features, and stories that took only one day to report were sometimes labeled "investigative." Local newscasts featured "watchdog" stories about a garbage problem at an apartment complex, a lost wedding reception deposit, and bartending schools that teach their students to control drunken patrons.

Yet the quality of some investigations was as good as ever, maybe better. Reporters used computers for deeper digging into a wider range of topics. Health, education, sports, religion, and charities joined government, crime, and business as subjects. For example, in 2000 the *Los Angeles Times* revealed how the Food and Drug Administration had approved seven unsafe prescription medicines. The following year, the *Washington Post* documented how neglect led to the deaths of 229 children placed in the District of Columbia's care. In 2002, the *Boston Globe* exposed the

Archdiocese of Boston's cover-up of widespread sexual abuse by priests. Within a year, Cardinal Bernard Law resigned, nine priests were charged with rape or molestation, and investigations of abuse by clergy were launched around the country.[9]

Other reporters turned to books to present lengthy investigations of social and economic problems. In *Nickel and Dimed: On (Not) Getting By in America,* Barbara Ehrenreich immersed herself in the lives of the country's working poor to describe how corporate and government policies made it difficult for them to survive. Eric Schlosser's *Fast Food Nation: The Dark Side of the All-American Meal* was a best-selling exposé of dangerous working conditions and unhealthy practices in the meat industry. Laurie Garrett documented the deteriorating public health system in *Betrayal of Trust: The Collapse of Global Public Health.* For *Newjack: Guarding Sing Sing,* Ted Conover spent a year working as a guard in one of America's most notorious prisons to reveal what life is like in a place hidden from most Americans.[10] IRE listed more than two hundred books by muckrakers in 2008 on topics including shady deals by banks, hazardous chemicals in consumer products, and brutal working conditions in Chinese factories. Large companies, however, increasingly dominated the book publishing industry, and it became harder to publish exposés of corporate wrongdoing.[11]

Most metropolitan and regional newspapers also limited their focus, confining their investigations to local matters. State governments received less attention as the number of newspaper reporters assigned to cover the fifty state capitols full-time dropped to 355 by 2009, a 31 percent decrease from eleven years earlier.[12] Coverage of Washington by regional newspapers also became thinner. By 1999, only one reporter watched the Social Security Administration, and no one covered the Department of the Interior full-time, even though both agencies affected millions of people.[13]

Much of the remaining Washington press corps had become members of the Washington establishment. In contrast to past generations of reporters who were more likely to have blue-collar backgrounds, many journalists now had degrees from the same colleges, lived in the same neighborhoods, and went to the same parties as the people they covered. Pressed for time and resources, reporters often depended on politicians and bureaucrats for their information. They were unlikely to challenge the actions and claims of these sources because they needed them for future stories and might move in the same social circles. Instead of investigating the information themselves, the press corps usually turned to opposing politicians or other Washington elites for contrasting viewpoints. Dissenters beyond the corridors of power were dismissed as renegades who should not be taken seriously. The result was remarkably homogenized news coverage from the networks, major magazines, and newspapers.[14]

When Bush took office, his administration was determined to keep the White House press corps busy. His staff fed reporters morsels of information on a daily basis to distract them from digging for information the president wanted to keep hidden. During its first term, the Bush administration hired 376 new public affairs officers at a cost of $50 million to package information. Borrowing a page from the Reagan White House, the administration excelled at creating prepackaged news events that played well on television news shows.[15]

Much of the Bush White House's press strategy focused on restricting the flow of information. It continued a program begun under Clinton to prevent the press and public from seeing thousands of previously declassified documents that were often embarrassing to the government. White House Counsel Alberto Gonzales ordered the national archivist to delay the release of files from the eight years when Ronald Reagan was president and Bush's father was vice president. Bush issued an executive order saying the president could stop the release of records from any prior administration. The executive order also allowed former presidents, their vice presidents, and their heirs to delay the release of their White House records forever.[16]

Cheney insisted the membership of an energy task force he created in early 2001 should remain secret. After Cheney's office refused a request by the General Accounting Office for records of the energy group's work and whom it met with, environmental and open government groups sued to make the information available. They cited the Freedom of Information Act and the Federal Advisory Committee Act (FACA), which requires public-private advisory committees to make records available for inspection. The case wound its way through the federal courts for nearly four years until Cheney's office won the right to withhold the information. FACA had been neutered and the Freedom of Information Act seriously weakened.[17]

Cheney was not the only one denying access to information. Federal, state, and local agencies were becoming increasingly adept at finding ways to delay fulfilling requests under the Freedom of Information Act. By 2007, according to one study, twenty-five federal agencies and departments had not responded to a third of FOIA requests within the twenty days required by law. And only 60 percent of requesters received all or some of the information they asked for, a record low. One *San Francisco Chronicle* reporter, Seth Rosenfeld, spent more than twenty-four years waiting for documents he requested about FBI covert activities at the University of California. As a result of the government's lengthy delays and refusal to turn over records, fewer reporters made public records requests.

The tide finally began to turn toward more information access. At the end of 2007, Congress passed and President Bush signed a bill requiring government agencies to meet twenty-day deadlines for responding to FOIA requests. It also made clear that journalists and the public should have access to government records held by private contractors. Government agencies, however, were slow to implement the new law during the last year of the Bush White House and the first months of Barack Obama's administration.[18]

Reporters also had difficulty getting information from the nation's courts, where judges increasingly used closed-door mediation as well as secret juries and dockets to hide cases. By 2008, fewer than 2 percent of cases in the federal courts went to a full and open trial. This meant that lawsuits involving medical malpractice, dangerous products, employment discrimination, and other matters of public interest were often hidden from reporters.[19]

White House information restrictions intensified after the September 11, 2001, terrorist attacks against the United States. As other administrations have done in times of war, Bush and his aides made secrecy a priority. Attorney General John Ashcroft encouraged agencies to withhold more documents from the press and public, and Chief of Staff Andrew Card ordered a review that removed at least six thousand pages from government Web sites. For the first time, the Environmental Protection Agency and the departments of Agriculture and Health and Human Services were given the power to classify their information.

In 2003, Bush issued an executive order delaying the declassification of some documents by three years and allowing the government to make secret again information it had previously declassified. Within the next three years, more than 25,000 documents were removed from public viewing at the National Archives and Records Administration. The number of government classification actions soared from nine million in fiscal year 2001 to sixteen million three years later. Many of the classified documents did indeed pertain to national security. Others included old budgets and other mundane matters as well as information that might prove embarrassing to government officials.[20]

Less access to records was not the only obstacle investigative reporters had to overcome. They also needed to ease the fears of federal employees who risked losing their jobs if they talked about corruption and public safety dangers. Whistle-blowers lost their jobs after raising concerns about airport security, tainted meat supplies, rapes at a Navy base, and falsified drug tests among Air Force personnel. Bush appointees fired Teresa Chambers, chief of the U.S. Park Police, after she told a *Washington Post* reporter that staffing shortages were leading to more crimes in national parks. The laws in place to protect whistle-blowers rarely worked. They could file complaints that they faced retaliation for speaking out, but between 1994 and 2007 they lost their cases nearly 97 percent of the time.[21]

The Bush White House took its efforts to manipulate the press even further when it spent $254 million during its first term on contracts to create fake news. The Department of Education paid syndicated columnist Armstrong Williams $186,000 through a public relations firm to write positive stories about the president's "No Child Left Behind" education policies. The Pentagon secretly hired retired military commanders to speak positively about Bush's conduct of the war on network news shows. The administration also created videos closely resembling broadcast news reports and sent them to television stations around the country. Many stations ran them uncut and unedited, as if their own reporters had done the stories. One of these videos featured a government employee, Karen Ryan, pretending to be a reporter who favorably describes Bush's signing of a Medicare prescription bill.

About fifty television stations ran the phony story, many without noting its origins.[22]

While the White House carefully scripted its message, the mainstream press rarely questioned Bush's policies during his first term. After the September 11 attacks, the president's approval rating soared to 90 percent (the highest a president ever had in a Gallup poll), and Bush's Republican supporters controlled both houses of Congress. Most Democrats, recognizing the president's popularity and wanting to appear tough on terrorism, avoided challenging him as U.S. forces prepared for war in Afghanistan and then Iraq. In this intimidating environment, most reporters did not want to seem unpatriotic. They also had a difficult time finding sources among Washington's elite who would provide information that countered the administration's policies.[23]

Bush, Cheney, and their aides began insisting in 2002 that war against Iraq was necessary. Reporters known for their skepticism did not investigate White House claims that the Iraqi government of Saddam Hussein had close links with al Qaeda terrorists and was developing weapons of mass destruction. Most journalists were content to use information leaked by the administration without fully probing it. "It took the kind of reporting that isn't done enough in Washington," said Deborah Nelson, former Washington investigations editor for the *Los Angeles Times*.[24] David Kaplan, an investigative reporter for *U.S. News & World Report* at the time, agreed that the press did not pursue the story aggressively enough. Most of their regular sources, he said, accepted the administration's evidence. Non-administration sources, such as United Nations weapons inspectors and some U.S. allies, questioned the rationale for war, but most journalists ignored them because they did not hold power within the United States.[25]

Some reporters, however, did investigate the White House's

case for war and its ability to protect the country from terrorist attacks. In a March 2002 *New Yorker* article, Seymour Hersh detailed the administration's determination to invade Iraq, its lack of preparation for governing the country once Saddam Hussein was toppled, and the $100 million it paid to a public relations firm to improve the reputations of Iraqi dissidents it championed. Bob Drogin of the *Los Angeles Times* revealed problems with the administration's evidence that Iraq possessed weapons of mass destruction.

ABC's Brian Ross showed the weakness of the Department of Homeland Security by easily smuggling fifteen pounds of depleted uranium from Eastern Europe to a Brooklyn warehouse in 2002. The uranium, while no longer dangerous in its depleted form, would have appeared the same as the lethal form to the human eye or an X-ray scanner and should have been detected by U.S. customs officers. A year later, Ross showed the nation's continued vulnerability to nuclear terrorism when he was able to ship depleted uranium from Indonesia past U.S. customs into Los Angeles.[26]

Members of Knight Ridder's Washington bureau were the journalists who most consistently investigated the argument that Hussein posed a mortal threat to the United States. Like Woodward and Bernstein during Watergate, Knight Ridder's reporters cultivated unglamorous sources in the depths of the government bureaucracy rather than rely on top officials. Many of the administration's statements about al Qaeda and Iraq made little sense, yet few other reporters bothered to investigate them. Led by bureau chief John Walcott, the Knight Ridder reporters kept digging. Their stories, however, received little attention from policy makers or other media because none of the chain's thirty-one newspapers was based in Washington or New York.[27]

The articles by Hersh, Drogin, and the Knight Ridder bureau were drowned out by stories on the network news shows and the front pages of the *New York Times* and *Washington Post* giving Bush's reasons for war. Some *Post* reporters investigated the White House's case for invading Iraq, but the newspaper failed to give their articles prominence. From the summer of 2002 through the winter of 2003, the *Post* ran more than 140 front-page stories about Bush's drive toward war. Most of them focused on the White House's rationale for fighting, with headlines such as "Cheney Says Iraqi Strike Is Justified." The *Post* buried on page A18 a story by Joby Warrick describing independent experts' doubts about the administration's claims that Hussein was building nuclear weapons.

In March 2003, the *Post*'s Walter Pincus probed allegations that Hussein was building weapons of mass destruction. Pincus discovered that the allegations had been challenged and sometimes disproved by U.S. intelligence reports, United Nations inspection records, and European governments. *Post* editors, however, ran the story on page A17, far from the front page. A follow-up story by Pincus and Dana Milbank ran on page A13. The *Post*'s executive editor, Leonard Downie, later said he and other editors were focused at the time on covering the war in Afghanistan and examining failures to prevent the September 11 attacks. They did not pay enough attention, Downie said, to how thin the evidence was that Hussein possessed weapons of mass destruction.[28]

A similar pattern held true at the *New York Times*. The newspaper's staff, particularly veteran foreign affairs reporter Judith Miller, tended to rely on the word of government sources and paid less attention to information and analysis provided by dissenters. Miller said her job as an investigative reporter on the intelligence beat did not include assessing government information or acting as an independent intelligence analyst. "My job is to tell readers of the *New York Times* what the government thought about Iraq's arsenal," she said.[29] After no weapons of mass destruction were found in Iraq following the invasion, the *Times* ran a front-page mea culpa acknowledging Miller's and other reporters' prewar stories did not adequately investigate White House claims. "Looking back, we wish we had been more aggressive in re-examining the claims as new evidence emerged or failed to emerge," the newspaper's editors wrote.[30]

The way Miller and many other reporters relied on information from top officials in the months leading up to the Iraq war resembled the performance of most journalists in the early days of Watergate. The lack of accurate statements from the White House was also similar. The nonprofit Center for Public Integrity found that Bush, Cheney, and six other top administration officials made 935 false statements in the two years following the September 11 attacks about possible weapons of mass destruction and links between Iraq and al Qaeda. But many reporters for the mainstream press avoided challenging administration claims because they did not want to appear too partisan. Challenges to Bush's justifications for war popped up in alternative newspapers and Web sites, but their stories were largely confined to their small audiences.[31]

Television news shows did not investigate Bush's case for war any better than most newspapers did. Katie Couric, then the host of NBC's *Today,* said that during the buildup to the war and its early days she felt pressure from "the corporations who own where we work and from the government itself to really squash any kind of dissent or any kind of questioning of it." She called the media's lack of skepticism about the White House's case for war "one of the most embarrassing chapters in American journalism." Jessica Yellin, a reporter for MSNBC in 2003, said her producers wanted her coverage to mirror the nation's patriotic fervor. Charles Gibson, a host of ABC's *Good Morning America* at the time, said television journalists did what they were supposed to do when interviewing White House officials. "It is not our job to debate them," Gibson said. "It is our job to ask the questions."[32]

One of the most persistent chroniclers of the Bush administration's war preparations and conduct was Bob Woodward. Since cowriting *The Final Days* and *The Brethren* in the 1970s, he had completed other best-selling and often controversial books about the death of actor John Belushi, the CIA, the Pentagon, the Federal Reserve Bank, the Persian Gulf War, Bill Clinton, and the 1996 presidential election. Along the way, he won extraordinary access to presidents and other leaders, gaining a closer look at the corridors of power than perhaps any reporter ever has. Although Woodward became famous during Watergate for exposing the lies of powerful people, his later books depended on some of the most influential people in the country telling the truth.

Woodward continued to use the same controversial, fly-on-the-wall narrative approach he used in *The Final Days* and *The Brethren,* re-creating scenes full of dialogue and emotions he had not witnessed himself. Because he frequently relied on anonymous sources and did not directly attribute his information, he asked his readers to put extraordinary trust in the veracity of his work. His book *Veil* came under special scrutiny because it contained a dramatic deathbed scene with CIA Director William Casey that some critics doubted ever occurred. Woodward's next book, *The Commanders,* explored how George H.W. Bush's administration decided to invade Panama and launch the Persian Gulf War. Bush accused Woodward of making up quotes in scenes the reporter did not witness.[33]

Woodward responds that his accuracy has withstood the test of time. Indeed, while critics have questioned the information in his books when they were first published, they have a hard time proving anything he wrote was incorrect. Woodward credits what he calls "saturation reporting," conducting background interviews to gather pieces of information that he verifies through other people and documents, using each bit of knowledge to pry more information from other sources. Woodward contends that by promising anonymity to his sources, he is able to get otherwise unavailable information.[34]

Woodward used this method to write four books about George W. Bush. The first of these books, *Bush at War,* portrayed the president as a firm, decisive leader responding to the September 11 terrorist attacks and directing the invasion of Afghanistan. The second Woodward book about Bush, *Plan of Attack,* was also largely sympathetic to the president as he prepared for the war against Iraq. Woodward faults himself for not aggressively pursuing tips he received that the Bush administration was exaggerating the threat of Iraqi weapons.[35] In his last two books about the war, *State of Denial* and *The War Within,* Woodward offered a scathing portrait of a Bush administration full of arrogance, incompetence, and infighting. Woodward said his reporting technique for these books did not vary greatly from what he did during Watergate, often scheduling interviews at night with people who did not want to be seen talking with him.[36]

While Woodward covered the war planning from Washington, dozens of reporters took advantage of a Pentagon policy allowing them to be embedded with American military units following the U.S. invasion of Iraq in 2003. This gave them a close-up view of the fighting from the troops' perspective but made it difficult to see the war from the viewpoint of Iraqi civilians. Some large news organizations created their own bureaus in Iraq, allowing them to cover the war independently. A few freelance reporters boldly traveled the country on their own. But reporting in Iraq was extremely expensive and dangerous, and few journalists stayed for long. As a result, information about the war came largely from Pentagon briefings.

The administration continued to tighten its secrecy during the Afghanistan and Iraq wars. The Pentagon banned photographers from taking pictures of the caskets of servicemen who died during the war. The names of people arrested or deported on terrorism charges were kept hidden. Federal court hearings were held with no public record of who was being tried or when and where the trial occurred. Terrorism suspects captured abroad were held in secret prisons without access to lawyers.

Carlotta Gall of the *New York Times* was one of the few reporters who penetrated this veil of secrecy. In late 2002, she painstakingly put together a story revealing that an Afghani taxi driver had been beaten to death while being held in a U.S. military prison. Gall's editors, however, held her story for a month, refusing to believe U.S. personnel could do such a brutal thing. After Gall gathered more evidence, they finally ran the story, burying it on page fourteen. Other news outlets also gave little attention to reports of prisoners being killed at the U.S. prison in Afghanistan. More than two years later, the *Times* printed a story disclosing that beatings, sexual humiliation, and sleep deprivation were routine practices at the prison.[37]

But the White House's ability to control press coverage waned as the fighting in Afghanistan and Iraq continued for months and then years, and as the death toll of U.S. soldiers climbed into the thousands. The *Post*'s Leonard Downie noted that every new administration comes to Washington determined to completely control information. With the exception of Carter and Clinton, whose top aides were inexperienced in the ways of the capital, recent presidents were successful in doing so during their first years. After rivalries develop and some aides quit, reporters start getting better information, which is what happened during Bush's second term.[38] David Kaplan, who wrote for *U.S. News & World Report* during the war, agreed that the longer the Bush administration was in office, the more sources reporters developed. "Generals, admirals, career intelligence officers were leaking us stuff in significant amounts, and it was going up, not down, because they were so frustrated with the level of incompetence and lack of integrity that they saw in the Iraq war and the Bush White House," Kaplan said.[39]

Those leaks gradually led to stronger investigations. Soon after the invasion, the Center for Public Integrity published a project disclosing that at least nine members of the Defense Policy Board, which advises the Pentagon, had connections with companies that won more than $76 billion in Pentagon contracts in the prior two years.[40] In March 2004, Bob Drogin and Greg Miller of the *Los Angeles Times* revealed that much of the evidence provided by the White House about Iraq's weapons of mass destruction "relied on the unconfirmed account of a dubious defector in Germany" who U.S. officials never bothered to interview.[41]

The next month, CBS's *60 Minutes II* and Seymour Hersh of the *New Yorker* produced the most powerful investigation of the war. Their stories divulged that American soldiers physically and sexually abused Iraqis held in the Abu Ghraib prison. Hersh included descriptions of the brutality that he obtained from a secret military review of the prison:

> Breaking chemical lights and pouring the phosphoric liquid on detainees; pouring cold water on naked detainees; beating detainees

with a broom handle and a chair; threatening male detainees with
rape; allowing a military police guard to stitch the wound of a
detainee who was injured after being slammed against the wall in
his cell; sodomizing a detainee with a chemical light and perhaps
a broom stick, and using military working dogs to frighten and
intimidate detainees with threats of attack, and in one instance
actually biting a detainee.[42]

Additional evidence for the stories came from the digital cameras
of soldiers who had taken photographs of prisoners threatened by
unmuzzled guard dogs, forced to simulate sex acts, and made to
form naked human pyramids. One photo showed a smiling guard
standing next to a prisoner's corpse.

Hersh documented how Abu Ghraib was, in the words of *New
Yorker* editor David Remnick, "a concerted attempt by the government and the military leadership to circumvent the Geneva
Conventions." The Bush White House claimed the abuse—which
it insisted did not count as torture—consisted of a few isolated
incidents by rogue soldiers. The administration attacked Hersh,
with one spokesman calling his stories "crap." Hersh's account of
the events at Abu Ghraib and their connection to Bush's policy
toward detainees, however, proved more accurate than the White
House's version. Less than three weeks after the initial Abu Ghraib
stories, a *Newsweek* report detailed the administration's policy decisions that had allowed the abuse.[43]

The watchdog press was regaining its bite. Two weeks after the
Abu Ghraib stories appeared, Dana Priest and Joe Stephens of the
Washington Post revealed that the CIA was running a network of
secret prisons abroad for terrorism suspects. For more than a year,
Priest detailed the abuses and detainee deaths that occurred at the
CIA prisons, which stretched from Eastern Europe to Thailand.

Priest won a Pulitzer Prize and several other journalism awards for her efforts. The administration responded by investigating who had given Priest information about the jails, making it more difficult for her to find sources for future stories. Accuracy in Media, a conservative watchdog of the press, said Priest was manipulated by former government officials "whose actions border on treason" and that her "completely misleading" stories could "undermine U.S. efforts to protect Americans from another major terrorist attack." Priest said the *Post* "got tons of hate mail and threats, calling our patriotism into question."[44]

In December 2005, James Risen and Eric Lichtblau of the *New York Times* exposed a secret National Security Agency program that eavesdropped, without warrants, on the electronic and telephone communications of U.S. citizens. When the White House learned Risen and Lichtblau were working on the story, it told the *Times* the program was legal and pressured the newspaper to hold the story, which it did for more than a year. Once the newspaper published the investigation, the administration and other GOP leaders attacked the *Times*'s patriotism, just as Nixon attacked it and the *Post* in 1971 for publishing the Pentagon Papers. The White House warned journalists they could be prosecuted under espionage laws, and a grand jury subpoenaed Risen to pressure him to divulge his confidential sources. In the summer of 2006, seventy-one congressmen tried to retaliate against the *Times* by demanding the Speaker of the House strip the newspaper of its congressional press credentials. In contrast with the 1970s, when Congress held extensive hearings on Watergate and the domestic spying scandals, the House and Senate did not investigate the revelations by the press. They did not want to be labeled as soft on terrorism.[45]

The administration's attacks continued when career diplomat

Joseph Wilson wrote a column in the *Times* poking holes in a Bush statement that Hussein had collected uranium for nuclear bombs from the African country of Niger. Wilson wrote that he had traveled to Niger and learned the Bush statement was untrue. Cheney's chief of staff, I. Lewis "Scooter" Libby, and other administration aides leaked to sympathetic reporters that Wilson's wife, Valerie Plame, was an undercover CIA agent who had arranged Wilson's trip. Federal prosecutors, searching for the leak's source, demanded that reporters Judith Miller of the *New York Times* and Matthew Cooper of *Time* identify who told them about Plame even though they never wrote stories about the case. After losing a court battle, *Time* cooperated with prosecutors. In contrast, Miller defied a court order to disclose her confidential source and spent eighty-five days in prison. Miller was only released after Libby freed her from her vow of confidentiality.

Miller was not the only reporter under pressure to divulge confidential sources. The days when a reporter like Woodward could easily protect the identity of a source like Deep Throat were over. Daily newspapers and network television affiliates received an estimated 744 federal subpoenas for information in 2006, nearly twice as many as five years earlier. Although thirty-five states had shield laws by 2009 that allowed reporters to protect the identity of their sources, there was no federal equivalent.[46] The lack of a shield law in some states and at the federal level allowed prosecutors to threaten reporters with jail time if they did not name their confidential sources. Reporters Lance Williams and Mark Fainaru-Wada of the *San Francisco Chronicle* faced eighteen months in federal prison when they refused to reveal their source for a story on a grand jury investigation into the sale of steroids to professional athletes. They avoided prison only after the source came forward to confess his role.

Journalists worried that these threats weakened their ability to do investigative stories. Reporter Jim Taricani of WJAR-TV in Providence was sentenced to six months of home confinement in 2004 after refusing to release the name of a source who gave him a videotape from an FBI corruption probe. Afterward, his station's management told Taricani he could only promise sources confidentiality until a case reached a court of appeals. After that, he would have to reveal their identities. Other reporters shunned e-mail, only met sources outdoors, and used disposable cell phones in order to avoid leaving a trail that prosecutors could follow.[47]

Legal threats, however, did not stop reporters from investigating corruption in Washington. In 2004, the *Washington Post* exposed the crooked practices of powerful lobbyist Jack Abramoff and his close ties to House Majority Leader Tom DeLay of Texas and Representative Bob Ney of Ohio. DeLay ended up resigning after being indicted on charges of fundraising irregularities; Ney pleaded guilty to charges of conspiracy and making false statements; and Abramoff pleaded guilty to fraud, conspiracy to commit bribery, and tax evasion. The *Los Angeles Times* revealed that two Russian firms and a Serbian family paid nearly $1 million to a lobbying firm owned by the daughter of Representative Curt Weldon, a Pennsylvania Republican. Representative Weldon then helped the Russian firms win U.S. government contracts. He also intervened to get the family, which had close ties to former Serbian autocrat Slobodan Milosevic, off a State Department blacklist for obtaining visas.[48]

In 2005, the *San Diego Union-Tribune* detailed how Representative Randy Cunningham, a California Republican, helped a defense contractor get Pentagon deals worth more than $100 million. The contractor had previously bought the congressman's house for $700,000 more than its market value. The *Union-Tribune*'s

stories described how other contractor favors helped Cunningham buy a mansion, a Rolls Royce, and luxury vacations. Cunningham was sentenced to more than eight years in prison, the
longest ever given to a congressman.[49] That same year, the *Toledo
Blade* revealed in its "Coingate" series that an Ohio state agency
had invested hundreds of millions of taxpayer dollars in risky rare
coin investments run by people who made large contributions to
the Republican Party.[50]

The watchdog press became even more aggressive after Hurricane Katrina devastated the Gulf Coast of Louisiana and Mississippi in the summer of 2005. With much of the administration
on summer vacation, reporters arrived at the scene of the massive
flooding before many federal officials. Their stories and live, unedited footage of the disaster made clear that the White House's
response was inept and its spin on events was inaccurate. While
Bush aides claimed they were handling the problems, desperate
people were shown clinging to the roofs of their New Orleans
homes, and thousands more were seen stranded in the city's convention center without food or other necessities.[51]

The Republican majority in Congress was further weakened
the following year when Brian Ross's investigative unit at ABC
heard from Capitol Hill sources that U.S. Representative Mark
Foley had sent an inappropriate e-mail to a sixteen-year-old congressional page. Foley, a Florida Republican, had asked the page
how old he was, what he wanted for his birthday, and whether he
could send the congressman a photo of himself. There was not
enough information for a story on the evening news, but reporter
Maddy Sauer and Rhonda Schwartz, ABC's chief of investigative projects, posted a short item on their Web site, known as
the *Blotter*.

Within a few hours, other former pages responded to that small story by sending ABC information about sexual advances they had received from Foley. Sauer, Schwartz, and the rest of Brian Ross's team were able to frequently update their Web posts and transform them into a story for the evening newscast. A day after the initial *Blotter* story, Foley resigned. The *Blotter* continued to pursue the scandal by presenting evidence that congressional leaders had received many warnings about Foley's conduct but failed to act. The Web format allowed the investigative unit to keep updating stories, which encouraged more sources to come forward with information. The Foley stories, many observers agreed, were partly responsible for the GOP losing its congressional majority in the 2006 midterm elections.[52]

The Foley stories demonstrated how technology was changing investigative journalism. If the ABC investigative unit had not posted the initial story on its Web site, the additional congressional pages probably would not have come forward with their own evidence, and the story would have quickly died. The rapidly increasing power of the Internet was allowing reporters to present news in more effective ways, spread stories quickly around the globe, and gather valuable information from readers and viewers. At the same time, journalists desperately searched for creative ways to pay for investigative reporting as newspapers, magazines, and television news programs struggled to survive.

—————◇—————

EIGHT

REVIVING THE IMPULSE

Think of how much faster Woodward and Bernstein would have toppled Nixon if Deep Throat had a Twitter account.
—Jon Klein, president of CNN/U.S., 2009

Investigative reporter Cal McAffrey was hot on the trail of discovering who murdered the young aide and lover of an ambitious congressman. Like the charismatic heroes of *All the President's Men,* McAffrey—played by Hollywood star Russell Crowe in the movie *State of Play*—worked for a major newspaper, the fictional *Washington Globe.* Unlike Woodward and Bernstein, McAffrey was not teamed with another skilled reporter as he unearthed the truth; instead he was ordered to work with an inexperienced blogger. And rather than receiving the full backing of a thriving, aggressive newspaper like the *Washington Post,* the frustrated McAffrey had to contend with a demoralized publisher who gave him little support as she looked for ways to cut costs.[1]

By the time *State of Play* appeared in 2009, many newsrooms were indeed frustrated and demoralized. Investigative reporters were still producing important stories, but staffing cutbacks had decimated their ranks. The economic meltdown of 2008 and the resulting recession devastated the finances of many media companies, who were already losing large portions of their audiences to the Internet. Advertisements on media companies' Web sites were not making up for the loss of more lucrative ones in print and on the air. Newspapers' highly profitable classified advertising was migrating to Web sites like Craigslist. As a result, newspaper revenues fell 23 percent between 2007 and 2009. Local television and network newsrooms also saw their profits drop and their reporting budgets reduced as the evening newscasts and prime-time newsmagazines lost viewers.[2]

Many media companies were still profitable, but they did not have money to pay off the debts accumulated while trying to expand during more optimistic years. The Tribune Company— owner of the *Chicago Tribune, Los Angeles Times, Baltimore Sun,* and other newspapers, broadcast outlets, and radio stations around the country—filed for bankruptcy protection. So did the owners of the *Minneapolis Star-Tribune* and *Philadelphia Inquirer.* The *Albuquerque Tribune, Cincinnati Post, Rocky Mountain News, Seattle Post-Intelligencer,* and *Tucson Citizen* stopped publishing or became Web-only operations. Most newsmagazines also lost readers and advertisers, and *Time, Newsweek,* and *U.S. News & World Report* shifted their focus away from original reporting.

Because of the economic downturn, reporters were fired, foreign bureaus closed, and the number of pages available for stories slashed. According to one count, more than 14,000 journalism jobs were eliminated in 2009. Short-staffed editors and news directors ordered the remaining reporters to crank out more stories, reducing the time they had to conduct in-depth research. Investigative reporting—the most expensive, controversial, and time-consuming kind of journalism—was often the first thing to be cut.[3]

Reporter Paul Giblin of the *East Valley Tribune* in suburban Phoenix learned this the hard way. He and reporting partner Ryan Gabrielson spent six months in 2008 investigating Maricopa County Sheriff Joe Arpaio. They discovered that while Arpaio was aggressively hunting for illegal immigrants to deport, the county's arrest rate was dropping, response times to emergency calls were slowing, and overtime pay for deputies was rising. Giblin and Gabrielson received a Pulitzer Prize for their efforts. But when the prize was announced in 2009, Giblin was no longer working for the *Tribune*. Nor was the project's editor, Patti Epler. They had been let go a few months earlier during a round of layoffs that had cut the newspaper's staff in half. By the end of 2009, the newspaper itself had shut down.[4] Giblin and Epler, however, were not ready to give up reporting. Along with two other journalists and a businessman, they launched arizonaguardian.com, an online publication devoted to keeping an eye on the state's government.

Giblin's move reflected a broader shift in investigative reporting. Other journalists like him were turning to the Internet to find creative ways to gather and distribute information. And they were experimenting with different models to pay for watchdog reporting. Some like arizonaguardian.com were small entrepreneurial start-ups struggling to survive. Other investigative reporters were finding financial support from nonprofit foundations, universities, private donors, and their readers and viewers. By the end of the decade, more journalists were collaborating, sometimes across borders, to enhance their muckraking. As a result, some of the most impressive investigative reporting in U.S. history was being done at the same time that newspapers, magazines, and broadcast outlets were gasping for air.

In its early days, the Internet did not produce much in the way of original investigative reporting. Instead, it served as a means to repackage and distribute stories originally developed for traditional print and broadcast media. But eventually journalists realized the Internet allowed them to present and report stories in completely new and often better ways. It offered nearly infinite capacity to provide text, photographs, videos, maps, documents, databases, audio clips of interviews, and interactive graphics. Readers could explore subjects further by clicking on links, and they could share information with reporters through comment sections and e-mails.

The Internet allowed muckraking stories to be more comprehensive because they no longer needed to fit the space available in a newspaper, magazine, or broadcast. In 2007, for example, the *Washington Post* ran "Citizen K Street," a twenty-seven-part series about one of the capital's most powerful lobbying firms. The Web package included a video, a photo slideshow, a review of the cast of characters, and an opportunity for reader feedback. Only small portions of the project appeared in the newspaper, but reporter Robert Kaiser was able to include the entire comprehensive series on the newspaper's Web site.[5]

Some investigative stories began to appear only on the Internet. The online news site *Salon* ran a series of articles by Mark Benjamin and Michael de Yoanna in 2009 detailing the Army's mistreatment of soldiers returning from the Iraq war with posttraumatic stress disorder. Benjamin and de Yoanna described the links between posttraumatic stress and a rash of suicides and homicides by returning soldiers. They discovered evidence that soldiers with mental illnesses did not receive adequate treatment and that the Army pressured its medical staff not to give posttraumatic stress diagnoses.[6] The *St. Petersburg Times* PolitiFact Web site used graphics rather than traditional story formats to present its probes of whether candidates and government officials were telling the truth. The PolitiFact graphics rated the politicians' statements on a scale ranging from "True" to "Pants on Fire."

By 2008, nearly three-quarters of all adults were active online. More than half used the Internet for research, and some of them searched through information in ways familiar to reporters. Government data that once might have taken weeks, months, or even years to get through a Freedom of Information Act request were now readily available to anyone with an online connection who wanted to do a little sleuthing. A new Web site, EveryBlock .com, allowed viewers in more than a dozen major cities to easily sift through local government information such as crime reports, building permits, and restaurant inspection reports. Comprehensive data about corporations and large nonprofit institutions were also only a mouse click away.[7]

People used this sea of information to publish stories without contending with the costs of printing plants, paper, or distribution. When Congress was debating a massive bailout of the financial system in the fall of 2008, thousands of people dug through the legislation's details after it was posted on the Web. Writers of Web logs (commonly known as blogs) identified the corporate contributors to congressmen who supported the bill, and they unearthed earmarks buried in the bill, including a special tax reduction for makers of wooden arrows. While the likelihood of errors expanded as more people without journalism training began posting stories, the Internet allowed for much quicker corrections.[8]

Journalists realized they could use their Web sites to gather information from their readers and viewers. When the *Washington Post* published stories about miserable conditions for veterans at Walter Reed Army Medical Center, the Internet magnified the response. The story quickly spread to readers around the world, some of whom shared their own experiences as injured veterans. "A good deal of our subsequent reporting has been based on information we've gotten from people responding to the initial articles," Executive Editor Leonard Downie said. When the *Post* ran a series in 2009 about the backgrounds of Obama White House appointees, readers responded with information of their own to help paint a clearer picture of the new administration.[9] Social networking sites such as Facebook made it even easier for reporters to find sources familiar with the people and topics they were investigating.

Asking the public to help gather news became known as crowdsourcing. Some journalists figured that a group of people can usually collect more information, and do it faster, than a single reporter. For example the Huffington Post Web site created "OffTheBus," a crowdsourcing effort between volunteers and veteran journalists during the 2008 presidential election campaign. Forty-four people contributed to an "OffTheBus" story on the extent of Bill Clinton's fundraising efforts on behalf of his wife, Democratic candidate Hillary Clinton. Organizing the efforts of inexperienced journalists could be difficult, however, and volunteers often could not give the same time to a story as a full-time reporter.[10]

Crowdsourcing helped the liberal-leaning Talking Points Memo become the first blog to win a major journalism prize. In 2008, it won a George Polk Award for revealing that the Bush administration had fired eight U.S. attorneys for political reasons. The blog's reporters used tips from readers around the country, links to articles from local newspapers, and their own digging to uncover a pattern of prosecutors being forced from office if they did not do the administration's bidding. Thousands of readers helped Talking Points Memo find information about the firings by combing through documents released by the administration.[11]

Crowdsourcing became crowd whistle-blowing with the creation of WikiLeaks.org in 2007. Started by journalists and other people concerned about the Chinese government's suppression of information, WikiLeaks allowed people around the world to post documents that had been classified, censored, or otherwise restricted. The documents could be used by journalists to write stories. A contemporary version of the Pentagon Papers, for example, could be posted by a whistle-blower on WikiLeaks and then downloaded by reporters and other people around the world before the government tried to prohibit publication. WikiLeaks's organizers said that by the start of 2010, the site had received 1.2 million documents, including an operations manual from the controversial U.S. military base at Guantánamo Bay and insider trading memos from the J.P. Morgan investment firm. In a typical week, people used WikiLeaks to share documents from Dubai, Iceland, Zambia, Canada, and the United States.[12]

While crowdsourcing and other Internet innovations helped reporters keep an eye on politicians, it also allowed the public to take a closer look at journalists. Blogs became a quick and easy way for people to share information about the media's factual errors, to focus attention on stories they thought had been ignored, and to question the news judgment of the mainstream press. By bringing together the collective knowledge and insights of the public, bloggers started serving as media watchdogs. They showed their ability to investigate the investigators after *60 Minutes II* broadcast a story two months before the 2004 election about President Bush's time in the Texas Air National Guard during the Vietnam War. Narrated by CBS anchorman Dan Rather, the story said Bush did not fulfill the terms of his service and that his commanding officer was pressured to give him positive evaluations.

Bloggers immediately attacked the authenticity of memos *60 Minutes II* said had been written in 1972 by Bush's commanding officer, since deceased. A comment on the conservative Web site Free Republic noted that the memos used fonts not commonly found on typewriters in the early 1970s. Bloggers on the Power Line, INDC Journal, and Little Green Footballs sites pounced on the opportunity to investigate the memos' authenticity, questioning the wording, spacing of letters, and use of superscript characters. Experts on typefaces and word processing declared that the documents were forgeries. One blogger interviewed a witness quoted in the *60 Minutes II* story and discovered he had no first-hand knowledge of the events.

Mainstream publications like the *Washington Post* eventually followed up on the bloggers' investigation, which they began calling "Rathergate." After defending the memos' validity for several weeks, CBS admitted that the man who supplied them had lied about their origins. Producer Mary Mapes and three CBS news executives were fired. Rather retired early under pressure from CBS. Although there was still substantial evidence Bush had received preferential treatment during Vietnam, the bloggers successfully shifted the debate to CBS's reporting techniques.[13]

The Internet was not the only technology changing investigative journalism. Small digital cameras made it easier for news teams to catch images of wrongdoing. Instead of going undercover, they could openly take photographs or shoot videos while looking like typical citizens or tourists. ABC News used this technique to gather footage of large donors wining and dining elected officials at the national political conventions. Brian Ross's investigative team also used simple cameras a tourist might carry to show

Department of Homeland Security officials snorkeling, lying on beaches, and partying at taxpayer expense during a 2006 Hawaii convention.[14]

Digital technology and the Internet were revolutionizing communications in the same way the invention of the printing press did more than five hundred years earlier. Because the Internet and portable devices such as cell phones made it easy for people to report a story, professional journalists no longer served as gatekeepers to the news. Instead, journalism was being produced by a mix of individuals, informal groups, and for-profit and nonprofit organizations, media scholar Clay Shirky observed. All of them could instantly transmit any information they wanted around the world for little or no cost.[15] But in-depth reporting still took weeks, months, or even years to complete. In reality, few amateurs had the time or inclination to spend day after day digging through documents and finding sources to interview. Professional investigative reporters were still necessary, but ways needed to be found to pay them as newspapers, magazines, and broadcast outlets cut their staffs.

One increasingly popular way to pay for investigative reporting was through nonprofit organizations, which have a long history in journalism. The Associated Press, the world's largest news organization, was founded as a cooperative and continued to operate as a nonprofit corporation. So did the *Christian Science Monitor, Delaware State News, Union-Leader* in Manchester, New Hampshire, and *Harper's, Mother Jones,* and *National Geographic* magazines. The *St. Petersburg Times* and *Governing* magazine were owned by the Poynter Institute for Media Studies. The nonprofit National Public Radio grew from approximately two million listeners in 1983 to about thirty million by 2007, and *Frontline* investigations were aired by the nonprofit Public Broadcasting

Service. The nonprofit *Chicago Reporter* magazine investigated discrimination in housing, education, employment, law enforcement, and city services.[16]

Inspired by the nonprofit Center for Investigative Reporting, Charles Lewis left his job as a producer for *60 Minutes* in 1988 to help launch the Center for Public Integrity. Since then the Center for Public Integrity has published more than 400 investigations, including seventeen books, on food safety, the hazards of the chemical industry, and other subjects. Every four years it puts together "The Buying of the President," a report detailing the economic interests behind each of the major presidential candidates. The Center broke the story of Bill Clinton swapping overnight stays in the White House Lincoln Bedroom for campaign cash. It also revealed that George W. Bush's campaign received big donations from Enron, a company that became infamous for financial misconduct.[17]

The oldest nonprofit group dedicated to investigations, the Better Government Association, was formed in Chicago in 1923 to fight the influence of gangster Al Capone. The BGA often worked with local media to uncover corruption in Chicago's political machine, including the *Mirage* tavern exposé of bribe taking by Chicago officials. The BGA also probed national issues such as crooked Navy shipbuilding contracts, government spying on American citizens, and Medicaid fraud.[18]

In the 1980s, former BGA investigator David Protess turned his attention away from political corruption and toward wrongdoing in the legal system. Protess became interested in wrongful conviction cases as a contributing editor at *Chicago Lawyer* magazine. One of his writers was covering the trial of Sandra Fabiano, a day care operator charged with molesting a child. Protess and *Chicago Lawyer* editor Rob Warden became convinced

Fabiano was innocent. Working with a private investigator and Paul Hogan, a reporter with NBC affiliate WMAQ TV, they independently dug into the evidence and found holes in the prosecution's case. Largely because of their efforts, the jury acquitted Fabiano.[19]

In the early 1990s, Protess, Warden, and Hogan worked on the case of David Dowaliby, convicted of murdering his seven-year-old stepdaughter, Jaclyn. They revealed mistakes in the original investigation and found witnesses the police and prosecutors had never questioned. Protess and Warden interviewed the only witness who had said Dowaliby was at the apartment complex where Jaclyn's body was found. The witness had based his identification on Dowaliby's large nose. When Protess and Warden showed him a photo of a painter with a similar nose who worked in the area, the witness recanted, admitting he could not positively identify Dowaliby. In response to the new evidence, a judge threw out Dowaliby's conviction. Protess and Warden later obtained a confession from a man who admitted killing Jaclyn.[20]

After Dowaliby was freed from prison, Protess knew he wanted to devote his career to overturning wrongful convictions. And he realized how much the students in his investigative reporting class at Northwestern University's Medill School of Journalism could learn from these cases. Some of them had volunteered to help with the Dowaliby investigation, and Protess began assigning his class to dig into other cases. He and his students proved the innocence of Steven Linscott, a Bible student convicted of murder based on a dream he described to police. Although police said Linscott's dream had remarkable similarities to the murder, Protess's students found more than seventy differences between the two. They also proved that DNA from the crime scene did not come from Linscott. When presented with the new information, prosecutors dropped the charges, and Linscott was released after more than three years in prison.[21]

Soon Protess and his students were getting innocent men not only out of prison but also off death row. In 1996, they worked with Warden and a private investigator to prove that four men, known as the "Ford Heights Four," did not murder a young couple. Two of the men were on death row at the time they were released by the courts.[22] Protess and his students also tackled the case of Anthony Porter, who was within two days of being executed for committing a double murder before his innocence was proven. The students examined trial testimony, police reports, and court documents, discovering that police had beat up the only witness who had identified Porter as the murderer. Following the trail of evidence, the students found a man who confessed to the killing.

In less than a decade, Protess and his students, working with other media outlets in the Chicago area, helped exonerate ten prisoners, including five on death row. Eric Zorn, Steve Mills, and Kenneth Armstrong of the *Chicago Tribune* revealed additional problems with the Illinois justice system. Their work persuaded Governor George Ryan to put a moratorium on executions in the state and commute the sentences of all 157 death row inmates in Illinois to life in prison. By 2009, about five hundred students had worked on investigations in Protess's class. "I used to think my goal was to free innocent prisoners," Protess said. "Now the goal is to turn out first-rate investigative reporters."[23]

While Protess and his students were busy in Illinois, Pete Shellem was finding evidence that proved the wrongful convictions of Pennsylvania prisoners. In one case, Shellem, a reporter for the *Patriot-News* in Harrisburg, gathered DNA evidence stored in a professor's refrigerator in Germany that exonerated a man convicted of murder. Another time, Shellem discovered an old briefcase in a deceased detective's attic that contained notes showing the state police had changed lab results to help convict an innocent man.[24]

Investigations of wrongful convictions began to spread around the country. Protess helped launch the national Innocence Network, which by 2010 included students at more than fifty journalism and law schools working on wrongful conviction cases. In 2001, William Moushey, a reporter for the *Pittsburgh Post-Gazette,* founded the Innocence Institute at Point Park University. Since then, Moushey has worked with students to investigate more than a dozen possible wrongful convictions in western Pennsylvania. In 2007, Steve Weinberg at the University of Missouri Journalism School helped start the Midwestern Innocence Project, which covers six states.[25]

University students were not just investigating wrongful convictions. Matt Kennard of the Toni Stabile Center for Investigative Journalism at Columbia University revealed in a story published in *Salon* that lax recruiting standards allowed neo-Nazis to join the U.S. Army and serve with American forces in Iraq. Georgetown University students investigated who kidnapped and murdered *Wall Street Journal* reporter Daniel Pearl. The New England Center for Investigative Reporting and the Wisconsin Center for Investigative Journalism both worked with students on local investigations. In 2005, Northwestern University students teamed with the Center for Public Integrity to examine the 23,000 privately funded trips, worth nearly $50 million, taken by Congress members and their aides over a five-year span. Their "Power Trips" series revealed thinly veiled attempts to influence legislation during junkets to vacation spots such as Paris, Hawaii, and Italy.[26]

In addition to universities, other nonprofits were assisting investigative journalists. An Alicia Patterson fellowship, for example, helped Ken Ward of the *Charleston Gazette* reveal that federal safety policies contributed to the deadly collapse of a West Virginia mine. The Pulitzer Center for Crisis Reporting sponsored stories on cocaine production in Bolivia, water shortages in East Africa, and political suppression in Burma. The Pulitzer Center and the Center for Investigative Reporting helped freelance reporter Loretta Tofani make five trips to China to investigate hazardous conditions for low-paid workers who manufacture products exported to the United States. Tofani visited twenty-five factories, interviewing sick workers and sifting through medical, shipping, and factory inspection records. She discovered workers routinely exposed to toxic chemicals and unsafe conditions that led to amputations and fatal diseases. Her four-part series, "American Imports: Chinese Deaths," won multiple prizes after appearing in the *Salt Lake Tribune* in 2007. But the grants only covered Tofani's travel costs; she ended up earning $5,000 for fourteen months of work.[27]

A few Web-based ventures found ways to pay their own investigative reporters. One of the most successful began in 2005 after the *San Diego Union-Tribune* fired Neil Morgan, a reporter and columnist for nearly fifty years. The newspaper, like so many others, was laying off reporters and editors to save costs. San Diego once had two daily newspapers plus heavy coverage from the *Los Angeles Times,* but by the time of Morgan's firing it had become a one-newspaper town—and that newspaper was shrinking fast. Buzz Woolley, a retired venture capitalist, decided it was time for some competition. He helped Morgan finance a new online-only publication, Voice of San Diego. Because they only had four employees at the start, the founders decided they needed to focus on one thing rather than trying to replicate a daily newspaper's broad coverage. That one thing was investigative journalism.

Voice of San Diego soon made a name for itself by uncovering corruption and incompetence in the city's government. For three years it investigated two local economic development agencies whose officials gave themselves large bonuses while allowing politically connected friends to make huge profits selling homes that were supposed to be affordable. The investigations led to reforms of the agencies and the resignations of their presidents, one of whom faced criminal charges and the other a grand jury investigation. Other stories exposed a local real-estate swindle, incorrect police department crime statistics, and the Mexican drug war's impact on the city. In 2009, Voice of San Diego won an IRE award, the first time one of the prizes went to a publication that exists only online. In four years, Voice of San Diego's staff and budget tripled despite operating during a recession. Woolley continued to make annual donations, but Voice of San Diego also received money from foundations, corporate sponsors, online advertisers, and more than 800 individual donors. "People in San Diego are understanding that this is a public service, and if they want it, they'll have to fund it," Editor Andrew Donohue said.[28]

The Web-only model was spreading. The New Haven Independent, St. Louis Beacon, and MinnPost in Minneapolis and St. Paul started sites similar to Voice of San Diego. They produced original stories, but their staffs remained a fraction of the size of a typical metropolitan newspaper's. In 2009, the Center for Investigative Reporting launched California Watch to expose corruption and problems with the state's education, health care, public safety, and environment. In addition to posting stories online, California Watch collaborates with local newspapers and broadcast outlets to distribute the results of its investigations.

David Cohn, a former *Wired* magazine writer, began the San Francisco–based Spot.us with the help of a $340,000 grant from the Knight Foundation. The Spot.us Web site allowed anyone to submit story ideas. The site's editors decided which of the ideas were most promising and then asked readers to contribute any amount they wanted toward reporting those ideas. If enough money was donated, freelance journalists covered the story. In its first year, Spot.us helped fund stories about the growth of California shantytowns and the impact of cement manufacturing plant emissions on global warming. The stories sometimes took months to get enough funding, however, limiting their timeliness. They also often had little depth, perhaps because they were usually written by freelancers who lacked experience with the topics they were covering.[29]

Spot.us was not the only journalism group receiving foundation support. In the second half of the decade, 180 American foundations gave nearly $128 million to news and information projects, not including public broadcasting. Half of that amount went toward muckraking. One of the biggest boosts occurred in 2008 with the launch of ProPublica, a Web site devoted to investigative reporting. It was founded by Marion and Herbert Sandler, a California couple who made billions of dollars as owners of the country's second largest savings and loan bank. The Sandlers committed $10 million annually for at least three years to ProPublica. Other foundations also chipped in. Instantly it became the biggest nonprofit investigative venture in the country. Without advertising job openings, Editor Paul Steiger, a former *Wall Street Journal* managing editor, was flooded with applications from 1,300 reporters seeking work. By 2009 ProPublica had hired thirty of them.

ProPublica collaborated on stories with reporters and editors from other newsrooms. Its first big story, "Lost in Translation" by Dafna Linzer, was broadcast on *60 Minutes*. It revealed that Alhurra, a U.S. government–backed Arabic television and radio network, had often run anti–American viewpoints. ProPublica worked with

ABC News and the *Los Angeles Times* on another story describing haphazard health care for contractors returning from Iraq. Other stories by ProPublica and the *Los Angeles Times* revealed that California nurses who committed crimes at work were allowed to keep their jobs for many years because of lax regulation. Because of the stories, most members of the California Board of Registered Nursing resigned or were replaced.[30]

Many of the stories appearing on investigative Web sites challenged the actions of the Bush administration and large corporations. Conservative groups, concerned that investigative reporting leaned to the left, looked for ways they could sponsor their own muckraking. K. Daniel Glover of Accuracy in Media, a journalism watchdog group, suggested in 2009 that conservatives launch their own investigative reporting teams. The Goldwater Institute, a think tank based in Arizona, took a step in that direction when it hired reporter Mark Flatten to monitor the state's government. In 2009, Flatten revealed that political insiders were winning lucrative Phoenix airport contracts meant for "disadvantaged" business owners. Although muckraking was not its primary mission, the Goldwater Institute previously sponsored an investigation into Arizona's standardized tests for high school students and discovered poor administration and inflated scores.[31]

Like the Goldwater Institute, other groups that did not have journalism as their main mission were doing their own investigations. The first information about mistreatment of Iraqi prisoners by U.S. forces came from Amnesty International, Human Rights Watch, and the International Committee of the Red Cross.[32] The American Civil Liberties Union used the Freedom of Information Act to obtain more than 100,000 pages of previously secret documents about U.S. treatment of detainees.[33] The Sunlight Foundation's blog, Real Time Investigations, compiled government data

such as federal contracts, lobbying disclosure forms, campaign finance contributions, and congressional earmarks. One of its posts
revealed that Representative Harold Rogers, a Kentucky Republican, had tucked $3.6 million into an appropriations bill to buy an
untested product from a company whose owners were longtime
campaign contributors.[34]

The nation's ethnic media were also doing more muckraking. In 1996, the Pacific News Service, an alternative press syndicate, created the New America Media network to help the
ethnic press produce and distribute stories. The network's more
than 2,000 publications and broadcast outlets had small staffs, but
some of them tackled investigative projects on immigration, health
care, education, and crime. For example, "Twenty-First Century
Slaves," by Claudia Núñez, in the Los Angeles newspaper *La Opinión,* exposed a human trafficking ring that used an evangelical
couple in Mexico to recruit its victims. Núñez's articles described
traffickers forcing at least thirty immigrants to work seventeen
hours a day without pay as they sold food on street corners and
cooked meals in restaurants.[35]

One of the ethnic media network's members, *Oakland Post*
editor Chauncey Bailey, was killed in broad daylight in August
2007 by a masked gunman firing a sawed-off shotgun. Bailey had
been probing the possible criminal actions of the controversial
Your Black Muslim Bakery; a former dishwasher at the bakery
was charged with his murder. Bay Area journalists, however, suspected a broader conspiracy behind Bailey's killing. They created
the Chauncey Bailey Project, the biggest collaborative investigative effort since the Arizona Project responded to the murder of
Don Bolles more than thirty years earlier. Working out of the
Oakland Tribune newsroom, the group included more than two
dozen reporters, editors, photographers, and journalism students

from around the region. Robert Rosenthal, executive director of the Center for Investigative Reporting, served as the project's chief editor.

Over the next two years, the Chauncey Bailey Project produced more than 140 stories and multimedia projects about the connection between Bailey's assassination and Your Black Muslim Bakery. The investigative team unearthed links between the bakery and two unsolved 1968 slayings, allegations that women who worked at the bakery had been raped and tortured by owner Yusuf Bey IV, evidence of real-estate fraud by Bey's former wife, and financial irregularities in the bakery's business practices. They revealed that the detective in charge of the case had a longstanding relationship with Bey. The reporters also discovered a jailhouse video, seemingly overlooked by police, which showed Bey bragging about being a part of the killing. The video's discovery was a factor leading to the resignation of Oakland's police chief. Bey was finally charged with murdering Bailey and two other men.[36]

Collaboration was also making a difference beyond U.S. borders. The collapse of totalitarian governments and rapid globalization in trade, transportation, and communication contributed to the spread of watchdog journalism to more countries. By 2007, thirty-nine nonprofit investigative reporting centers were muckraking in cities around the world, more than double the number seven years earlier. Hundreds of journalists from more than eighty countries were attending annual Global Investigative Journalism Conferences. By working together, these journalists could investigate issues that transcend borders such as terrorism, drug trafficking, global warming, food safety, pollution, organized crime, and infectious diseases.[37]

To promote reporting across borders, the Center for Public Integrity founded the International Consortium of Investigative

Journalists in 1997. Within a decade, the Consortium included about one hundred journalists from fifty countries. Consortium members cooperated on stories about human rights abuses, the global arms trade, and the monopolization of the world's water resources. In 2008, thirty Consortium reporters and editors produced a multimedia investigation detailing the smuggling of billions of dollars' worth of tobacco across borders and the resulting corruption, violence, addiction, and loss of government revenue. They uncovered illegal tobacco deals involving counterfeiters in China, warlords in North Africa, factories in Russia, and criminal gangs in Canada. Big tobacco companies were shown to be involved in the illicit trade, prompting Japan Tobacco International and Philip Morris International to pay a combined $1.65 billion to the European Union and ten countries to settle lawsuits. Two other companies pleaded guilty to smuggling and were fined $1.1 billion.[38]

Collaboration reached a higher level the next year when leaders of nonprofit newsgroups met at Pocantico—oil baron John D. Rockefeller's old estate—to form the Investigative News Network. Representatives from more than a dozen news organizations, including National Public Radio, IRE, the Center for Public Integrity, Pacific News Service, the Center for Investigative Reporting, and Voice of San Diego helped create the network. In what became known as the Pocantico Declaration, nonprofit news publishers agreed for the first time to look for ways to help each other report investigative projects, raise money, and share administrative costs. The organizers understood this would not be easy. "None of us harbors any illusions about the grubby logistics of building a new institution," said one of the founders, Charles Lewis of the Investigative Reporting Workshop. "The staff sizes, annual budgets, and editorial capacities of the various non-profit publishers in the U.S. vary widely, as does, frankly, the quality and quantity of their work and the actual extent to which they do investigative reporting."[39]

Muckraking received more help in 2009 when the John S. and James L. Knight Foundation announced it was contributing $15 million in grants toward promoting investigative reporting in the digital age. That same year, the Associated Press agreed to distribute investigative stories from four other nonprofit groups: ProPublica, the Center for Public Integrity, the Center for Investigative Reporting, and the Investigative Reporting Workshop at American University. The deal allowed stories that once might have appeared in only one publication to be seen in up to 1,500 newspapers.[40]

By the end of the decade, investigative reporters could see signs of hope: increased collaboration, creative Web-based ventures, new nonprofits, growing university support, and more help from foundations. But would it be enough to replace the amount of investigative reporting once done by the mainstream press? Most big-city newspapers and televisions stations, not to mention national publications and the networks, had bigger budgets and reporting staffs than any of the new groups popping up. Freelancers and reporters working on investigative stories for start-up companies or small nonprofits were likely to receive less pay than their counterparts in large news organizations. They were also likely to have fewer resources available to them if they were sued, detained while covering a foreign country, denied access to government information, or pressured by prosecutors to reveal a source. "When you lose big institutions, you lose not only money but also clout," observed Deborah Nelson, the *Los Angeles Times*'s former Washington investigations editor.[41]

Fortunately, some leaders of mainstream news organizations

were reemphasizing investigative work. In a media environment with more than 180 million blogs around the world, they used muckraking as a way to make their news products distinctive.[42] Amid severe staff cutbacks in broadcast news, WFOR-TV in Miami kept nine people on its investigative team in 2009. "It's what sets you apart from all the other noise out there," News Director Adrienne Roark said. The *Seattle Times* grabbed readers' attention by running stories revealing that crimes by members of the 2001 University of Washington football team went unreported and that hundreds of medical professionals were allowed to practice even after sexually abusing patients. Whenever the *Times* did a good investigative series, Executive Editor David Boardman noted, more readers bought the newspaper and visited its Web site. "It's what they care about passionately," he said. "They value this more than anything else we do."[43]

In 2007, the *Milwaukee Journal-Sentinel* created a ten-person watchdog team, one of the largest of any newspaper its size in the country. Within a year, the team, working with daily beat reporters, had published more than fifty investigative stories and created two muckraking blogs. Soon they were winning national awards. A series on the health dangers of bisphenol A, a chemical compound used in some children's products, won several prizes and led to congressional hearings. The *Journal-Sentinel* also posted corporate records, lobbying reports, and campaign contribution data on its new Citizen Watchdog site, allowing readers to do their own digging. All of this muckraking did not hurt the *Journal-Sentinel's* bottom line. One study showed its Sunday edition ranking first among those in the nation's fifty largest metropolitan areas for percentage of adults in the community reading the newspaper. Its daily edition ranked second.[44]

The 2008 Pulitzer Prizes proved that investigative reporting was alive and kicking. The *Journal-Sentinel*'s Dave Umhoefer won an award for uncovering illegal pension deals costing taxpayers $50 million. Jake Hooker and Walt Bogdanich of the *New York Times* also received a prize for their stories detailing how China exports medicines and other products containing toxic ingredients. And the *Washington Post* earned three Pulitzers for investigative projects: exposés of misconduct by private contractors in Iraq, revelations of mistreatment at Walter Reed Hospital, and an investigatory profile of Vice President Cheney.

That same year, the *Chicago Tribune* won a Pulitzer for documenting faulty government regulation of dangerous toys and other hazardous children's products.[45] Even after its parent company filed for bankruptcy protection, the *Tribune* emphasized muckraking. Its marketing material trumpeted recent investigations: doctors who sold dubious yet expensive cures for autism, a University of Illinois admissions list that gave applicants with clout preference over other students, and a Chicago suburb that knowingly distributed drinking water contaminated with cancer-causing chemicals.

Despite all the economic problems, legal worries, political cynicism, and emphasis on celebrities and sensationalism, great investigative reporting was still being done, and the Internet was allowing it to go deeper and spread wider. As in other eras, muckraking was done by only a small minority of reporters, but the work they did made a difference. It did not seem to matter what economic model supported their work—corporate ownership, nonprofit foundation, small Internet start-up, a network of volunteers—they still investigated. The same has been true for more than a century. Ida B. Wells revealed the truth about lynchings for a struggling African American newspaper, Ida Tarbell sifted through Standard Oil's secret deals for an upstart magazine, Edward R. Murrow broadcast *Harvest of Shame* on a national network, I. F. Stone exposed government lies about atomic testing in his own small newsletter, Seymour Hersh discovered the truth about My Lai as a freelance reporter relying on grant money, and Bob Woodward and Carl Bernstein uncovered Nixon's crimes while working for a large metropolitan newspaper.

As these reporters demonstrated, the investigative impulse that has existed since the dawn of American journalism is too strong to disappear. Investigative reporting has changed dramatically since the glory days of Watergate, but it will endure for a few simple reasons. People are curious about the world around them. They want to make sure no one is taking advantage of them. They like a good story. And they want to know the truth.

PREFACE

1. Michael Schudson, *Watergate in American Memory: How We Remember, Forget, and Reconstruct the Past* (New York: Basic Books, 1992), 103–4.

2. Robert W. Greene, foreword to first edition of John Ullmann and Jan Colbert, eds., *The Reporter's Handbook: An Investigator's Guide to Documents and Techniques,* Investigative Reporters & Editors, Inc. (New York: St. Martin's Press, 1991), vii. James L. Aucoin writes that "serious reporters" define investigative journalism as "original reporting on an issue of significant public concern that reveals information not previously known and perhaps even hidden" (James L. Aucoin, *The Evolution of American Investigative Journalism* [Columbia: University of Missouri Press, 2005], 3); W. Lance Bennett and William Serrin use a similar definition of investigative reporting: "enterprise reporting on important public issues involving the discovery and documentation of previously hidden information." See "The Watchdog Role," in Geneva Overholser and Kathleen Hall Jamieson, eds., *The Press* (Oxford: Oxford University Press, 2005), 178.

3. Aucoin, *The Evolution of American Investigative Journalism,* 180–81.

4. Leonard Downie Jr., *The New Muckrakers* (Washington, D.C.: New Republic Book Company, 1976), 190.

5. Gerry Lanosga and Jason Martin, "The Investigative Reporting Agenda in America: 1979–2007." Paper presented to the Association for Education in Journalism and Mass Communication, Chicago, August 6–9, 2008, 22.

CHAPTER ONE

1. Wm. David Sloan and Julie Hedgepeth Williams, *The Early American Press, 1690–1783*. The History of American Journalism, ed. James D. Startt and Wm. David Sloan, no. 1 (Westport, Conn.: Greenwood Press, 1994), 76–77.

2. Ibid., 205–9.

3. *Publick Occurrences, Both Forreign and Domestick;* Aucoin, *The Evolution of American Investigative Journalism,* 19–20; Sloan and Williams, *The Early American Press,* 3–5.

4. *Publick Occurrences, Both Forreign and Domestick;* Charles E. Clark, *The Public Prints: The Newspaper in Anglo-American Culture, 1665–1740* (New York: Oxford University Press, 1994), 71–73; Sloan and Williams, *The Early American Press,* 3–5.

5. Aucoin, *The Evolution of American Investigative Journalism,* 20.

6. Sloan and Williams, *The Early American Press, 1690–1783,* 5.

7. Clarke, *The Public Prints,* 92–97; Sloan and Williams, *The Early American Press,* 20–21.

8. Rosemary Armao, "The History of Investigative Reporting," *The Big Chill: Investigative Reporting in the Current Media Environment,* Marilyn Greenwald and Joseph Bernt, eds. (Ames: Iowa State University Press, 2000), 36; Aucoin, *The Evolution of American Investigative Journalism,* 20–21; David L. Protess et al., *The Journalism of Outrage: Investigative Reporting and Agenda Building in America* (New York: Guilford Press, 1991), 30–31; Sloan and Williams, *The Early American Press,* 60–67.

9. Louis L. Snyder and Richard B. Morris, eds. *A Treasury of Great Reporting: "Literature under Pressure" from the Sixteenth Century to Our Own Time,* 2nd ed. (New York: Simon & Schuster, 1962), 20–25; and Sloan and Williams, *The Early American Press,* 85–90.

10. Sloan and Williams, *The Early American Press,* 100–101.

11. Ibid., 148–51, 154.

12. Ibid., *The Early American Press,* 171–91; Armao, "The History of Investigative Reporting," 37; Bruce Shapiro, ed., *Shaking the Foundations: 200 Years of Investigative Journalism in America* (New York: Thurnder's Mouth Press/Nation Books, 2003), 3–8; Carol Sue Humphrey, *The Press of the Young Republic, 1783–1833.* The History of American Journalism,

ed. James D. Startt and Wm. David Sloan, no. 2 (Westport, Conn.: Greenwood Press, 1996), 2–47; and Aucoin, *The Evolution of American Investigative Journalism,* 22.

13. Humphrey, *The Press of the Young Republic,* 57–68, 75–76, 159; Aucoin, *The Evolution of American Investigative Journalism,* 22–23.

14. Humphrey, *The Press of the Young Republic,* 2, 133–35, 140, 145, 156.

15. Clint C. Wilson II, Félix Gutiérrez, and Lena M. Chao, *Racism, Sexism, and the Media: The Rise of Class Communication in Multicultural America,* 3rd ed. (Thousand Oaks, Calif.: Sage Publications, 2003), 270–72; Jacqueline Bacon, *Freedom's Journal: The First African-American Newspaper* (Lanham, Md.: Lexington Books, 2007), 76–77; Humphrey, *The Press of the Young Republic,* 144–45; Patrick S. Washburn, *The African American Newspaper: Voice of Freedom,* Medill School of Journalism Visions of the American Press, ed. David Abrahamson (Evanston, Ill.: Northwestern University Press, 2006), 17–23. William E. Huntzicker, *The Popular Press 1833–1865.* The History of American Journalism, ed. James D. Startt and Wm. David Sloan, no. 3 (Westport, Conn.: Greenwood Press, 1999), 74–75, 174.

16. Humphrey, *The Press of the Young Republic,* 133–35; Aucoin, *The Evolution of American Investigative Journalism,* 23–25; William E. Huntzicker, *The Popular Press,* 1; and Michael Schudson, *Discovering the News: A Social History of American Newspapers* (New York: Basic Books, 1978), 14–18, 22–23.

17. Serrin and Serrin, *Muckraking!,* 307–9; Huntzicker, *The Popular Press,* 19–21; Margaret H. DeFleur, *Computer-Assisted Investigative Reporting* (Mahwah, N.J.: Lawrence Erlbaum Associates, 1997), 10.

18. Caleb Crain, "A Star is Born," *New York Review of Books* 49, no. 9 (May 23, 2002); Agnes Hooper Gottlieb, "Women and Exposé: Reform and Housekeeping," in Robert Miraldi, ed., *The Muckrakers: Evangelical Crusaders* (Westport, Conn.: Praeger, 2000), 77.

19. Huntzicker, *The Popular Press,* 21–22.

20. "The Swill Milk Trade of New York and Brooklyn," *Frank Leslie's Illustrated Weekly* (May 8, 1958), in Serrin and Serrin, *Muckraking!,* 47–50.

21. Huntzicker, *The Popular Press,* 142, 148–49, 151–53, 156–57; W. Joseph Campbell, *The Year That Defined American Journalism: 1897 and the Clash of Paradigms* (New York: Routledge, 2006), 14–15; Leonard

Ray Teel, *The Public Press, 1900–1945*. The History of American Journalism, James D. Startt and Wm. David Sloan, eds., no. 5 (Westport, Conn.: Praeger, 2006), 3; David E. Sumner, "Makers of the Modern Magazine Model: *Munsey's, McClure's* and *Cosmopolitan* in the 1890s." Paper presented at the Joint Journalism Historians Conference, New York City, March 14, 2009, 3; Ted Curtis Smythe, *The Gilded Age Press, 1865–1900*. The History of American Journalism, James D. Startt and Wm. David Sloan, eds., no. 4 (Westport, Conn.: Praeger, 2003), x, 208.

22. Smythe, *The Gilded Age Press*, x, 57, 65, 71–74; James T. Hamilton, *All the News That's Fit to Sell* (Princeton: Princeton University Press, 2004), 46–48; Phyllis Kaniss, *Making Local News* (Chicago: University of Chicago Press, 1991), 19–20; Michael Dillon, "Anatomy of a Crusade: The *Buffalo News'* Campaign for Immigrants," in Miraldi, ed., *The Muckrakers: Evangelical Crusaders,* 26–28; and Aucoin, *The Evolution of American Investigative Journalism,* 25–27.

23. "More Ring Villainy." *New York Times,* 8 July 1871, 4; Aucoin, *Evolution of American Investigative Journalism,* 26–28; Shapiro, *Shaking the Foundations,* 26–39; Smythe, *Gilded Age Press,* 10–13.

24. Serrin and Serrin, *Muckraking!,* 99–102; Suzanne Garment, *Scandal: The Crisis of Mistrust in American Politics* (New York: Times Books, 1991), 3; Smythe, *The Gilded Age Press,* 51.

25. Smythe, *The Gilded Age Press,* 71, 79–80, 206.

26. Richard Digby-Junger, *The Journalist as Reformer: Henry Demarest Lloyd and* Wealth Against Commonwealth (Westport, Conn.: Greenwood Press, 1996), 62.

27. Dillon, "Anatomy of a Crusade," 25–46.

28. Denis Brian, *Pulitzer: A Life* (New York: John Wiley & Sons, 2001), 5, 31–62; Smythe, *Gilded Age Press,* 84–86; Aucoin, *Evolution of American Investigative Journalism,* 28.

29. Smythe, *Gilded Age Press,* 132–39.

30. "The Journalism That Does Things," *New York Journal,* 13 October 1897, cited in Campbell, *The Year That Defined American Journalism,* 87; Campbell, *The Year That Defined American Journalism,* 25, 87; Teel, *The Public Press,* 7; Bruce W. Sanford, *Don't Shoot the Messenger: How Our Growing Hatred of the Media Threatens Free Speech for All of Us* (Lanham,

Md.: Rowman & Littlefield, 1999), 47–49; Smythe, *Gilded Age Press,* 173–83.

31. David Randall, *The Great Reporters* (London: Pluto Press, 2005), 93–100; Shapiro, *Shaking the Foundations,* 45–49.

32. Nellie Bly, "Ten Days in a Mad-House," *New York World,* 16 October 1887; Serrin and Serrin, *Muckraking!,* 142–46; Randall, *Great Reporters,* 100–103.

33. Randall, *Great Reporters,* 103–5; Serrin and Serrin, *Muckraking!,* 145–46.

34. Agnes Hooper Gottlieb, "Women and Exposé: Reform and Housekeeping," in Miraldi, *The Muckrakers,* 80; Serrin and Serrin, *Muckraking!,* 146.

35. Bonnie Yochelson, *Jacob Riis* (London: Phaidon Press, 2001), 3–15; Serrin and Serrin, *Muckraking!,* 1–3; Steve Weinberg, "The Accidental Icon: How Jacob Riis Went from the Muck to Muckraker," *Columbia Journalism Review* 47, no. 3 (September/October 2008): 61–62.

36. Rodger Streitmatter, *Voices of Revolution: The Dissident Press in America* (New York: Columbia University Press, 2001), 81–87; Serrin and Serrin, *Muckraking!,* 179–80.

37. Protess et al., *The Journalism of Outrage,* 33–34.

38. David Mark Chalmers, *The Muckrake Years* (New York: D. Van Nostrand, 1974), 4–12; Mark Feldstein, "A Muckraking Model: Investigative Reporting Cycles in American History," *Harvard International Journal of Press/Politics* 11, no. 2 (Spring 2006): 109; Sumner, "Makers of the Modern Magazine Model," 1–15; Robert Miraldi, "Introduction: Why the Muckrakers Are Still with Us," in *The Muckrakers,* xii–xiv; Protess et al., *The Journalism of Outrage,* 35–36; Teel, *The Public Press,* 240–41; Carey McWiliams, "Is Muckraking Coming Back?" *Columbia Journalism Review* 9, no. 3 (Fall 1970): 8.

39. Lincoln Steffens, *The Shame of the Cities* (New York, 1904) in Chalmers, *The Muckrake Years,* 82–83; Steve Weinberg, *Taking on the Trust: The Epic Battle of Ida Tarbell and John D. Rockefeller* (New York: W. W. Norton & Company, 2008), 159, 195–97; Chalmers, *The Muckrake Years,* 17–19, 171; Louis Filler, *Crusaders for American Liberalism* (Yellow Springs, Ohio: Antioch Press, 1939), 81, 86; Teel, *The Public Press,* 240.

40. S. S. McClure, "Concerning Three Articles in this Number of

McClure's, and a Coincidence that May Set Us Thinking," *McClure's* 20 (January 1903): 336 in Chalmers, *The Muckrake Years,* 79–82; Steve Weinberg, author interview, 6 June 2008; Weinberg, *Taking on the Trust,* xiv, 211–13, 224, 266; Kathleen Brady, *Ida Tarbell: Portrait of a Muckraker* (New York: Seaview/Putnam, 1984), 120–38.

41. Weinberg, *Taking on the Trust,* 222, 224, 227, 249–50, 254; Kathleen Brady, "Remembering Ida Tarbell," *IRE Journal* 31, no. 1 (January/February 2008): 13; Chalmers, *The Muckrake Years,* 21–24.

42. Chalmers, *The Muckrake Years,* 38–42.

43. Ibid., 61.

44. Charles Edward Russell, "The Tenements of Trinity Church," *Everybody's* 19 (July 1908): 47 in Chalmers, *The Muckrake Years,* 146–47; Robert Miraldi, "Muckraking the World's Richest Church," in Miraldi, ed., *The Muckrakers,* 53–67.

45. Samuel Hopkins Adams, "The Great American Fraud," *Collier's* 36 (October 7, 1905): 14–15, 29 in Chalmers, *The Muckrake Years,* 102–7; Serrin and Serrin, *Muckraking!* 309–15; Robert Miraldi, *Muckraking and Objectivity: Journalism's Colliding Traditions* (New York: Greenwood Press, 1990), 29, 34–35; Teel, *The Public Press,* 22.

46. Upton Sinclair, *The Jungle* (New York, 1906), in Chalmers, *The Muckrake Years,* 107–9; Samuel P. Winch, "Ethical Challenges for Investigative Journalists," in Greenwald and Bernt eds., *The Big Chill,* 126.

47. David Graham Phillips, "New York's Misrepresentatives," *Cosmopolitan* (March 1906) in Serrin and Serrin, *Muckraking!* 105–9.

48. Filler, *Contemporaries,* x; Chalmers, *The Muckrake Years,* 43–46; Miraldi, *Muckraking and Objectivity,* 23–29, 38.

49. Hermann Hagedorn, ed., *The Works of Theodore Roosevelt,* 16 (New York, 1926) in Chalmers, *The Muckrake Years,* 125–30; Weinberg, *Taking on the Trust,* 241; Teel, *The Public Press,* 17–18, 22–23.

50. Protess et al., *The Journalism of Outrage,* 40; Chalmers, *The Muckrake Years,* 31–37; Teel, *The Public Press,* 21–24.

51. Winch, "Ethical Challenges for Investigative Journalists," 126; Edwin Markham, "The Hoe-Man in the Making," *Cosmopolitan* 41 (September 1906): 480–84 in Chalmers, *The Muckrake Years,* 133–36; Chalmers, *The Muckrake Years,* 52–58; John A. Fitch, "Old Age at Forty," *American Magazine* (March 1911), in Serrin and Serrin, *Muckraking!,* 25–28; Will

Irwin, "The American Newspaper, A Study of Journalism in Its Relation to the Public," *Collier's* 47 (June 17, 1911): 18 in Chalmers, *The Muckrake Years,* 147–49.

52. Miraldi, *Muckraking and Objectivity,* 62–71; Thomas Leonard, "Did the Muckrakers Muck Up Progress?" in Miraldi, ed., *The Muckrakers,* 146; Protess et al., *The Journalism of Outrage,* 42–44; Chalmers, *The Muckrake Years,* 60–63; Bennett and Serrin, "The Watchdog Role," 177.

53. Aucoin, *The Evolution of American Investigative Journalism,* 64; Teel, *The Public Press,* 74–79; Michael S. Sweeney, *The Military and the Press: An Uneasy Truce,* Medill School of Journalism Visions of the American Press, ed. David Abrahamson (Evanston, Ill.: Northwestern University Press, 2006), 35–59.

CHAPTER TWO

1. Feldstein, "A Muckraking Model," 110; DeFleur, *Computer-Assisted Investigative Reporting,* 14; Miraldi, *Muckraking and Objectivity,* 19; Bennett and Serrin, "The Watchdog Role," 177.

2. Campbell, *The Year That Defined American Journalism,* 6, 94; Miraldi, *Muckraking and Objectivity,* 47; Aucoin, *The Evolution of American Investigative Journalism,* 37–38.

3. Roy J. Harris Jr., *Pulitzer's Gold: Behind the Prize for Public Service Journalism* (Columbia: University of Missouri Press, 2007), 171–73, 390, 396, 397.

4. Walter Lippmann, *Public Opinion* (New York: Harcourt, Brace and Company, 1922), 363–65, 409–10; Schudson, *Discovering the News,* 120–59; Robert Karl Manoff and Michael Schudson, eds., *Reading the News* (New York: Pantheon Books, 1986), 20.

5. Curtis D. MacDougall, *Interpretative Reporting* (New York: Macmillan, 1938), 594–95; Robert W. Jones, *Journalism in the United States* (New York: E. P. Dutton, 1947); Edwin Emery and Henry Ladd Smith, *The Press and America* (Englewood Cliffs, N.J.: Prentice-Hall, 1954).

6. Hamilton, *All the News That's Fit to Sell,* 26; Paul N. Williams, *Investigative Reporting and Editing* (Englewood Cliffs, N.J.: Prentice-Hall, 1978), 5–6.

7. James Aronson, *The Press and the Cold War* (New York: Monthly Review Press, 1970), 14–15, 19; Protess et al., *The Journalism of Outrage,* 35; Teel, *The Public Press,* 2, 28–29; Robert W. McChesney, *The Political Economy of Media: Enduring Issues, Emerging Dilemmas* (New York: Monthly Review Press, 2008), 28–29.

8. Donna L. Halper, "Dangerous Ideas: Censorship in Broadcasting's First Two Decades." Paper presented to Joint Journalism Historians Conference, New York City, March 14, 2009.

9. David R. Davies, *The Postwar Decline of American Newspapers, 1945–1965.* The History of American Journalism, ed. James D. Startt and Wm. David Sloan, no. 6 (Westport, Conn.: Praeger, 2006), 36; Schudson, *Discovering the News,* 139–40, 144, 167.

10. Harris, *Pulitzer's Gold,* 13, 122–35; Serrin and Serrin, *Muckraking!,* 188–92.

11. Aucoin, 35–36; Serrin and Serrin, *Muckraking!,* 37–39; Shapiro, *Shaking the Foundations,* 201–44; Teel, *The Public Press, 1900–1945,* 105.

12. Jack Anderson with James Boyd, *Confessions of a Muckraker: The Inside Story of Life in Washington during the Truman, Eisenhower, Kennedy and Johnson Years* (New York: Random House, 1979), 12, 19; Teel, *The Public Press,* 139.

13. Anderson, *Confessions of a Muckraker,* 9, 10, 13, 21–23.

14. Ibid., 7, 31, 110–21.

15. Davies, *The Postwar Decline of American Newspapers,* 34–37.

16. Anthony Lewis, "The Richard S. Salant Lecture on Freedom of the Press," The Joan Shorenstein Center on the Press, Politics and Public Policy, Cambridge, Mass., 1 October 2008, 13.

17. Loren Ghiglione, *CBS's Don Hollenbeck: An Honest Reporter in the Age of McCarthyism* (New York: Columbia University Press, 2008), 112–13; "Brother Crawford," *Time,* 16 August 1948; Bill Steigerwald, "Sprigle's Secret Journey," *Pittsburgh Post-Gazette,* 2 August 1998, G10.

18. James Brian McPherson, *Journalism at the End of the American Century, 1965–Present.* The History of American Journalism, James D. Startt and Wm. David Sloan, eds., no. 7 (Westport, Conn.: Praeger, 2006), 8.

19. Ghiglione, *CBS's Don Hollenbeck,* 113.

20. Rodger Streitmatter, *Raising Her Voice: African-American Women*

Journalists Who Changed History (Lexington: The University Press of Kentucky, 1994), 121.

21. Teel, *The Public Press,* 177–78; Gene Roberts, author interview, Evanston, Ill., 8 October 2007, tape recording.

22. Patricia Bradley, *Women and the Press: The Struggle for Equality,* Medill School of Journalism Visions of the American Press, ed. David Abrahamson (Evanston, Ill.: Northwestern University Press, 2005), 193; Shapiro, *Shaking the Foundations,* 245–53; Streitmatter, *Raising Her Voice,* 91–94.

23. McPherson, *Journalism at the End of the American Century,* 10–14; Bradley, *Women and the Press,* 241.

24. Shapiro, *Shaking the Foundations,* 137–56; Bradley, *Women and the Press,* 191–92.

25. Bernard Allen, "Two Thousand Dying on a Job," *New Masses* (15 January 1935), in Serrin and Serrin, *Muckraking!,* 34–37.

26. James F. Tracy, "A Historical Case Study of Alternative Media and Labor Activism: The *Dubuque Leader* 1935–1939," *Journalism & Communication Monographs* (Columbia, S.C.: Association for Education in Journalism and Mass Communication, 2007), 269–304.

27. Shapiro, *Shaking the Foundations,* 193–200.

28. Downie, *The New Muckrakers,* 202–11; McWilliams, "Is Muckraking Coming Back?" 11.

29. Randall, *The Great Reporters,* 72.

30. Randall, *The Great Reporters,* 71–91.

31. Jackson Lears, "Paper Trail," *New York Times Book Review,* 5 July 2009, 12; Streitmatter, *Voices of Revolution,* 186–88; Downie, *The New Muckrakers,* 188.

32. D. D. Guttenplan, *American Radical: The Life and Times of I. F. Stone* (New York: Farrar, Straus and Giroux, 2009), 338; Jack Lule, "I. F. Stone: The Practice of Reporting," *Journalism & Mass Communication Quarterly* 72, no. 3 (Autumn 1995): 500–502, 504; Downie, *The New Muckrakers,* 183–91.

33. Lule, "I. F. Stone," 499; Downie, *The New Muckrakers,* 182–83, 189; Paul Berman, "The Watchdog," *New York Times Book Review,* 1 October 2006, 12.

34. Aucoin, *The Evolution of American Investigative Journalism,* 50;

Davies, *The Postwar Decline of American Newspapers,* 41–47; Serrin and Serrin, *Muckraking!,* 119–22.

35. Bob Edwards, *Edward R. Murrow and the Birth of Broadcast Journalism* (Hoboken, N.J.: John Wiley & Sons, 2004), 110–18; Fred W. Friendly, *Due to Circumstances Beyond Our Control* (New York: Random House, 1967), 3–60; Serrin and Serrin, *Muckraking!,* 122–26.

36. Davies, *The Postwar Decline of American Newspapers,* 51–52, 56, 60–62.

37. Gerry Lanosga, "'God Help Our Democracy': Investigative Reporting in America, 1946–1960." Paper presented to the Association for Education in Journalism and Mass Communication, Boston, 6 August 2009; John Hohenberg, "New Patterns in Public Service," *Columbia Journalism Review* 1, no. 2 (Summer 1962): 17.

38. Gene Gleason and Fred J. Cook, "Few Homes Built by Title 1 Billion," *World-Telegram and Sun,* 30 July 1956, in Serrin and Serrin, *Muckraking!,* 158–60; Downie, *The New Muckrakers,* 211–13.

39. Gene Roberts and Hank Klibanoff, *The Race Beat: The Press, the Civil Rights Struggle, and the Awakening of a Nation* (New York: Alfred A. Knopf, 2006), 101–6.

40. Matt Marrone, "Oral History Interview with Jack Nelson." Defining Civil Rights & the Press Symposium, 24 April 2004. civilrightsand thepress.syr.edu/pdfs/jacknelson.pdf.

41. Jack Nelson, "Orangeburg Students Unarmed, Study Shows," *Los Angeles Times,* 18 February 1968, A3; Roberts and Klibanoff, *The Race Beat,* 402–3; Marrone, "Oral History Interview with Jack Nelson."

42. Ralph Nader, *Unsafe at Any Speed: The Designed-in Dangers of the American Automobile* (New York: Grossman Publishers, 1965); Serrin and Serrin, *Muckraking!,* 56–59.

43. Michael Harrington, *The Other America: Poverty in the United States* (New York: Simon & Schuster, 1962; Touchstone, 1997); Jessica Mitford, *The American Way of Death* (New York: Simon & Schuster, 1963); Rachel Carson, *Silent Spring* (Boston: Houghton Mifflin, 1962); Lisa Budwig, "Breaking Nature's Silence: Pennsylvania's Rachel Carson," The Rachel Carson Homestead, www.rachelcarsonhomestead.org/Education/Featured StoriesandReports/BreakingNaturesSilence/tabid/86/Default.aspx.

44. *New York Times Co. v Sullivan,* cited in Anthony Lewis, *Make*

No Law: The Sullivan Case and the First Amendment (New York: Random House, 1991), 270; Lewis, *Make No Law,* 157–58; Jane Kirtley, "Is It a Crime? An Overview of Recent Legal Actions Stemming from Investigative Reports," in Greenwald and Bernt, *The Big Chill,* 138.

45. McPherson, *Journalism at the End of the American Century,* 50–51; Aucoin, *The Evolution of American Investigative Journalism,* 76–77; Gerry Lanosga, "God Help Our Democracy."

46. Joseph C. Spear, *Presidents and the Press* (Cambridge, Mass.: MIT Press, 1984), 39; Martin Linsky, *Impact: How the Press Affects Federal Policymaking* (New York: W.W. Norton, 1986), 44–45.

47. Aronson, *The Press and the Cold War,* 190, 297–98; Aucoin, *The Evolution of American Investigative Journalism,* 59; Miles Maguire, "Richard Critchfield: 'Genius' Journalism and the Fallacy of Verification." Paper presented to the International Conference for Literary Journalism Studies, Evanston, Ill., 15 May 2009; Herbert J. Gans, *Deciding What's News: A Study of "CBS Evening News," "NBC Nightly News," "Newsweek," and "Time"* (New York: Random House, 1979; Evanston, Ill.: Northwestern University Press, 2004), 135; Schudson, *Discovering the News,* 174–75.

48. David Halberstam, *The Powers That Be* (New York: Alfred A. Knopf, 1979), 488–90.

49. Davies, *The Postwar Decline of American Newspapers,* 125–27; Leonard Downie Jr. and Robert G. Kaiser, *The News about the News: American Journalism in Peril* (New York: Alfred A. Knopf, 2002), 131.

50. Chad Raphael, *Investigated Reporting: Muckrakers, Regulators, and the Struggle over Television Documentary* (Urbana: University of Illinois Press, 2005), 2–4; Tom Mascaro, "Documentary," The Museum of Broadcast Communication, www.museum.tv/archives/etv/D/htmlD/documentary/documentary.htm.

51. Miraldi, *Muckraking and Objectivity,* 87–99; Raphael, *Investigated Reporting,* 18–26.

52. Raphael, *Investigated Reporting,* 3–4, 26–47, 111; Gans, *Deciding What's News,* 256.

53. John Hohenberg, "Public Service: A 1964 Honor Roll," *Columbia Journalism Review* 3, no. 2 (Summer 1964): 11–12.

54. McWilliams, "Is Muckraking Coming Back?" 12; Eddith Dashiell, "For Mainstream Audiences Only," in Greenwald and Bernt, eds.,

The Big Chill, 182; Clark R. Mollenhoff, *Investigative Reporting: From Courthouse to White House* (New York: Macmillan Publishing, 1981), 259–304; Schudson, *Discovering the News,* 189–91; Donald L. Barlett and James B. Steele, "Reporting Is Only Part of the Investigative Story," *Nieman Reports* 62, no. 1 (Spring 2008): 50–52.

55. Aucoin, *The Evolution of American Investigative Journalism,* 77–78; McPherson, *Journalism at the End of the American Century,* 24–25, 51.

56. Richard G. Gray, "Introduction" in Robert J. Glessing, *The Underground Press in America* (Bloomington: Indiana University Press, 1970), xii; Glessing, *The Underground Press in America,* 6, 10, 16.

57. Todd Gitlin, "An Unexpected Aeration: A Crisis of Conscience Breathed Life into American Journalism," *Media Studies Journal* 12, no. 3 (Fall 1998): 151; Abe Peck, *Uncovering the Sixties: The Life and Times of the Underground Press* (New York: Citadel Press, 1991), 201.

58. Streitmatter, *Voices of Revolution,* 191–93; Aucoin, *The Evolution of American Investigative Journalism,* 57–58; Downie, *The New Muckrakers,* 175–80, 191–201, 219.

59. David Halberstam, "Justified Doubts," *Media Studies Journal* 12, no. 3 (Fall 1998): 11; Melissa Guthrie, "Investigative Journalism Under Fire," *Broadcast & Cable,* 22 June 2008; Schudson, *Discovering the News,* 176–81; Samuel P. Huntington, "The Democratic Distemper," *Public Interest* 41 (Fall 1975): 9–10.

60. Downie, *The New Muckrakers,* 50–82; John Hyde, "When a Few Dollars Make a Big Difference," *Nieman Reports* 62, no. 1 (Spring 2008): 38–39.

61. Seymour M. Hersh, *Cover-up* (New York: Random House, 1972); Seymour M. Hersh, *My Lai 4: A Report on the Massacre and Its Aftermath* (New York: Random House, 1970); Downie, *The New Muckrakers,* 50–82.

CHAPTER THREE

1. Richard Reeves, *President Nixon: Alone in the White House* (New York: Simon & Schuster, 2001), 14; Rick Perlstein, *Nixonland: The Rise of a President and the Fracturing of America* (New York: Scribner, 2008), xii.

2. Perlstein, *Nixonland,* 358–59; Richard M. Nixon, *In the Arena: A Memoir of Victory, Defeat, and Renewal* (New York: Simon & Schuster,

1990), 254; Joan Hoff, *Nixon Reconsidered* (New York: Basic Books, 1994), 277.

3. Richard E. Neustadt, *Presidential Power and the Modern Presidents: The Politics of Leadership from Roosevelt to Reagan* (New York: The Free Press, 1990), 218; Reeves, *President Nixon,* 11–12; Spear, *Presidents and the Press,* 93–94; Hugh Sidey, "The Man and Foreign Policy," in Kenneth W. Thompson, ed., *The Nixon Presidency: Twenty-Two Intimate Perspectives of Richard M. Nixon* (Lanham, Md.: University Press of America, 1987), 312.

4. Theodore H. White, *Breech of Faith: The Fall of Richard Nixon* (New York: Atheneum Publishers, 1975), 80, 113.

5. James Keogh, *President Nixon and the Press* (New York: Funk and Wagnalls, 1972), 2–3.

6. Stephen E. Ambrose, *Nixon: The Education of a Politician 1913–1962* (New York: Simon & Schuster, 1987), 668–71; Sidey, "The Man and Foreign Policy," 301–4; H. R. Haldeman notes of 15 May 1972, released by the Nixon Presidential Library & Museum, http://nixon.archives.gov/virtuallibrary/documents/dec08.php; William Safire, *Before the Fall: An Inside View of the Pre-Watergate White House* (Garden City, N.Y.: Doubleday, 1975), 343.

7. White, *Breech of Faith,* 68–69, 82–96; David Greenberg, *Nixon's Shadow: The History of an Image* (New York: W. W. Norton & Company, 2003), 137; Robert Shogan, "Enemas for Elephants," *Media Studies Journal* 12, no. 3 (Fall 1998): 50–54.

8. Spear, *Presidents and the Press,* 31–32; J. Anthony Lukas, *Nightmare: The Underside of the Nixon Years* (Athens: Ohio University Press, 1973), 11.

9. Charles Colson memorandum for H. R. Haldeman, 4 November 1971, released by the Nixon Presidential Library & Museum, http://nixon.archives.gov/virtuallibrary/documents/jun09.php; Louis W. Liebovich, *Richard Nixon, Watergate, and the Press: A Historical Retrospective* (Westport, Conn.: Praeger, 2003), 24; Spear, *Presidents and the Press,* 42, 66, 73, 77–78.

10. Daniel Schorr, *Clearing the Air* (Boston: Houghton Mifflin, 1977), 41; Greenberg, *Nixon's Shadow,* 128–29, 140; Perlstein, *Nixonland,* 360.

11. Richard M. Nixon, *RN: The Memoirs of Richard Nixon* (New York: Grosset & Dunlap, 1978), 354–55.

12. Liebovich, *Richard Nixon, Watergate, and the Press,* 1–12; Lukas, *Nightmare,* 23–24.

13. Schudson, *Watergate in American Memory,* 115–17; Ambrose, *Nixon: The Education of a Politician,* 673.

14. McChesney, *The Political Economy of Media,* 31.

15. James Rosen, *The Strong Man: John Mitchell and the Secret of Watergate* (New York: Doubleday, 2008), 116; Bob Woodward and Scott Armstrong, *The Brethren: Inside the Supreme Court* (New York: Simon & Schuster, 1979; Avon Books, 1981), 14–17.

16. Hoff, *Nixon Reconsidered,* 284.

17. Nixon, *RN,* 390.

18. Nixon, *RN,* 387–89; Keith W. Olson, *Watergate: The Presidential Scandal That Shook America* (Lawrence: University Press of Kansas, 2003), 10–12.

19. Olson, *Watergate,* 10–12.

20. Ibid., 8–9, 12; White, *Breech of Faith,* 120–21.

21. Leonard Garment, "The Guns of Watergate," *Commentary* 83, no. 4 (April 1987): 16–17.

22. "List of White House 'Enemies' and Memorandums Relating to Those Named," *New York Times,* 28 June 1973, 38.

23. Greenberg, *Nixon's Shadow,* 145–46; Liebovich, *Richard Nixon, Watergate, and the Press,* 1–8, 10; Perlstein, *Nixonland,* 730; Raphael, *Investigated Reporting,* 90–91; Schorr, *Clearing the Air,* 36–40.

24. Spiro Agnew, "On the National Media," speech, Des Moines, Iowa, 13 November 1969; Stephen E. Ambrose, *Nixon: The Triumph of a Politician 1962–1972* (New York: Simon & Schuster, 1989), 163.

25. Liebovich, *Richard Nixon, Watergate, and the Press,* 8–9.

26. Greenberg, *Nixon's Shadow,* 147; Schorr, *Clearing the Air,* 40.

27. Liebovich, *Richard Nixon, Watergate, and the Press,* ix, 8, 17–18.

28. Agnew, "On the National Media."

29. Liebovich, *Richard Nixon, Watergate, and the Press,* 14; Schorr, *Clearing the Air,* 40.

30. Raphael, *Investigated Reporting,* 5–6, 11.

31. Liebovich, *Richard Nixon, Watergate, and the Press,* 22–24; Schorr, *Clearing the Air,* 41–47; Katharine Graham, *Personal History* (New York: Alfred A. Knopf, 1997), 478–79.

32. John W. Dean III, *Blind Ambition: The White House Years* (New York: Simon & Schuster, 1976), 32–38.

33. Lukas, *Nightmare*, 1–2, 10; Olson, *Watergate*, 26; Liebovich, *Richard Nixon, Watergate, and the Press*, 26–29; Perlstein, *Nixonland*, xii; Richard M. Nixon, interview by David Frost in *Frost/Nixon: The Original Watergate Interviews*, originally broadcast as "The Nixon Interviews" by David Paradine Productions, Inc., on 5 May 1977.

34. Raphael, *Investigated Reporting*, 76–105.

35. Nixon, *RN*, 508–11; Aronson, *The Press and the Cold War*, 292–93; Kathryn S. Olmsted, *Challenging the Secret Government* (Chapel Hill: University of North Carolina Press, 1996), 32; Spear, *Presidents and the Press*, xi; Aucoin, *The Evolution of American Investigative Journalism*, 72–73.

36. Ben Bradlee, author interview, 13 May 2009.

37. H. R. Haldeman, *The Haldeman Diaries: Inside the Nixon White House* (New York: G. P. Putnam's Sons, 1994), 309.

38. Reeves, *President Nixon*, 339; Liebovich, *Richard Nixon, Watergate, and the Press*, 37; Nixon, *RN*, 512; Kutler, *Abuse of Power*, 8.

39. Lawrence Higby memorandum for H. R. Haldeman, 8 July 1971, released by the Nixon Presidential Library & Museum, http://nixon.archives.gov/virtuallibrary/documents/jun09.php; Dean, *Blind Ambition*, 44–47; Tape of Nixon, Haldeman, and Colson Oval Office conversation of 2 July 1971 in Kutler, *Abuse of Power*, 16.

40. Stanley I. Kutler, *The Wars of Watergate: The Last Crisis of Richard Nixon* (New York: Alfred A. Knopf, 1990), 108.

41. Nixon, *RN*, 513.

42. Jack Caulfield memorandum for John Ehrlichman, 31 July 1969, released by the Nixon Presidential Library & Museum, http://nixon.archives.gov/virtuallibrary/documents/jun09.php; Kutler, *The Wars of Watergate*, 111–16; Olson, *Watergate*, 18–20.

43. Hoff, *Nixon Reconsidered*, 294; Barry Sussman, *The Great Coverup: Nixon and the Scandal of Watergate* (New York: Signet Classics, 1974), 213–18.

44. Tape of Nixon and Ehrlichman Oval Office conversation of 8 September 1971 in Kutler, *Abuse of Power*, 28.

45. J. Edgar Hoover letter to John W. Dean III, 20 December 1971, released by the Nixon Presidential Library & Museum, http://nixon

.archives.gov/virtuallibrary/documents/dec08.php; Schorr, *Clearing the Air,* 70–76; David R. Young undated memorandum for Richard Nixon, released by the Nixon Presidential Library & Museum, http://nixon .archives.gov/virtuallibrary/documents/jun09.php; Daniel Schorr, remarks at "Watergate—35 Years Later." Society of Professional Journalists Convention & National Journalism Conference in Washington, D.C., 6 October 2007; Joseph C. Spear, *Presidents and the Press,* 134–39; Scott Carlson, "In Jack Anderson's Papers, a Hidden History of Washington," *The Chronicle of Higher Education* 16 March 2007, A18; Lukas, *Nightmare,* 104–5.

46. Greenberg, *Nixon's Shadow,* 126–27.

47. Nixon, *RN,* 542; Ambrose, *Nixon: The Triumph of a Politician,* 552–54; Olson, *Watergate,* 22, 29–30; Liebovich, *Richard Nixon, Watergate, and the Press,* 46–50.

48. Dean, *Blind Ambition,* 72–73; Nixon, *RN,* 774–75; Perlstein, *Nixonland,* 630–32; Olson, *Watergate,* 30–34, 40–41.

49. Nixon, *RN,* 774–75; Carl Bernstein, "Watergate's Last Chapter," *Vanity Fair,* October 2005.

50. "Historian Decries Watergate as 'Cult of Personality,'" William B. Dickinson, ed., *Watergate: Chronology of a Crisis,* vol. 1 (Washington, D.C.: Congressional Quarterly, 1973), 170.

51. Olson, *Watergate,* 19; Dean, *Blind Ambition,* 76–79: Liebovich, *Richard Nixon, Watergate, and the Press,* 46.

52. Rosen, *The Strong Man,* 262–75; Olson, *Watergate,* 36–38.

53. Olson, *Watergate,* 38–40; Sussman, *The Great Coverup,* 218.

54. Schudson, *Watergate in American Memory,* 25–26; Edward D. Berkowitz, *Something Happened: A Political and Cultural Overview of the Seventies* (New York: Columbia University Press, 2006), 21; Olson, *Watergate,* 38–39; W. Mark Felt and John O'Connor, *A G-Man's Life: The FBI, Being "Deep Throat," and the Struggle for Honor in Washington* (New York: Public Affairs, 2006), 195.

55. "Watergate Scandal: A Senate Search for Truth," in Dickinson, ed., *Watergate: Chronology of a Crisis,* 3; Carl Bernstein and Bob Woodward, *All the President's Men* (New York: Simon & Schuster, 1974; Pocket Books, 2005), 15–16; Sussman, *The Great Coverup,* 3–9; Olson, *Watergate,* 39–40.

56. Kutler, *Abuse of Power,* xx; Ambrose, *Nixon: The Triumph of a Politician,* 561; Jim Hougan, *Secret Agenda: Watergate, Deep Throat and the CIA* (New York: Random House, 1984), xvii–xix; Len Colodny and Robert Gettlin, *Silent Coup: The Removal of a President* (New York: St. Martin's Press, 1991), 142–72; Steve Weinberg, "Was Nixon Duped? Did Woodward Lie?" *Columbia Journalism Review* 30, no. 4 (November/December 1991): 88–94; Hoff, *Nixon Reconsidered,* 304–5; Sussman, *The Great Coverup,* 25; Rick Perlstein, *Nixonland,* 665–66.

57. Olson, *Watergate,* 41–44.

CHAPTER FOUR

1. Bob Woodward, author interview, 20 May 2009; Barry Sussman, author interview, 11 September 2008; Alicia Shepard, *Woodward and Bernstein: Life in the Shadow of Watergate* (Hoboken, N.J.: John Wiley & Sons, 2007), 22–23; Sussman, *The Great Coverup,* 22; Bradlee, *A Good Life,* 323.

2. Sussman, author interview.

3. Ibid.; Bradlee, *A Good Life,* 325; Downie, *The New Muckrakers,* 2; Bernstein and Woodward, *All the President's Men,* 13–16; Shepard, *Woodward and Bernstein,* 7–17; Bob Woodward, *The Secret Man* (New York: Simon & Schuster, 2005), 27–34.

4. Sussman, *The Great Coverup,* 15–18; Woodward, *The Secret Man,* 53–55; Shepard, *Woodward and Bernstein,* 32; Bernstein and Woodward, *All the President's Men,* 13–20.

5. Years later Woodward wrote that eight *Post* reporters worked on the first day's coverage, but Sussman, the editor in charge, said in his 1974 book that it was ten. Sussman, *The Great Coverup,* 17.

6. Woodward, *The Secret Man,* 55–56; Bob Woodward, remarks at "Watergate—35 Years Later."

7. Sussman, author interview; Bradlee, author interview; Timothy Crouse, *The Boys on the Bus* (New York: Random House, 1973), 291; Downie, *The New Muckrakers,* 3–6; Graham, *Personal History,* 462; Shepard, *Woodward and Bernstein,* 17–29, 32; David Segal, "Carl Bernstein, Back on the Beat," *Washington Post,* 20 June 2007, C01; Sussman, *The Great Coverup,* 54–55.

8. Bernstein and Woodward, *All the President's Men,* 23–25; Bradlee, *A Good Life,* 325–26; Shepard, *Woodward and Bernstein,* 33–34.

9. W. Mark Felt, *The FBI Pyramid from the Inside,* 12–13; Woodward, *The Secret Man,* 15–22, 57–58; Woodward, author interview, 20 May 2009.

10. Woodward, *The Secret Man,* 63–67; Woodward, author interview, 20 May 2009.

11. John D. O'Connor, "'I'm the Guy they Called Deep Throat,'" *Vanity Fair,* July 2005.

12. Woodward, *The Secret Man,* 85–87.

13. Bernstein and Woodward, *All the President's Men,* 71; Woodward, *The Secret Man,* 4.

14. Sussman, author interview; Bradlee, *A Good Life,* 364–65; Carl Bernstein, "A Reporter's Assessment," in Woodward, *The Secret Man,* 230.

15. Bernstein, "Watergate's Last Chapter."

16. Liebovich, *Richard Nixon, Watergate, and the Press,* 63–64; Olson, *Watergate,* 49–50.

17. Woodward, *The Secret Man,* 58; Sussman, *The Great Coverup,* 13; Reeves, *President Nixon,* 506.

18. George W. Johnson, ed. *The Nixon Presidential Press Conferences* (New York: Earl M. Coleman Enterprises, 1978), 247–82.

19. Dean, *Blind Ambition,* 118, 128–30.

20. Bradlee, *A Good Life,* 327; Shepard, *Woodward and Bernstein,* 34–35.

21. Bernstein and Woodward, *All the President's Men,* 51; Shepard, *Woodward and Bernstein,* 35–36.

22. Carl Bernstein and Bob Woodward, "Bug Suspect Got Campaign Funds," *Washington Post,* 1 August 1972, A1; Shepard, *Woodward and Bernstein,* 36–40; Sussman, *The Great Coverup,* 55–59.

23. Sussman, *The Great Coverup,* 59–60, 85–100; Olson, *Watergate,* 66.

24. Bob Schieffer, remarks at "Watergate—35 Years Later."

25. Crouse, *Boys on the Bus,* 15; Mark Feldstein, "Watergate Revisited," *American Journalism Review* 26, no. 4 (August/September 2004): 67; Ambrose, *Nixon: The Triumph of a Politician,* 577; Halberstam, *Powers That Be,* 667–69.

26. Shepard, *Woodward and Bernstein,* 45–46; Crouse, *Boys on the Bus,* 297; Liebovich, *Richard Nixon, Watergate, and the Press,* 70.

27. Dean, *Blind Ambition,* 127–28.

28. Seymour M. Hersh, "Watergate Days," *New Yorker,* 13 June 2005; Robert M. Smith, "Before Deep Throat," *American Journalism Review* 31, no. 3 (June/July 2009): 14–15; Richard Pérez-Peña, "2 Ex-Timesmen Say They Had a Tip on Watergate First," *New York Times,* 25 May 2009, B4.

29. Woodward, author interview, 20 May 2009.

30. Dean, *Blind Ambition,* 133–36; Sussman, *The Great Coverup,* 106; Kutler, *Abuse of Power,* 146.

31. Carl Bernstein and Bob Woodward, "Spy Funds Linked to GOP Aides," *Washington Post,* 17 September 1972, A1; Carl Bernstein and Bob Woodward, "Watergate Data Destruction Charged," *Washington Post,* 20 September 1972, A1; Carl Bernstein and Bob Woodward, "Mitchell Controlled Secret GOP Fund," *Washington Post,* 29 September 1972, A1; Rosen, *The Strong Man,* 334–35; Graham, *Personal History,* 464–65.

32. "The Watergate Three," *Time,* 7 May 1973.

33. Ibid.

34. Sussman, *The Great Coverup,* 112.

35. Bradlee, author interview.

36. Carl Bernstein and Bob Woodward, "FBI Finds Nixon Aides Sabotaged Democrats," *Washington Post,* 10 October 1972, A1; Bernstein and Woodward, *All the President's Men,* 127; Bradlee, *A Good Life,* 336–37.

37. Dean, *Blind Ambition,* 144; Carl Bernstein and Bob Woodward, "Key Nixon Aide Named as 'Sabotage' Contact," *Washington Post,* 15 October 1972, A1; Bob Woodward and Carl Bernstein, "Lawyer for Nixon Said to Have Used GOP's Secret Spy Fund," *Washington Post,* 16 October 1972, A1; "Watergate Scandal: A Senate Search for Truth," in Congressional Quarterly, *Watergate: Chronology of a Crisis,* 8; Shepard, *Woodward and Bernstein,* 42–43.

38. Nixon, *RN,* 713; Tape of Nixon and Haldeman Oval Office conversation of 8 September 1972 in Kutler, *Abuse of Power,* 135; Liebovich, *Richard Nixon, Watergate, and the Press,* 64–65; Graham, *Personal History,* 464.

39. Tape of Nixon and Colson Executive Office Building conversation of 14 September 1972 in Kutler, *Abuse of Power,* 144; Graham, *Personal History,* 479–82, 496–97.

40. Graham, *Personal History,* 483.

41. Ibid., 499.

42. Sussman, author interview.

43. Graham, *Personal History,* 484; Bradlee, *A Good Life,* 371.

44. "Watergate Scandal: A Senate Search for Truth," in Congressional Quarterly, *Watergate: Chronology of a Crisis,* 13; Graham, *Personal History,* 465–67, 476.

45. Bob Woodward, "Accountability Reporting and Digging Deep," panel discussion, Investigative Reporters & Editors Conference, Baltimore, 12 June 2009.

46. Gladys Engel Lang and Kurt Lang, *The Battle for Public Opinion: The President, the Press, and the Polls During Watergate* (New York: Columbia University Press, 1983), 28–29, 38–39; Liebovich, *Richard Nixon, Watergate, and the Press,* 68–70; Tom Wicker, "American Political Institutions after Watergate—A Discussion," 13 September 1974, symposium transcript in *Political Science Quarterly* 89, no. 4: 720.

47. Lang and Lang, *The Battle for Public Opinion,* 28–29, 32–34.

48. Carl Bernstein, remarks at "Watergate—35 Years Later."

49. Sussman, author interview.

50. Sussman, *The Great Coverup,* 120.

51. Philip Meyer, author interview, 12 June 2008.

52. Graham, *Personal History,* 471.

53. Ben Bradlee, remarks at "Watergate—35 Years Later."

54. Woodward, *The Secret Man,* 89–91; Graham, *Personal History,* 467–68; Bernstein and Woodward, *All the President's Men,* 184–92.

55. Bob Woodward speech to the National Press Club, cited in Shepard, "Woodward and Bernstein Uncovered," washingtonian.com, 1 September 2003.

56. Graham, *Personal History,* 506.

57. Bradlee, *A Good Life,* 364.

58. "Watergate Scandal: A Senate Search for Truth," 4, 9; Liebovich, *Richard Nixon, Watergate, and the Press,* 69; Jack Nelson and Ronald J. Ostrow, "Wiretap Witness Says He Gave Logs to Official," *Los Angeles Times,* 5 October 1972, A1; Robert L. Jackson, "Fifth Person Tells of Support from Segretti," *Los Angeles Times,* 24 October 1972, A21; Shepard, *Woodward and Bernstein,* 42–43.

59. Schorr, *Clearing the Air,* 18, 23; James A. Capo, "Network Watergate Coverage Patterns in Late 1972 and Early 1973," *Journalism Quarterly* 60, no. 4 (1983): 595, 599; Lang and Lang, *The Battle for Public Opinion,* 29–30.

60. Carl Bernstein, remarks at "Watergate—35 Years Later."

61. Daniel Schorr, remarks at "Watergate—35 Years Later"; Schorr, *Clearing the Air,* 31–34, 53–59; Alicia Shepard, *Woodward and Bernstein,* 52.

62. Liebovich, *Richard Nixon, Watergate, and the Press,* 54–55; Olson, *Watergate,* 65–66.

63. Kutler, *Abuse of Power,* 176–77, 192; Graham, *Personal History,* 475; Sussman, *The Great Coverup,* 133.

64. Graham, *Personal History,* 474–75; Bernstein and Woodward, *All the President's Men,* 207–11; Shepard, *Woodward and Bernstein,* 64–65.

65. Seymour M. Hersh, "Pressure to Plead Guilty Alleged in Watergate Case," *New York Times,* 14 January 1973, 1; Hersh, "Watergate Days"; Dean, *Blind Ambition,* 181–82; Olson, *Watergate,* 69–70; Sussman, *The Great Coverup,* 140–41; Kutler, *The Wars of Watergate,* 253–54.

66. Sussman, *The Great Coverup,* 163–74; Olson, *Watergate,* 72–73, 82; Congressional Quarterly, *Watergate: Chronology of a Crisis,* 22.

67. Sussman, *The Great Coverup,* 176–79; Bernstein and Woodward, *All the President's Men,* 275–77; Nixon, *RN,* 803.

68. Olson, *Watergate: The Presidential Scandal That Shook America,* 75–76; David Greenberg, "Nabobs Revisited: What Watergate Reveals about Today's Washington Press Corps," *Washington Monthly* 35, no. 10 (October 2003): 45–48.

69. Carl Bernstein and Bob Woodward, "McCord: 'Hush' Money Came from Hunt's Wife," *Washington Post,* 10 April 1973, A1; Bob Woodward and Carl Bernstein, "Mitchell Aide Got $70,000 of Bug Fund," *Washington Post,* 11 April 1973, A1.

70. Downie, *The New Muckrakers,* 97; Philip Greer, "Ehrlichman Said to Agree to Aid Vesco," *Washington Post,* 28 April 1973, A1.

71. Sussman, *The Great Coverup,* 199.

72. Nixon, interview by David Frost; Reeves, *President Nixon,* 600–602.

73. Shepard, *Woodward and Bernstein,* 70.

74. Seymour M. Hersh, "6 May Be Indicted," *New York Times,* 1 May

1973, 1; Hersh, "Teams of Agents," *New York Times*, 2 May 1973, 1; Hersh, "President Linked to Taps on Aides," *New York Times*, 15 May 1973, 1; Hersh, "White House Unit Reportedly Spied on Radicals in '70," *New York Times*, 20 May 1973, 1.

75. Hersh, "Watergate Days."

76. Capo, "Network Watergate Coverage Patterns in Late 1972 and Early 1973," 599–602; Lang and Lang, *The Battle for Public Opinion*, 44–52; Alexander, "Culture and Political Crisis," 206.

77. Woodward, author interview, 8 June 2009; Bernstein and Woodward, *All the President's Men*, 246–50.

78. Ben H. Bagdikian, "Newspapers: Learning (Too Slowly) to Adapt to TV," *Watergate and the American Political Process*, Ronald E. Pynn, ed. (New York: Praeger, 1975), 82–84; Olson, *Watergate*, 90–92, 94–95; Lang and Lang, *The Battle for Public Opinion*, 62–63, 70–71.

79. Liebovich, *Richard Nixon, Watergate, and the Press*, 88–89; Schorr, *Clearing the Air*, 106–7; Greenberg, *Nixon's Shadow*, 256; Congressional Quarterly, *Watergate: Chronology of a Crisis*, 51.

80. William Proxmire, 8 May 1973 speech on the floor of the U.S. Senate, in Congressional Quarterly, *Watergate: Chronology of a Crisis*, 51; Greenberg, "Nabobs Revisited," 45–48.

81. Olson, *Watergate*, 103–5.

82. Lang and Lang, *The Battle for Public Opinion*, 103.

83. Ibid., 92–105; Alexander, "Culture and Political Crisis," 207.

84. Olson, *Watergate*, 114–16.

85. Lang and Lang, *The Battle for Public Opinion*, 2; Johnson, ed., *The Nixon Presidential Press Conferences*, 369; Liebovich, *Richard Nixon, Watergate, and the Press*, 99.

86. *National Review*, 16 November 1973, B173 cited in Greenberg, *Nixon's Shadow*, 174.

87. Haldeman, *The Haldeman Diaries*, 473; Woodward and Bernstein, *The Final Days*, 94–95; Olson, *Watergate*, 127–28, 131; Sussman, *The Great Coverup*, 283–84.

88. Berkowitz, *Something Happened*, 29; Jeffrey C. Alexander, "Culture and Political Crisis," 208; Olson, *Watergate*, 143–47.

89. Graham, *Personal History*, 494.

90. Articles of Impeachment Adopted by the Committee on the Judiciary, 27 July 1974.

91. Nixon, interview by David Frost, 5 May 1977; "The Nation: A Gallery of the Guilty," *Time,* 13 January 1975; Hoff, *Nixon Reconsidered,* 301–2; Kutler, *The Wars of Watergate,* 575–76.

92. Edward Jay Epstein, "Did the Press Uncover Watergate?" *Commentary* 58, no. 1 (July 1974): 23.

93. Woodward, *The Secret Man,* 120–21.

94. Shepard, "The Myth of Watergate, Woodward and Bernstein," *Poynteronline,* 15 June 2007, http://www.poynter.org/content/content_print.asp?id=124751.

95. Olson, *Watergate,* 44.

96. Felt, *The FBI Pyramid,* 258; Felt and O'Connor, *A G-Man's Life,* 204–6, 212–13.

97. Carl Bernstein, "The Idiot Culture," *New Republic,* 8 June 1992, 22.

98. John Dean conversation with Richard Nixon and H. R. Haldeman, 21 March 1973, in Kutler, *Abuse of Power,* 252.

99. Felt and O'Connor, *A G-Man's Life,* 213; Sussman, *The Great Coverup,* 77–83, 144, 222–26; Woodward, *The Secret Man,* 82–83, 92–94; Olson, *Watergate,* 55–57, 80–81.

CHAPTER FIVE

1. Paul Gronke and Timothy E. Cook, "Disdaining the Media: The American Public's Changing Attitudes Toward the News," *Political Communication* 24, no. 3 (July 2007): 259.

2. Robert A. McCaughey, "American Political Institutions after Watergate," 719.

3. Victor Lasky, *It Didn't Start with Watergate* (New York: Dial Press, 1977), 3.

4. Huntington, "The Democratic Distemper," 28.

5. Schudson, *Watergate in American Memory,* 99–100; McPherson, *Journalism at the End of the American Century,* 47; Garment, *Scandal,* 39–40.

6. "The Pulitzer Flap," *Time,* 20 May 1974.

7. Bradlee, *A Good Life,* 369; Shepard, *Woodward and Bernstein,* 71–73.

8. Shepard, *Woodward and Bernstein,* 77, 89–92.

9. Greene, foreword to *The Reporter's Handbook,* vii; David E. Kaplan, author interview, 6 June 2008.

10. Schudson, *Watergate in American Memory,* 110–11; Anderson and Benjaminson, *Investigative Reporting*; Mollenhoff, *Investigative Reporting*; Williams, *Investigative Reporting and Editing.*

11. Greenberg, *Nixon's Shadow,* 162–63; Shepard, *Woodward and Bernstein,* 154.

12. Mollenhoff, *Investigative Reporting,* 6, 259–304.

13. Steven Hess, *The Washington Reporters* (Washington, D.C.: The Brookings Institution, 1981), 19–20.

14. Bernstein, "Watergate's Last Chapter."

15. Leonard Downie Jr., author interview, 9 August 2007.

16. Bob Woodward and Carl Bernstein, *The Final Days* (New York: Simon & Schuster, 1976), 12–13. Although Bernstein's name was on the cover, most sources say he conducted few of the interviews and contributed less to the writing than Woodward and researchers Scott Armstrong and Al Kamen.

17. Shepard, *Woodward and Bernstein,* 145–47; Adrian Havill, *Deep Truth: The Lives of Bob Woodward and Carl Bernstein* (New York: Birch Lane Press, 1993), 108–12.

18. Richard Reeves, "Lots of Footwork, No Footnotes," *New York Times,* 18 April 1976, 174.

19. Bradlee, *A Good Life,* 405; Shepard, *Woodward and Bernstein,* 84–85, 124–25, 142–44, 154–55, 210–12; Schudson, *Watergate in American Memory,* 133.

20. Scott Armstrong, author interview, 3 June 2008; Woodward and Armstrong, *The Brethren*; Shepard, *Woodward and Bernstein,* 168–76, 188–92, 210–18.

21. Lasky, *It Didn't Start with Watergate,* 1–2.

22. Paul Johnson, "In Praise of Richard Nixon," *Commentary* 86, no. 4 (October 1988): 52.

23. Gerald Ford, *A Time to Heal* (New York: Harper & Row, 1979), 156–57; Lang and Lang, *The Battle for Public Opinion,* 235.

24. Ford, *A Time to Heal*, 176–80; Kutler, *The Wars of Watergate*, 553–54.

25. Nixon, *RN*, 996.

26. Berkowitz, *Something Happened*, 2–3, 6, 28.

27. Fred T. Smoller, "The Six O'Clock Presidency: Patterns of Network News Coverage of the President," Doris A. Graber, ed., *Media Power in Politics*, 3rd ed. (Washington: Congressional Quarterly Press, 1994), 233–35; Spear, *Presidents and the Press*, 31–32, 237.

28. Liebovich, *Richard Nixon, Watergate, and the Press*, 114–15.

29. "Carter Press Aide Asks a New Start, With Some Open Cabinet Meetings," *New York Times*, 24 November 1976, 14.

30. James T. Patterson, *Restless Giant: The United States from Watergate to Bush v. Gore* (New York: Oxford University Press, 2005), 112.

31. William Safire, "Lancegate," *New York Times*, 11 August 1977, 17; Schudson, *Watergate in American Memory*, 75–80; Garment, *Scandal*, 43–46.

32. Anthony Lewis, "Lowering the Gate," *New York Times*, 15 November 1979, A31; Larry J. Sabato, *Feeding Frenzy: How Attack Journalism Has Transformed American Politics* (New York: Free Press, 1991), 11; Garment, *Scandal*, 47–49.

33. Michael Schudson, *The Power of News* (Cambridge: Harvard University Press, 1995), 159; Garment, *Scandal*, 49–56; Aucoin, *Evolution of American Investigative Journalism*, 119–20.

34. Joseph Kraft, "The Imperial Media," *Commentary* 71, no. 5 (May 1981): 41.

35. "Discretion Urged in Press Power; A.P. Manager Says Freedom is 'Not a Hunting License,'" *New York Times*, 4 May 1976, 14.

36. Sissela Bok, *Lying* (New York: Vintage Books, 1979), 127–28.

37. James S. Ettema and Theodore L. Glasser, *Custodians of Conscience: Investigative Reporting and Public Virtue* (New York: Columbia University Press, 1998), 37–39.

38. Zay N. Smith and Pamela Zekman, *The Mirage* (New York: Random House, 1979); "Bribes Were Only Real Thing at Mirage," *Chicago Sun-Times*, 17 February 2008, 15A; David Protess, author interview, 15 July 2009.

39. Philip Meyer, author interview, 12 June 2008; Philip Meyer, *Precision Journalism: A Reporter's Introduction to Social Science Methods*, 4th ed.

(Lanham, Md.: Rowman & Littlefield, 2002), 14–15; "The 43 Who Died," *Detroit Free Press,* 3 September 1967, in Serrin and Serrin, *Muckraking!,* 196–200; Melisma Cox, "The Development of Computer-Assisted Reporting." Paper presented to the Newspaper Division of the Association for Education in Journalism and Mass Communication, Southeast Colloquium, Chapel Hill, N.C., 17–18 March 2000.

40. Meyer, author interview; Meyer, *Precision Journalism,* 191–92.

41. DeFleur, *Computer-Assisted Investigative Reporting,* 74–75.

42. Meyer, *Precision Journalism,* 3–5.

43. Donald Barlett and James Steele, author interview, 13 June 2009; Steve Weinberg, *Telling the Untold Story: How Investigative Reporters Are Changing the Craft of Biography* (Columbia: University of Missouri Press, 1992), 105–10.

44. Barlett and Steele, author interview; Downie, *The New Muckrakers,* 93–95, 103–5; Weinberg, *Telling the Untold Story,* 110–12.

45. Downie, *The New Muckrakers,* 93–95, 103–5.

46. Weinberg, *Telling the Untold Story,* 112–16.

47. Ibid., 7, 14–16, 40–44, 100–103.

48. Downie, *The New Muckrakers.*

49. John C. Behrens, *The Typewriter Guerrillas: Closeups of 20 Top Investigative Reporters* (Chicago: Nelson-Hall, 1977), 155–66.

50. Kathryn Olmsted, "An American Conspiracy: The Post-Watergate Press and the CIA," *Journalism History* 19, no. 2 (Summer 1993): 53–56; Olmsted, *Challenging the Secret Government,* 4, 30, 39.

51. Schorr, *Clearing the Air,* 130–78; Schudson, *Watergate in American Memory,* 43–46.

52. Schorr, *Clearing the Air,* 186–258; Spear, *Presidents and the Press,* 22.

53. Sabato, *Feeding Frenzy,* 10; Downie, *The New Muckrakers,* 136–38, 152–55, 165–72.

54. Steve Weinberg, author interview, 6 June 2008; Aucoin, *The Evolution of American Investigative Journalism,* 120–24, 136–37.

55. Michael F. Wendland, *The Arizona Project: How a Team of Investigative Reporters Got Revenge on Deadline* (Kansas City: Sheed Andrews and McMeel, 1977), 26–27.

56. Ibid., 1–14, 28; Tatiana Hensley, "Cautious Man, Dedicated Journalist," *In the Pursuit of Justice,* an *Arizona Republic* special section produced

by the Walter Cronkite School of Journalism and Mass Communication, May 2006, 3–6; Investigative Reporters & Editors, "The Arizona Project," http://www.ire.org/history/arizona.html.

57. Wendland, *The Arizona Project*, 24–32; Aucoin, *Evolution of American Investigative Journalism*, 143–44; Investigative Reporters & Editors, "IRE: 1975–1985," http://www.ire.org/history/30years/decade1_pr.html; Myrta Pulliam, "His Leadership Built IRE," *IRE Journal* 31, no. 3 (May/June 2008): 22.

58. Anthony Marro, "A Larger-Than-Life Reporter," *Columbia Journalism Review* 40, no. 6 (March/April 2002): 18.

59. Wendland, *The Arizona Project*, 109; Investigative Reporters and Editors, Inc., "The Arizona Project" and "The Desert Rats," http://www.ire.org/history/desertrats.html; Aucoin, *Evolution of American Investigative Journalism*, 140–49.

60. Aucoin, *Evolution of American Investigative Journalism*, 149–53; Wendland, *The Arizona Project*, 43, 224–25, 252–64; Kenneth C. Killebrew, "Don Bolles: News Martyr of the 1970s, Enigma of the 1990s." Paper presented August 1995 to the History Division at the Association for Education in Journalism and Mass Communication.

61. Aucoin and Killebrew, "Don Bolles"; Wendland, *The Arizona Project*, 256–57.

62. Aucoin, *Evolution of American Investigative Reporting*, 164–66; Weinberg, author interview, 6 June 2008; Investigative Reporters & Editors, "IRE: 1975–1985," http://www.ire.org/history/30years/decade1_pr.html; Deborah Nelson, author interview, 19 June 2009.

63. Kaplan, author interview, 6 June 2008; David Armstrong, *A Trumpet to Arms* (Los Angeles: J. P. Tarcher, 1981), 348–49; Philip F. Lawler, *The Alternative Influence: The Impact of Investigative Reporting Groups on America's Media* (Lanham, Md.: University Press of America, 1984), 15–18.

64. Adam Hochschild, "The First 25 Years," *Mother Jones* 26, no. 3 (May/June 2001): 50; Armstrong, *A Trumpet to Arms*, 335–37.

65. Kaplan, author interview; Hochschild, "The First 25 Years"; Armstrong, *A Trumpet to Arms*, 327; David Weir and Mark Schapiro, *Circle of Poison: Pesticides and People in a Hungry World* (San Francisco: Institute for Food and Development Policy, 1981), x–xi, 3–5; Sarah Schaffer,

"Muckraking and Fundraising," *American Journalism Review* 24, no. 10 (December 2002): 16.

66. Aucoin, *Evolution of American Investigative Journalism,* 193; Downie, *The New Muckrakers,* 218–23, 247–48; Lawler, *The Alternative Influence,* 25–28.

67. Rodger Streitmatter, *Unspeakable: The Rise of the Gay and Lesbian Press in America* (Boston: Faber and Faber, 1995), 234–36.

68. Richard Campbell, *60 Minutes and the News: A Mythology for Middle America* (Urbana: University of Illinois Press, 1991), 1–4, 15–16, 22, 31, 160–61; Adam Bernstein, "'60 Minutes' Creator Turned TV News Profitable," *Washington Post,* 20 August 2009, B5.

69. Don Hewitt quoted in William A. Henry, "Don Hewitt: Man of the Hour," *Washington Journalism Review* 8 (May 1986): 26 in Campbell, *60 Minutes and the News,* 45–46.

70. Campbell, *60 Minutes and the News,* 48–50.

71. Mike Wallace and Gary Paul Gates, *Close Encounters: Mike Wallace's Own Story* (New York: Berkley Books, 1984), 380, in Richard Campbell, *60 Minutes and the News,* 160.

72. David Blum, *Tick ... Tick ... Tick ... The Long Life and Turbulent Times of 60* Minutes (New York: HarperCollins, 2004), 1; Campbell, *60 Minutes and the News,* 1–4; Downie and Kaiser, *The News about the News,* 132.

73. Raphael, *Investigated Reporting,* 219–20, 228–30.

74. Douglass K. Daniel, *Lou Grant: The Making of TV's Top Newspaper Drama* (Syracuse: Syracuse University Press, 1996), xv–xvi, 2–17, 159, 173–217.

75. Janet Maslin, "Absence of Malice," *New York Times,* 19 November 1981; Schudson, *Watergate in American Memory,* 120.

76. Bradlee, *A Good Life,* 435; Bradlee, author interview; Shepard, *Woodward and Bernstein,* 195–200; Sandra Borden, "Janet Cooke in Hindsight: Reconsideration of a Paradigmatic Case in Journalism Ethics," *Journal of Communication Inquiry* 26, no. 2 (2002): 155–70.

77. Woodward, author interview, 20 May 2009.

78. David R. Simon, "Watergate and the Nixon Presidency: A Comparative Ideological Analysis," in Leon Friedman and William F. Levantrosser, eds., *Watergate and Afterward: The Legacy of Richard M. Nixon* (Westport, Conn.: Greenwood Press, 1992), 19; *ANPA Public Affairs Newsletter*

(January 1977) and Gallup Opinion Index (September 1976) cited in Lee B. Becker, Robin E. Cobbey, and Idowu A. Sobowale, "Public Support for the Press," *Journalism Quarterly* 55, no. 3 (1978): 422; Herbert J. Gans, *Democracy and the News* (Oxford: Oxford University Press, 2003), 34; Rosemary Armao, "The History of Investigative Reporting," in Greenwald and Bernt, eds., *The Big Chill,* 41.

79. Jimmy Carter, "Crisis of Confidence," speech, Washington, D.C., 15 July 1979. Transcript from www.cartercenter.org; Patterson, *Restless,* 125–27.

CHAPTER SIX

1. Mark Hertsgaard, *On Bended Knee: The Press and the Reagan Presidency* (New York: Farrar Straus Giroux, 1988), 38, 44, 47; Spear, *Presidents and the Press,* 26, 263–65.

2. Hertsgaard, *On Bended Knee,* 52.

3. Eleanor Clift and Bill Hendrick, "Jordan and Powell: Literary Voices," *Newsweek,* 17 August 1981, 16B.

4. Smoller, "The Six O'Clock Presidency," 236; Hertsgaard, *On Bended Knee,* 3–4, 17, 27, 205–21; McPherson, *Journalism at the End,* 89; Spear, *Presidents and the Press,* 4–5, 30, 260, 292.

5. Garment, *Scandal,* 60–64.

6. McPherson, *Journalism at the End,* 88–89.

7. Scott Armstrong, "Was the Press Any Match for All the President's Men?" *Columbia Journalism Review* 29, no. 1 (May/June 1990): 28–29; Hertsgaard, *On Bended Knee,* 303–4.

8. *Report of the Congressional Committees Investigating the Iran/Contra Affair* (Washington, D.C.: U.S. Senate Select Committee on Secret Military Assistance to Iran and the Nicaraguan Opposition; U.S. House of Representatives Select Committee to Investigate Covert Arms Transactions with Iran, 1987), xv, 3–9, 160–70; Patterson, *Restless Giant,* 209–10; Sabato, *Feeding Frenzy,* 19–20.

9. Alan F. Westin, "Information, Dissent, and Political Power: Watergate Revisited," in Friedman and Levantrosser, eds., *Watergate and Afterward,* 53–54.

10. Schudson, *Watergate in American Memory,* 171.

11. Armstrong, "Was the Press Any Match," 30; Hugh Sidey, "An Interview with the President," *Time,* 8 December 1986.

12. Armstrong, "Was the Press Any Match," 29–31; Sussman, author interview; Schudson, *Watergate in American Memory,* 173.

13. Armstrong, "Was the Press Any Match," 31–35; McPherson, *Journalism at the End,* 103–4.

14. McPherson, *Journalism at the End,* 121–25.

15. Bob Woodward, *Shadow: Five Presidents and the Legacy of Watergate* (New York: Simon & Schuster, 1999), 175–80, 207–8.

16. Ibid., 222.

17. Garment, *Scandal,* 3–4.

18. Donald A. Ritchie, *Reporting from Washington: The History of the Washington Press Corps* (Oxford: Oxford University Press, 2009), 238.

19. Timothy J. Conlan, "Federal, State, or Local? Trends in the Public's Judgment," *The Public Perspective,* January/February 1993, 4, cited in Joseph N. Cappella and Kathleen Hall Jamieson, *Spiral of Cynicism: The Press and the Public Good* (Oxford: Oxford University Press, 1997), 18.

20. Sanford, *Don't Shoot the Messenger,* 19–20; Greenwald and Bernt, *The Big Chill,* 3; Bennett and Serrin, "The Watchdog Role," 180.

21. David Broder, "War on Cynicism: Politicians and the Media Badly Need a Dialogue about the Deterioration of Public Discourse," *Washington Post,* 6 July 1994, A19.

22. Ettema and Glasser, *Custodians of Conscience,* 105.

23. Robert D. Putnam, *Bowling Alone,* 32, 38, 41, 46–47.

24. Donald L. Barlett and James B. Steele, "The Great Tax Giveaway," *Philadelphia Inquirer,* 10 April 1988, 1; Barlett and Steele, author interview; James B. Steele, "Unsung Documents," panel at Investigative Reporters & Editors Conference, Baltimore, 12 June 2009; Steve Weinberg, "Profile: Donald Barlett and James Steele," *Investigative Reporting: Advanced Methods and Techniques,* ed. John Ullman (New York: St. Martin's Press, 1995), 14–24; Mark Tatge, "Taking CAR for a Spin: Conventional News Gathering Goes High-Tech," in *The Big Chill,* 218–20.

25. Barlett and Steele, author interview; Donald Barlett and James Steele, "Building the Story: From Getting Started to Knowing When to

Stop," panel discussion, Investigative Reporters & Editors Conference, Baltimore, 13 June 2009; Donald Barlett and James Steele, "America: Who Stole the Dream?" *Philadelphia Inquirer,* 22 September 1996, 1.

26. Gene Roberts, author interview.

27. Barlett and Steele, author interview, 13 June 2009; Aucoin, *The Evolution of American Investigative Journalism,* 189–90.

28. DeFleur, *Computer-Assisted Investigative Reporting,* 78.

29. Ibid., 3–5; Tatge, "Taking CAR for a Spin," 214–15; Ezra Bowen, "New Paths to Buried Treasure," *Time,* 7 July 1986, 56.

30. DeFleur, *Computer-Assisted Investigative Reporting,* 34–36; Rose Ciotta, "Baby You Should Drive This CAR," *American Journalism Review* 18, no. 2 (March 1996): 34; Bruce Garrison, "Newspaper Size as a Factor in Use of Computer-Assisted Reporting," paper presented to Communication Technology and Policy Division of the Association for Education in Journalism and Mass Communication, Baltimore, August 1998; Meyer, author interview.

31. Tatge, "Taking CAR for a Spin," 215–17.

32. Stephen K. Doig, "Reporting with Tools of Social Science," *Nieman Reports* 62, no. 1 (Spring 2008): 47–49.

33. Meyer, *Precision Journalism,* 15–16.

34. Ciotta, "Baby You Should Drive This CAR," 34; Sarah Cohen, author interview, 12 June 2009.

35. Ullmann, *Investigative Reporting,* viii.

36. Lewis, *Make No Law,* 201; Shepard, *Woodward and Bernstein,* 193–95; Aucoin, *The Evolution of American Investigative Journalism,* 198–99.

37. Jane Kirtley, "Is It a Crime?" in Greenwald and Bernt, *The Big Chill,* 139; Michael Massing, "The Libel Chill: How Cold Is It Out There?" *Columbia Journalism Review* 24, no. 1 (May/June 1985): 33; Raphael, *Investigated Reporting,* 221, 227.

38. Lewis, *Make No Law,* 216–17; Aucoin, *Evolution of American Investigative Journalism,* 199–201.

39. Richard E. Labunski and John V. Pavlik, "The Legal Environment of Investigative Reporters: A Pilot Study," *Newspaper Research Journal* 5, no. 3 (1985): 13–16; Douglass K. Daniel, "Best of Times and Worst of Times: Investigative Reporting in Post-Watergate America," *The Big Chill,* 20; Lewis, *Make No Law,* 202–3, 220; Raphael, *Investigated Reporting,*

220–22; Aucoin, *Evolution of American Investigative Journalism,* 201–2; Michael Massing, "The Libel Chill," 31–43; Lewis, *Make No Law,* 202–3.

40. Guthrie, "Investigative Journalism Under Fire," 10–26; Raphael, *Investigated Reporting,* 224–25.

41. Susan K. Opt and Timothy Delaney, "Public Perceptions of Investigative Reporting," in *The Big Chill,* 81; Tom Goldstein, *Journalism and Truth: Strange Bedfellows,* Medill School of Journalism: Visions of the American Press, ed. David Abrahamson (Evanston, Ill.: Northwestern University Press, 2007), 31; Jane Kirtley, "Is It a Crime?" 139–40; Winch, "Ethical Challenges for Investigative Journalists," 127–30.

42. "Phillip Morris, Reynolds Settle with ABC," *Los Angeles Times,* 22 August 1995; Guthrie, "Investigative Journalism Under Fire"; Raphael, *Investigated Reporting,* 227; Blum, *Tick . . . Tick . . . Tick . . . ,* 208.

43. Blum, *Tick . . . Tick . . . Tick . . . ,* 206–12; Guthrie, "Investigative Journalism Under Fire," 10–26; Sanford, *Don't Shoot the Messenger,* 6–7.

44. Cameron McWhirter, "Saved by the Shield," *Columbia Journalism Review* 47, no. 1 (May/June 2008): 23; Sanford, *Don't Shoot the Messenger,* 1.

45. Brant Houston, author interview, 6 June 2008; Charles Lewis, "Investigative Journalism Doesn't Win Many Friends," *Nieman Reports* 60, no. 2 (Summer 2006): 82; Bill Moyers, "Journalism Under Fire," speech, annual conference of the Society of Professional Journalists, New York City, 11 September 2004.

46. Daniel, "Best of Times and Worst of Times," 21; Schudson, *Discovering the News,* 189.

47. Joseph Bernt, Marilyn Greenwald, and Mark Tatge, "Enterprise and Investigative Reporting in Three Metropolitan Papers: 1980 and 1995 Compared," presentation, Council of Affiliates and Investigative Reporters and Editors, Association for Education in Journalism and Mass Communication annual meeting, Anaheim, Calif., 12 August 1996.

48. Ben H. Bagdikian, *The Media Monopoly,* 5th ed. (Boston: Beacon Press, 1997), ix, xi–xii.

49. Ibid., xiii; Ben H. Bagdikian, *The New Media Monopoly* (Boston: Beacon Press, 2004), 3.

50. McPherson, *Journalism at the End of the American Century,* 109; David Pearce Demers, *The Menace of the Corporate Newspaper: Fact or Fiction?* (Ames: Iowa State University Press, 1996), viii–ix, 16–19, 222, 294.

51. Gans, *Democracy and the News*, 22; Bill Hickey, "Money Lust: How Pressure for Profit Is Perverting Journalism," *Columbia Journalism Review* 37, no. 2 (Summer 1998): 28–36.

52. Downie and Kaiser, *News about the News*, 79; James D. Squires, *Read All About It! The Corporate Takeover of America's Newspapers* (New York: Times Books, 1993), 140–41.

53. Downie and Kaiser, *News about the News*, 79–83; Roberts, author interview.

54. Squires, *Read All About It!*, 147–49.

55. Barlett and Steele, author interview; Donald L. Barlett and James B. Steele, "Soaked by Congress," *Time*, 15 May 2000; Katharine Q. Seelye, "An Established Reporting Team Moves to Vanity Fair," *New York Times*, 7 August 2006.

56. Downie and Kaiser, *News about the News*, 23.

57. McPherson, *Journalism at the End of the American Century*, 105–6, 113; Gans, *Democracy and the News*, 23; Hamilton, *All the News That's Fit to Sell*, 22.

58. Downie and Kaiser, *News about the News*, 145–46; McPherson, *Journalism at the End of the American Century*, 34–35; Sussman, author interview.

59. Bagdikian, *The Media Monopoly*, xiv–xx; Alec Foege, *Right of the Dial: The Rise of Clear Channel and the Fall of Commercial Radio* (New York: Faber and Faber, 2008), 6, 11.

60. Dashiell, "For Mainstream Audiences Only," in *Big Chill*, 178.

61. Deborah Nelson, author interview, 19 June 2009.

62. Hamilton, *All the News*, 71–120; Michael Emery, Edwin Emery, and Nancy L. Roberts, *The Press and America: An Interpretive History of the Mass Media*, 9th ed. (Boston: Allyn and Bacon, 2000), 482–83.

63. Nicholas Lemann, "Anchors Away," *Atlantic Monthly* 261, no. 5 (May 1988): 89; Jim Rutenberg, "Anchor's Pay Package May Change Standards," *New York Times*, 20 December 2001, C5; Hickey, "Money Lust," 28–36.

64. Rhonda Schwartz, author interview, 16 July 2009; "Wal-Mart," *Dateline NBC*, 22 December 1992.

65. Raphael, *Investigated Reporting*, 228–29; Downie and Kaiser, *News about the News*, 238; Matthew C. Ehrlich, "Not Ready for Prime Time:

Tabloid and Investigative TV Journalism," in *Big Chill,* 103; Tom Mascaro, "NBC Reports," The Museum of Broadcast Communications, www .museum.tv/archives/etv/N/htmlN/nbcreports/nbcreports.htm.

66. Marion Just, Rosalind Levine, and Kathleen Regan, "Investigative Reporting Despite the Odds: Watchdog Reporting Continues to Decline," Project for Excellence in Journalism, 1 November 2002.

67. Robert W. McChesney, *The Problem of the Media: U.S. Communication Politics in the Twenty-First Century* (New York: Monthly Press, 2004), 81; Raphael, *Investigated Reporting,* 230.

68. Downie and Kaiser, *News about the News,* 185.

69. Project for Excellence in Journalism, "Changing Definitions of News," 6 March 1998; Sabato, *Feeding Frenzy,* 13–14.

70. Carl Bernstein, *A Woman in Charge: The Life of Hillary Rodham Clinton* (New York: Alfred A. Knopf, 2007), 348–75; Ritchie, *Reporting from Washington,* 238, 277–80; Woodward, *Shadow,* 234.

71. Bill Kovach and Tom Rosenstiel, *Warp Speed: America in the Age of Mixed Media* (New York: Century Foundation Press, 1999), 4, 6–7, 17–21, 28; Baym, "Strategies of Illumination," 644.

72. Bill Kovach, "Report from the Ombudsman," *Brill's Content* 1, no. 2 (September 1998): 18–21; Bartholomew H. Sparrow, *Uncertain Guardians: News Media as a Political Institution* (Baltimore: Johns Hopkins University Press, 1999), xiii.

73. Sherri Cavan, "Richard Nixon and the Idea of Rehabilitation," in *Watergate and Afterward,* 300–310; Ambrose, *Nixon: Triumph of a Politician,* 558–59; Kutler, *Abuse of Power,* xiv.

CHAPTER SEVEN

1. Greg Palast, "Silence of the Lambs: An American in Journalistic Exile," *Into the Buzzsaw,* 65–75; Greg Palast, "U.S. Media Have Lost the Will to Dig Deep," *Los Angeles Times,* 27 April 2007, A33.

2. Clint Hendler, "What We Didn't Know Has Hurt Us," *Columbia Journalism Review* 47, no. 5 (January/February 2009): 28.

3. Murrey Marder, "The Press and the Presidency," 8–10.

4. Ibid.

5. Pew Research Center for the People & the Press, *Views of Press Values and Performance: 1985–2007,* Washington, D.C., 2007, 2.

6. Megan Garber, "The Big Picture," *Columbia Journalism Review* 46, no. 4 (November/December 2007): 12.

7. Michele Weldon, *Everyman News: The Changing American Front Page* (Columbia: University of Missouri Press, 2008), 8; Pew Research Center for People and the Press, "Internet Sapping Broadcast News Audience," 11 June 2000; Downie and Kaiser, *The News about the News,* 78.

8. Chelsea Ide and Kanupriya Vashisht, "The State of Investigative Reporting: Resources Don't Match Interest," *In the Pursuit of Justice,* an *Arizona Republic* special section produced by the Walter Cronkite School of Journalism and Mass Communication, May 2006, 22–24; Lanosga and Martin, "The Investigative Reporting Agenda in America."

9. David Willman, "New FDA: How a New Policy Led to Seven Deadly Drugs," *Los Angeles Times,* 20 December 2001, A1; Sari Horwitz, Scott Higham, and Sarah Cohen, "'Protected' Children Died as Government Did Little," *Washington Post,* 9 September 2001, A1; "Abuse in the Catholic Church," *Boston Globe,* www.boston.com/globe/spotlight/abuse/.

10. Cecilia Tichi, *Exposés and Excess: Muckraking in America, 1900/2000* (Philadelphia: University of Pennsylvania Press, 2004), 2, 5, 115–16, 129–47, 168–87.

11. Steve Weinberg, "Investigative Books of 2008," *IRE Journal* 32, no. 1 (Winter 2009): 6–10; Gerald Colby, "The Price of Liberty," in Kristina Borjesson, ed., *Into the Buzzsaw: Leading Journalists Expose the Myth of a Free Press* (Amherst, NY: Prometheus Books, 2002), 15–35.

12. Jennifer Dorroh, "Statehouse Exodus," *American Journalism Review* 31, no. 2 (April/May 2009): 22–23.

13. Ritchie, *Reporting from Washington,* ix; Gene Roberts, ed., *Leaving Readers Behind: The Age of Corporate Newspapering* (Fayetteville: University of Arkansas Press, 2001), 10.

14. W. Lance Bennett, Regina G. Lawrence, and Steven Livingston, *When the Press Fails: Political Power and the News Media from Iraq to Katrina* (Chicago: University of Chicago Press, 2007), 149; Smoller, "The Six O'Clock Presidency," 232.

15. Scott Armstrong, remarks at "Watergate—35 Years Later"; Charles

Lewis, "Seeking New Ways to Nurture the Capacity to Report," *Nieman Reports* 62, no. 1 (Spring 2008): 23–27.

16. Hendler, "What We Didn't Know Has Hurt Us," 29.

17. Ibid., 28–29, 31; Pete Weitzel, "Keeping Secrets," *The American Editor* (May/June/July 2004), 5–9.

18. Coalition of Journalists for Open Government, "An Opportunity Lost: An In-depth Analysis of FOIA Performance from 1998 to 2007," 3 July 2008; Hendler, "What We Didn't Know Has Hurt Us," 31; Weitzel, "Keeping Secrets," 5–9; Martha Mendoza, "*San Francisco Chronicle* Reporter's FOIA Dates Back to 1981," Associated Press, 14 March 2005; Daniel J. Metcalfe, "Sunshine Not So Bright: FOIA Implementation Lags Behind," *Administrative and Regulatory Law News* 34, no. 4 (Summer 2009): 5.

19. Ted Gup, "Investigative Reporting about Secrecy," *Nieman Reports* 62, no. 1 (Spring 2008): 21–23.

20. Hendler, "What We Didn't Know Has Hurt Us," 29–30; Coalition of Journalists for Open Government, "The Card Memo," http://www.cjog.org/background_the_card_memo.html; Stven Aftergood, "The Age of Missing Information," *Slate,* 17 March 2005; Steven Aftergood, "Classified Documents: Secrecy vs. Citizenship," *Nieman Reports* 62, no. 1 (Spring 2008): 19–20.

21. James Sandler, "The War on Whistle-Blowers," *Salon,* 1 November 2007.

22. Lewis, "Seeking New Ways," 23–27; United States Government Accountability Office, *Department of Education—Contract to Obtain Services of Armstrong Williams,* no. B-305368, Washington, D.C., 30 September 2005; Bennett, Lawrence, and Livingston, *When the Press Fails,* 143–45.

23. "A Nation Challenged: A Snapshot Gives Bush 90% Approval," *New York Times,* 24 September 2001, B6; Deborah Nelson, author interview.

24. Deborah Nelson, author interview.

25. David E. Kaplan, author interview; Bennett, Lawrence, and Livingston, *When the Press Fails,* 7, 21.

26. Seymour M. Hersh, "The Debate Within: The Objective is Clear—Topple Saddam. But How?" *New Yorker,* 11 March 2002, 34; Bob Drogin, "Determining the Reliability of a Key CIA Source," *Nie-*

man Reports 62, no. 1 (Spring 2008): 12–14; Rhonda Schwartz, author interview; Brian Ross, Rhonda Schwartz, and David Scott, "Customs Fails to Detect Depleted Uranium," *ABC News,* 11 September 2002; "How Secure Are U.S. Borders?" *ABC News,* 10 September 2003.

27. Michael Massing, "Now They Tell Us," *New York Review of Books* 51, no. 3 (February 26, 2004); Russell Baker, "Goodbye to Newspapers?" *New York Review of Books* 54, no. 13 (August 16, 2007): 8; Sweeney, *Military and the Press,* 218–19.

28. Howard Kurtz, "The Post on WMDs: An Inside Story; Prewar Articles Questioning Threat Often Didn't Make Front Page," *Washington Post,* 12 August 2004, A1; Michael Massing, "Now They Tell Us"; Downie, "Accountability Reporting and Digging Deep," panel discussion, Investigative Reporters & Editors Conference, Baltimore, 12 June 2009.

29. Michael Massing, "Now They Tell Us"; Goldstein, *Journalism and Truth,* 8–9.

30. "The Times and Iraq," *New York Times,* 26 May 2004, A10.

31. Charles Lewis, "Selling the War: Unearthing False Advertising," *Nieman Reports* 62, no. 1 (Spring 2008): 26; Charles Lewis, "Investigative Journalism Doesn't Win Many Friends," 82; Bennett, Lawrence, and Livingston, *When the Press Fails,* 8, 57.

32. Brian Stelter, "Was Press a War 'Enabler'?" *New York Times,* 30 May 2008, A18.

33. Doyle McManus, "Casey and Woodward: Who Used Whom?" *Los Angeles Times,* 11 October 1987, B1; Bruce M. Swain and J. Michael Robertson, "The *Washington Post* and the Woodward Problem," *Newspaper Research Journal* 16, no. 1 (Winter 1995): 11, 15; Shepard, *Woodward and Bernstein,* 227–28.

34. Bob Woodward, author interview, 8 June 2009.

35. Woodward, author interview, 20 May 2009; Downie and Woodward, "Accountability Reporting and Digging Deep," panel discussion, Investigative Reporters & Editors Conference, Baltimore, 12 June 2009.

36. Woodward, author interviews, 20 May 2009 and 8 June 2009.

37. Eric Umansky, "Failures of Imagination: American Journalists and the Coverage of American Torture," *Columbia Journalism Review* 45, no. 3 (September/October 2006): 17–18.

38. Downie, author interview, 9 August 2007.

39. Kaplan, author interview.

40. Charles Lewis, "Selling the War," 26; Charles Lewis, "Investigative Journalism Doesn't Win Many Friends," 82.

41. Drogin, "Determining the Reliability," 12–13.

42. Seymour Hersh, "Torture at Abu Ghraib," *New Yorker,* 10 May 2004.

43. David Remnick, introduction to Seymour M. Hersh, *Chain of Command: The Road from 9/11 to Abu Ghraib* (New York: Harper Collins, 2004), xvii–xix; Eric Umansky, "Failures of Imagination," 22–23.

44. Dana Priest and Joe Stephens, "Secret World of U.S. Interrogation: Long History of Tactics in Overseas Prisons Is Coming to Light," *Washington Post,* 11 May 2004, A1; Dana Priest, "CIA Avoids Scrutiny of Detainee Treatment," *Washington Post,* 3 March 2005, A1; Dana Priest, "CIA Holds Terror Suspects in Secret Prisons," *Washington Post,* 2 November 2005, A1; Downie, author interview; "AIM Report: Treason, Plagiarism and The Washington Post," a report by Accuracy in Media, 4 December 2007; Michael Massing, "Now They Tell Us."

45. James Risen and Eric Lichtblau, "Bush Lets U.S. Spy on Callers without Courts," *New York Times,* 16 December 2005, A1; Laura Rozen, "Hung out to Dry: The National-Security Press Dug up the Dirt, but Congress Wilted," *Columbia Journalism Review* 47, no. 5 (January/February 2009): 33.

46. RonNell Andersen Jones, "Avalanche or Undue Alarm? An Empirical Study of Subpoenas Received by the News Media," *Minnesota Law Review* 93, no. 101 (November 17, 2008): 142, 154; Dean C. Smith, "Journalist Privilege in 1929: Sen. Arther Capper and the Start of the Shield Law Movement in America," paper presented at the Association for Education in Journalism and Mass Communication conference, Boston, 5 August 2009.

47. Lori Robertson, "Kind of Confidential," *American Journalism Review* 29, no. 3 (June/July 2007): 27; Max Frankel, "The Washington Back Channel," *New York Times Magazine,* 25 March 2007, 47, 66; Jones, "Avalanche or Undue Alarm?" 131–32.

48. Howard Kurtz, "Tightened Belts Could Put Press in a Pinch," *Washington Post,* 23 October 2006, C01; Ken Silverstein and Chuck Neu-

bauer, "Lucrative Deals for a Daughter of Politics," *Los Angeles Times,* 20 February 2004, A1.

49. Marcus Stern, "Digital Records Reveal Corruption on Capitol Hill," *Nieman Reports* 62, no. 1 (Spring 2008): 15–16.

50. Steve Eder, "Ohio Will Get $54.9M from Noe's Rare Coins," *Toledo Blade,* 25 July 2008.

51. Bennett, Lawrence, and Livingston, *When the Press Fails,* 10.

52. Brian Ross, "Doing Great Work in Tough Times," panel discussion, Investigative Reporters & Editors Conference, Baltimore, 12 June 2009; Rhonda Schwartz, author interview.

CHAPTER EIGHT

1. Simon Dumenco, "The Last Hurrah of Hollywood's Hero Journalist?" *Advertising Age,* 13 April 2009, 16.

2. Ibid., 9–10, 22.

3. The Pew Research Center's Project for Excellence in Journalism, *The State of the News Media 2009: An Annual Report on American Journalism* (Washington, D.C., 2009), 3, 7, 9–10; Erica Smith, "Paper Cuts," http://newspaperlayoffs.com/maps/2009-layoffs/.

4. Paul Giblin, "Journalism at the Crossroads: After Newspapers, Then What?" panel discussion, Association for Education in Journalism and Mass Communication Annual Convention, Boston, 6 August 2009; Richard Pérez-Peña, "At Papers, New Levels of Job Insecurity," *New York Times,* 27 April 2009, B6.

5. Jeff Leen, "Citizen K Street: A Case Study in Investigative Journalism," washingtonpost.com, 21 March 2007, www.washingtonpost.com/wp-dyn/content/discussion/2007/03/20/DI2007032000705_pf.html.

6. Mark Benjamin and Michael de Yoanna, "Coming Home: The Army's Fatal Neglect," *Salon,* 9 February to 16 July 2009, http://dir.salon.com/topics/coming_home/; *St. Petersburg Times,* PolitiFact, http://www.politifact.com/truth-o-meter/.

7. Sydney Jones and Susannah Fox, "Generations Online in 2009," data memo for Pew Internet & American Life Project, 28 January 2009, 5; http://www.everyblock.com/; http://www.corpwatch.org/; http://

www.sharesleuth.com/; Micah Sifry, "A See-Through Society," *Columbia Journalism Review* 47, no. 5 (January/February 2009): 43–47.

8. Sifry, "A See-Through Society," 43.

9. Downie, author interview; Sarah Cohen, "Future CAR: Emerging Trends and Strategies," panel discussion, Investigative Reporters & Editors Conference, Baltimore, 11 June 2009.

10. John McQuaid, "Critical Mass: Crowdsourcing Projects Evolve at NewsAssignment.net," *IRE Journal* 31, no. 2 (March/April 2008): 24–26.

11. Noam Cohen, "Blogger, Sans Pajamas, Rakes Muck and a Prize," *New York Times,* 25 February 2008, C1.

12. WikiLeaks http://www.wikileaks.org/; Mark Feldstein, "The Challenges and Opportunities of 21st Century Muckraking," *Nieman Reports* 63, no. 2 (Summer 2009): 50–53.

13. Stephen D. Cooper, *Watching the Watchdog: Bloggers as the Fifth Estate* (Spokane: Marquette Books, 2006), 54–77; Raphael, *Investigated Reporting,* 232–33; Jesse Sunenblick, "Murrow's Boy: Dan Rather in High Definition," *Columbia Journalism Review* 47, no. 4 (November/December 2008): 48.

14. Schwartz, author interview; Brian Ross and Avni Patel, "Money Trail: Big Business Means Big Fun for Congress Members at RNC," ABC News, 4 September 2008, http://abcnews.go.com/Blotter/story?id=5719036&page=1; ABC News, "Aloha Al Qaeda," 23 April 2006, http://abcnews.go.com/US/Video/playerIndex?id=1879346.

15. Clay Shirky, *Here Comes Everybody: The Power of Organizing Without Organizations* (London: Allen Lane, 2008), 66–73, 77.

16. Charles Lewis, "The Nonprofit Road," *Columbia Journalism Review* 46, no. 3 (September/October 2007): 32–36.

17. Ibid.; Lewis, "Investigative Journalism Doesn't Win Many Friends," 82; Anath Hartmann, "Center of Attention," *American Journalism Review* 29, no. 26 (December 2007/January 2008): 10–11; Charles Lewis, "Keeping Investigative Journalism Thriving: Strategies for the Future," panel discussion, Investigative Reporters & Editors Conference, Phoenix, 8 June 2007.

18. Protess et al., *The Journalism of Outrage,* 69; Lawler, *The Alternative Influence,* 5–8.

19. Protess, author interview, 15 July 2009; Lynn Sweet, "Fabiano Cleared," *Chicago Sun-Times,* 31 March 1989.

20. Protess, author interview, 15 July 2009; David Protess and Rob Warden, *Gone in the Night: The Dowaliby Family's Encounter with Murder and the Law* (New York: Delacorte Press, 1993).

21. Protess, author interview, 15 July 2009; Bob Secter, "Slaying Charge Dropped, Ending 12-Year Ordeal," *Chicago Sun-Times,* 16 July 1992.

22. David Protess and Rob Warden, *A Promise of Justice* (New York: Hyperion, 1998).

23. Protess, author interview, 15 July 2009; Shapiro, *Shaking the Foundations,* 474–87; Serrin and Serrin, *Muckraking!,* 367–69.

24. Mario F. Catabiani, "The Sleuth," *American Journalism Review* 29, no. 3 (June/July 2007): 45–47; Dennis Hevesi, "Peter Shellem, Investigative Reporter Who Wrote about Wrongful Convictions, Dies at 49," *New York Times,* 1 November 2009, 35.

25. Protess, author interview, 15 July 2009; Innocence Network, http://www.innocencenetwork.org/members.html; Lewis, "The Non-profit Road," 32–36; Weinberg, author interview, 6 June 2008.

26. Brant Houston, "Consider the Alternative: Independence and Innovation Drive Nonprofits' Work," *IRE Journal* 31, no. 2 (March/April 2008): 18; Toni Stabile Center, http://www.stabilecenter.org/; Asra Q. Nomani with Margo Humphries, "The Pearl Project: Wikis and Social Network Software Used to Track Daniel Pearl's Killers," *IRE Journal* 31, no. 2 (March/April 2008): 29–31; Center for Public Integrity, "Power Trips," http://projects.publicintegrity.org/powertrips/report .aspx?aid=799.

27. Carol Guensburg, "Nonprofit News," *American Journalism Review* 30, no. 1 (February/March 2008): 30; Carol Guensburg, "Funding for Foreign Forays," *American Journalism Review* 30, no. 1 (February/March 2008): 32; Christine Russell, "The Survival of Investigative Journalism," *Columbia Journalism Review* online, 24 March 2008; Houston, "Consider the Alternative," 18; Pulitzer Center on Crisis Reporting www.pulitzer center.org.

28. Andrew Donohue, author interview, 18 June 2009; Andrew Donohue, "Doing Great Work in Tough Times," panel discussion, Investigative Reporters & Editors Conference, Baltimore, 12 June 2009; Rachel

Smolkin, "Cities Without Newspapers," *American Journalism Review* 31, no. 3 (June/July 2009): 20.

29. Scott Leadingham, "David Cohn," *Quill* 97, no. 6 (August 2009): 14–15; Sarah Kershaw, "A Different Way to Pay for the News You Want," *New York Times,* 24 August 2008, WK4.

30. Jan Schaffer, "New Media Makers," Institute for Interactive Journalism, May 2009, 2; Paul Steiger, "Doing Great Work in Tough Times"; Carol Guensburg, "Nonprofit News," 27; Joe Nocera, "Self-Made Philanthropists," *New York Times Magazine,* 9 March 2008, 59–61; www.pro publica.org/series.

31. K. Daniel Glover, "The Future of Conservative Journalism," *Accuracy in Media,* 15 June 2009; Mark Flatten, "High Fliers," *Goldwater Institute,* 13 October 2009, http://www.goldwaterinstitute.org/highfliers; Rhonda Bodfield, "AIMS Test May Have No Future in Schools," *Arizona Daily Star,* 15 July 2008; Goldwater Institute Annual Report, 2008.

32. Raphael, *Investigated Reporting,* 230–31.

33. Scott Shane, "A.C.L.U. Lawyers Mine Documents for Truth about Detainees and Interrogations," *New York Times,* 30 August 2009, A4.

34. Bill Allison, "Real-Time Watchdogs: Sunlight Foundation Bloggers Chip Away at Government Secrets," *IRE Journal* 31, no. 2 (March/April 2008): 20–22.

35. Claudia Núñez, "Twenty-First Century Slaves," *La Opinión,* 16–18 June 2008, http://expo.newamericamedia.org/winners/stories/best_in _depth_and_investigative_in_language#a_hell_in_paradise.

36. Tim Arango, "Articles on Editor's Killing Made a Difference," *New York Times,* 23 February 2009, B1; Sherry Ricchiardi, "The Oakland Project," *American Journalism Review* 30, no. 4 (August/September 2008): 30–37; Tim Reiterman, "Journalists Press on for a Slain Colleague," *Los Angeles Times,* 6 April 2008, B1; http://www.chaunceybaileyproject.org/.

37. Kaplan, author interview; David E. Kaplan, *Global Investigative Journalism: Strategies for Support,* Washington, D.C.: Center for International Media Assistance, 5 December 2007; Brant Houston, "Beacons of Hope: Investigative Journalism Centers," *Nieman Reports* 62, no. 1 (Spring 2008): 67–71.

38. Marina Walker Guevara, "Tobacco Underground: The Booming Global Trade in Smuggled Cigarettes," International Consortium for

Investigative Journalism, 19 October 2008, http://www.publicintegrity.org/investigations/tobacco/.

39. *The Pocantico Declaration: Creating a Nonprofit Investigative News Network,* 1 July 2009; Charles Lewis, "Great Expectations: An Investigative News Network Is Born. Now What?" *Columbia Journalism Review* (September/October 2009): 17.

40. Steve Myers, "ProPublica, *NY Times* Team Wins Knight News Challenge Grant for Investigative Document Site," *Poynter Online,* 17 June 2009, www.poynter.org; Richard Pérez-Peña, "A.P. in Deal to Deliver Nonprofits' Journalism," *New York Times,* 13 June 2009, B3.

41. Brian Stelter, "A World of Risk for a Brand New Journalist," *New York Times,* 15 June 2009; Nelson, author interview, 19 June 2009.

42. Bree Nordenson, "Overload! Journalism's Battle for Relevance in an Age of Too Much Information," *Columbia Journalism Review* 47, no. 4 (November/December 2008): 30–37, 40; "State of the Blogosphere 2008," http://technorati.com/blogging/article/state-of-the-blogosphere-introduction/; Deborah Potter, "Endangered I-Teams," *American Journalism Review* 30, no. 2 (April/May 2009), 58.

43. David Boardman, "Editors: Keeping Investigative Reporting Alive with Fewer People, Resources, Space and Time," panel discussion, 2009 Investigative Reporters & Editors Conference, Baltimore, 13 June 2009; David Boardman, "Making Firm a Newspaper's Focus on Investigative Reporting," *Nieman Reports* 62, no. 3 (Fall 2008).

44. Kevin Rector, "Watchdogs with Teeth," *American Journalism Review* 30, no. 3 (June/July 2008): 10–11; Mark Katches, "Investing in Watchdog Reporting," *Nieman Reports* 62, no. 3 (Fall 2008).

45. Dean Starkman, "Pulitzers a Triumph for Investigations," *Columbia Journalism Review Online,* 8 April 2008, www.cjr.org/the_audit/post_111.php?page=all&print=true.

BIBLIOGRAPHY

PERSONAL INTERVIEWS BY AUTHOR

Armstrong, Scott. Interview by author, June 3, 2008. Tape recording.
Barlett, Donald L., and James B. Steele. Interview by author, June 13, 2009. Tape recording.
Bradlee, Ben. Interview by author, May 13, 2009. Tape recording.
Cohen, Sarah. Interview by author, June 12, 2009. Tape recording.
Donohue, Andrew. Interview by author, June 18, 2009. Tape recording.
Downie, Leonard Jr. Interview by author, August 9, 2007. Tape recording.
Hersh, Seymour M. Interview by author, August 9, 2007. Tape recording.
Houston, Brant. Interview by author, June 6, 2008. Tape recording.
Kaplan, David. Interview by author, June 6, 2008. Tape recording.
Meyer, Philip. Interview by author, June 12, 2008. Tape recording.
Nelson, Deborah. Interview by author, June 19, 2009. Tape recording.
Protess, David. Interview by author, July 15, 2009. Tape recording.
Roberts, Gene. Interview by author, October 8, 2007. Tape recording.
Schwartz, Rhonda. Interview by author, July 16, 2009. Tape recording.
Sussman, Barry. Interviews by author, September 11, 2008, and August 6, 2009. Tape recording.
Weinberg, Steve. Interview by author, June 6, 2008. Tape recording.
Woodward, Bob. Interviews by author, May 20, 2009, and June 8, 2009. Tape recording.

BOOKS AND MONOGRAPHS

Alexander, Jeffrey C., ed. *Durkheimian Sociology: Cultural Studies.* Cambridge: Cambridge University Press, 1988.

Ambrose, Stephen E. *Nixon: Ruin and Recovery 1973–1990*. New York: Simon & Schuster, 1991.

———. *Nixon: The Triumph of a Politician 1962–1972*. New York: Simon & Schuster, 1989.

———. *Nixon: The Education of a Politician 1913–1962*. New York: Simon & Schuster, 1987.

Anderson, David, and Peter Benjaminson. *Investigative Reporting*. Bloomington: Indiana University Press, 1976.

Anderson, Jack, with James Boyd. *Confessions of a Muckraker: The Inside Story of Life in Washington during the Truman, Eisenhower, Kennedy and Johnson Years*. New York: Random House, 1979.

Armstrong, David. *A Trumpet to Arms: Alternative Media in America*. Los Angeles: J. P. Tarcher, 1981.

Aronson, James. *The Press and the Cold War*. New York: Monthly Review Press, 1970.

Aucoin, James L. *The Evolution of American Investigative Journalism*. Columbia: University of Missouri Press, 2005.

Bacon, Jacqueline. *Freedom's Journal: The First African-American Newspaper*. Lanham, Md.: Lexington Books, 2007.

Bagdikian, Ben H. *The New Media Monopoly*. Boston: Beacon Press, 2004.

———. *The Media Monopoly*, 5th ed. Boston: Beacon Press, 1997.

Behrens, John C. *The Typewriter Guerillas: Closeups of 20 Top Investigative Reporters*. Chicago: Nelson-Hall, 1977.

Bennett, W. Lance, Regina G. Lawrence, and Steven Livingston. *When the Press Fails: Political Power and the News Media from Iraq to Katrina*. Chicago: University of Chicago Press, 2007.

Berkowitz, Edward D. *Something Happened: A Political and Cultural Overview of the Seventies*. New York: Columbia University Press, 2006.

Bernstein, Carl. *A Woman in Charge: The Life of Hillary Rodham Clinton*. New York: Alfred A. Knopf, 2007.

Bernstein, Carl, and Bob Woodward. *All the President's Men*. New York: Simon & Schuster, 1974; Pocket Books, 2005.

Blum, David. *Tick . . . Tick . . . Tick . . . : The Long Life and Turbulent Times of 60 Minutes*. New York: HarperCollins, 2004.

Bok, Sissela. *Lying: Moral Choice in Public and Private Life*. New York: Vintage Books, 1979.

Borjesson, Kristina, ed. *Into the Buzzsaw: Leading Journalists Expose the Myth of a Free Press*. Amherst, N.Y.: Prometheus Books, 2002.

Bradlee, Ben. *A Good Life: Newspapering and Other Adventures*. New York: Simon & Schuster, 1995.

Bradley, Patricia. *Women and the Press: The Struggle for Equality*. Medill School of Journalism Visions of the American Press. David Abrahamson, ed. Evanston, Ill.: Northwestern University Press, 2005.

Brady, Kathleen. *Ida Tarbell: Portrait of a Muckraker*. New York: Seaview/Putnam, 1984.

Brasch, Walter M., and Dana R. Ulloth. *Social Foundations of the Mass Media*. Lanham, Md.: University Press of America, 2001.

Brian, Denis. *Pulitzer: A Life*. New York: John Wiley & Sons, 2001.

Campbell, Richard. *60 Minutes and the News: A Mythology for Middle America*. Urbana: University of Illinois Press, 1991.

Campbell, W. Joseph. *The Year That Defined American Journalism: 1897 and the Clash of Paradigms*. New York: Routledge, 2006.

Cappella, Joseph N., and Kathleen Hall Jamieson. *Spiral of Cynicism: The Press and the Public Good*. Oxford: Oxford University Press, 1997.

Carson, Rachel. *Silent Spring*. Boston: Houghton Mifflin, 1962.

Chalmers, David Mark. *The Muckrake Years*. New York: D. Van Nostrand Company, 1974.

Clark, Charles E. *The Public Prints: The Newspaper in Anglo-American Culture, 1645–1740*. New York: Oxford University Press, 1994.

Colodny, Len, and Robert Gettlin. *Silent Coup: The Removal of a President*. New York: St. Martin's Press, 1991.

Cooper, Stephen D. *Watching the Watchdogs: Bloggers as the Fifth Estate*. Spokane: Marquette Books, 2006.

Copeland, David A. *The Idea of a Free Press: The Enlightenment and Its Unruly Legacy*. Medill School of Journalism Visions of the American Press. David Abrahamson, ed. Evanston, Ill.: Northwestern University Press, 2006.

Crouse, Timothy. *The Boys on the Bus*. New York: Random House, 1973.

Daniel, Douglass K. *Lou Grant: The Making of TV's Top Newspaper Drama*. Syracuse: Syracuse University Press, 1996.

Davies, David R. *The Postwar Decline of American Newspapers, 1945–1965*.

The History of American Journalism, no. 6. James D. Startt and Wm. David Sloan, eds. Westport, Conn.: Praeger, 2006.

Dean, John W. III. *Blind Ambition: The White House Years.* New York: Simon & Schuster, 1976.

de Burgh, Hugo, ed. *Investigative Journalism: Context and Practice.* London: Routledge, 2000.

DeFleur, Margaret H. *Computer-Assisted Investigative Reporting: Development and Methodology.* Mahwah, N.J.: Lawrence Erlbaum Associates, 1997.

Demers, David Pearce. *The Menace of the Corporate Newspaper: Fact or Fiction?* Ames: Iowa State University Press, 1996.

Dickinson, William B. *Watergate: Chronology of a Crisis.* Washington, D.C.: Congressional Quarterly, 1973.

Downie, Leonard Jr. *The New Muckrakers.* Washington, D.C.: The New Republic Book Co., 1976.

Downie, Leonard Jr., and Robert G. Kaiser. *The News about the News: American Journalism in Peril.* New York: Alfred A. Knopf, 2002.

Edwards, Bob. *Edward R. Murrow and the Birth of Broadcast Journalism.* Hoboken, N.J.: John Wiley & Sons, 2004.

Einstein, Daniel. *Special Edition: A Guide to Network Television Documentary Series and Special News Reports, 1955–1979.* Metuchen, N.J.: Scarecrow Press, 1987.

Emery, Michael, Edwin Emery, and Nancy L. Roberts. *The Press and America: An Interpretive History of the Mass Media,* 9th ed. Boston: Allyn and Bacon, 2000.

Ettema, James S., and Theodore L. Glasser. *Custodians of Conscience: Investigative Journalism and Public Virtue.* New York: Columbia University Press, 1998.

Felt, Mark, with John O'Connor. *A G-Man's Life: The FBI, Being "Deep Throat," and the Struggle for Honor in Washington.* New York: Public Affairs, 2006.

Felt, W. Mark. *The FBI Pyramid from the Inside.* New York: G. P. Putnam's Sons, 1979.

Filler, Louis, ed. *Contemporaries: Portraits in the Progressive Era by David Graham Phillips.* Westport, Conn.: Greenwood Press, 1981.

————. *Crusaders for American Liberalism.* Yellow Springs, Ohio: Antioch Press, 1939.

Foege, Alec. *Right of the Dial: The Rise of Clear Channel and the Fall of Commercial Radio.* New York: Faber & Faber, 2008.

Ford, Gerald R. *A Time to Heal.* New York: Harper & Row, 1979.

Friedman, Leon, and William F. Levantrosser, eds. *Watergate and Afterward: The Legacy of Richard M. Nixon.* Westport, Conn.: Greenwood Press, 1992.

Friendly, Fred W. *Due to Circumstances Beyond Our Control.* New York: Random House, 1967.

Gans, Herbert J. *Deciding What's News: A Study of "CBS Evening News," "NBC Nightly News," "Newsweek," and "Time."* Medill School of Journalism Visions of the American Press. David Abrahamson, ed. Evanston, Ill.: Northwestern University Press, 2004. First published 1979 by Random House.

————. *Democracy and the News.* Oxford: Oxford University Press, 2003.

Garment, Suzanne. *Scandal: The Crisis of Mistrust in American Politics.* New York: Times Books, 1991.

Ghiglione, Loren. *CBS's Don Hollenbeck: An Honest Reporter in the Age of McCarthyism.* New York: Columbia University Press, 2008.

Gillmor, Dan. *We the Media: Grassroots Journalism by the People, for the People.* Sebastopol, Calif.: O'Reilly Media, 2006.

Glessing, Robert J. *The Underground Press in America.* Bloomington: Indiana University Press, 1970.

Goldstein, Tom. *Journalism and Truth: Strange Bedfellows.* Medill School of Journalism Visions of the American Press. David Abrahamson, ed. Evanston, Ill.: Northwestern University Press, 2007.

Graber, Doris A., ed. *Media Power in Politics,* 3rd ed. Washington, D.C.: CQ Press, 1994.

Graham, Katharine. *Personal History.* New York: Alfred A. Knopf, 1997.

Greenberg, David. *Nixon's Shadow: The History of an Image.* New York: W. W. Norton & Company, 2003.

Greenwald, Marilyn, and Joseph Bernt, eds. *The Big Chill: Investigative Reporting in the Current Media Environment.* Ames: Iowa State University Press, 2000.

Guttenplan, D. D. *American Radical: The Life and Times of I. F. Stone.* New York: Farrar, Straus & Giroux, 2009.

Halberstam, David. *The Powers That Be.* New York: Alfred A. Knopf, 1979.

Haldeman, H. R. *The Haldeman Diaries: Inside the Nixon White House.* New York: G. P. Putnam's Sons, 1994.

Hamilton, James T. *All the News That's Fit to Sell: How the Market Transforms Information into News.* Princeton: Princeton University Press, 2004.

Harrington, Michael. *The Other America: Poverty in the United States.* New York: Simon & Schuster, 1962; Touchstone, 1997.

Harris, Roy Jr. *Pulitzer's Gold: Behind the Prize for Public Service Journalism.* Columbia: University of Missouri Press, 2007.

Havill, Adrian. *Deep Truth: The Lives of Bob Woodward and Carl Bernstein.* New York: Birch Lane Press, 1993.

Hench, John B., ed. *Three Hundred Years of the American Newspaper.* Worcester, Mass.: American Antiquarian Society, 1991.

Herman, Edward S., and Noam Chomsky. *Manufacturing Consent: The Political Economy of the Mass Media.* New York: Pantheon Books, 1988.

Hersh, Seymour M. *Chain of Command: The Road from 9/11 to Abu Ghraib.* New York: HarperCollins, 2004.

———. *Cover-up.* New York: Random House, 1972.

———. *My Lai 4: A Report on the Massacre and Its Aftermath.* New York: Random House, 1970.

Hertsgaard, Mark. *On Bended Knee: The Press and the Reagan Presidency.* New York: Farrar, Straus & Giroux, 1988.

Hess, Stephen. *The Washington Reporters.* Washington, D.C.: The Brookings Institution, 1981.

Hoff, Joan. *Nixon Reconsidered.* New York: Basic Books, 1994.

Hougan, Jim. *Secret Agenda: Watergate, Deep Throat and the CIA.* New York: Random House, 1984.

Houston, Brant, Len Bruzzese, and Steve Weinberg. *The Investigative Reporter's Handbook: A Guide to Documents, Databases and Techniques,* 4th ed. Boston: Bedford/St. Martin's, 2002.

Huntzicker, William E. *The Popular Press, 1833–1865.* The History of American Journalism, no. 3. James D. Startt and Wm. David Sloan, eds. Westport, Conn.: Greenwood Press, 1999.

Johnson, George W., ed. *The Nixon Presidential Press Conferences.* New York: Earl M. Coleman Enterprises, 1978.

Jones, Robert W. *Journalism in the United States.* New York: E. P. Dutton & Company, 1947.

Kaniss, Phyllis. *Making Local News.* Chicago: University of Chicago Press, 1991.

Kennedy, George, and Daryl Moen. *What Good Is Journalism?: How Reporters and Editors Are Saving America's Way of Life.* Columbia: University of Missouri Press, 2007.

Keogh, James. *President Nixon and the Press.* New York: Funk & Wagnalls, 1972.

Kovach, Bill, and Tom Rosenstiel. *Warp Speed: America in the Age of Mixed Media.* New York: Century Foundation, 1999.

Kutler, Stanley I., ed. *Abuse of Power: The New Nixon Tapes.* New York: The Free Press, 1997.

———. *The Wars of Watergate: The Last Crisis of Richard Nixon.* New York: Alfred A. Knopf, 1990.

Lang, Gladys Engel, and Kurt Lang. *The Battle for Public Opinion: The President, the Press, and the Polls during Watergate.* New York: Columbia University Press, 1983.

Lasky, Victor. *It Didn't Start with Watergate.* New York: The Dial Press, 1977.

Lawler, Philip F. *The Alternative Influence: The Impact of Investigative Reporting Groups on America's Media.* Lanham, Md.: University Press of America, 1984.

Lewis, Anthony. *Make No Law: The Sullivan Case and the First Amendment.* New York: Random House, 1991.

Liebovich, Louis W. *Richard Nixon, Watergate, and the Press: A Historical Perspective.* Westport, Conn.: Praeger, 2003.

Linsky, Martin. *Impact: How the Press Affects Federal Policymaking.* New York: W. W. Norton, 1986.

Lippmann, Walter. *Pubic Opinion.* New York: Harcourt, Brace and Company, 1922.

Lyons, Gene, and the editors of *Harper's* magazine. *Fools for Scandal: How the Media Invented Whitewater.* New York: Franklin Square Press, 1996.

MacDougall, Curtis D. *Interpretative Reporting.* New York: The Macmillan Company, 1938.

Manoff, Robert Karl, and Michael Schudson, eds. *Reading the News.* New York: Pantheon Books, 1986.

McChesney, Robert W. *The Political Economy of Media: Enduring Issues, Emerging Dilemmas.* New York: Monthly Review Press, 2008.

———. *The Problem of the Media: U.S. Communication Politics in the 21st Century.* New York: Monthly Review Press, 2004.

McPherson, James Brian. *Journalism at the End of the American Century, 1965–Present.* The History of American Journalism, no. 7. James D. Startt and Wm. David Sloan, eds. Westport, Conn.: Praeger, 2006.

Meyer, Philip. *Precision Journalism: A Reporter's Introduction to Social Science Methods,* 4th ed. Lanham, Md.: Rowman & Littlefield Publishers, 2002.

———. *The New Precision Journalism.* Bloomington: Indiana University Press, 1991.

Miraldi, Robert, ed. *The Muckrakers: Evangelical Crusaders.* Westport, Conn.: Praeger, 2000.

———. *Muckraking and Objectivity: Journalism's Colliding Traditions.* New York: Greenwood Press, 1990.

Mitford, Jessica. *Poison Penmanship: The Gentle Art of Muckraking.* New York: Alfred A. Knopf, 1979.

———. *The American Way of Death.* New York: Simon & Schuster, 1963.

Mollenhoff, Clark R. *Investigative Reporting: From Courthouse to White House.* New York: Macmillan Publishing, 1981.

Mosher, Frederick C. *Watergate: Implications for Responsible Government.* National Academy of Public Administration Report to the Senate Select Committee on Presidential Campaign Activities. New York: Basic Books, 1974.

Nader, Ralph. *Unsafe at Any Speed: The Designed-in Dangers of the American Automobile.* New York: Grossman Publishers, 1965.

Nelson, Deborah. *The War Behind Me: Vietnam Veterans Confront the Truth about U.S. War Crimes.* New York: Basic Books, 2008.

Neustadt, Richard E. *Presidential Power and the Modern Presidents: The Politics of Leadership from Roosevelt to Reagan.* New York: The Free Press, 1990.

Nimmo, Dan D., and Chevelle Newsome. *Political Commentators in the United States in the 20th Century: a Bio-critical Sourcebook.* Westport, Conn.: Greenwood Press, 1997.

Nixon, Richard M. *In the Arena: A Memoir of Victory, Defeat, and Renewal.* New York: Simon & Schuster, 1990.

———. *RN: The Memoirs of Richard Nixon.* New York: Grosset & Dunlap, 1978.

Olmsted, Kathryn S. *Challenging the Secret Government: The Post-Watergate Investigations of the CIA and FBI.* Chapel Hill: University of North Carolina Press, 1996.

Olson, Keith W. *Watergate: The Presidential Scandal That Shook America.* Lawrence: University Press of Kansas, 2003.

Overholser, Geneva, and Kathleen Hall Jamieson, eds. *The Press.* Oxford: Oxford University Press, 2005.

Patterson, James T. *Restless Giant: The United States from Watergate to Bush v. Gore.* New York: Oxford University Press, 2005.

Patterson, Margaret Jones, and Robert H. Russell. *Behind the Lines: Case Studies in Investigative Reporting.* New York: Columbia University Press, 1986.

Peck, Abe. *Uncovering the Sixties: The Life and Times of the Underground Press.* New York: Citadel Press, 1985.

Perlstein, Rick. *Nixonland: The Rise of a President and the Fracturing of America.* New York: Scribner, 2008.

Pilger, John, ed. *Tell Me No Lies: Investigative Journalism That Changed the World.* New York: Thunder's Mouth Press, 2005.

Protess, David L. *Muckraking Matters: The Societal Impact of Investigative Reporting.* The Institute for Modern Communications' Research Monograph Series and Center for Urban Affairs and Policy Research's Research and Policy Reports Series. Evanston, Ill.: Northwestern University, 1987.

Protess, David L., Fay Lomax Cook, Jack C. Doppelt, et al. *The Journalism of Outrage: Investigative Reporting and Agenda Building in America.* New York: Guilford Press, 1991.

Protess, David, and Rob Warden. *A Promise of Justice: The Eighteen-Year Fight to Save Four Innocent Men.* New York: Hyperion, 1998.

———. *Gone in the Night: The Dowaliby Family's Encounter with Murder and the Law.* New York: Delacorte Press, 1993.

Putnam, Robert D. *Bowling Alone: The Collapse and Revival of American Community.* New York: Simon & Schuster, 2000.

Pynn, Ronald E., ed. *Watergate and the American Political Process.* New York: Praeger, 1975.

Randall, David. *The Great Reporters.* London: Pluto Press, 2005.

Raphael, Chad. *Investigated Reporting: Muckrakers, Regulators, and the Struggle over Television Documentary.* Urbana: University of Illinois Press, 2005.

Reeves, Richard. *President Nixon: Alone in the White House.* New York: Simon & Schuster, 2001.

Ritchie, Donald A. *Reporting from Washington: The History of the Washington Press Corps.* Oxford: Oxford University Press, 2005.

Roberts, Gene, ed. *Leaving Readers Behind: The Age of Corporate Newspapering.* Fayetteville: University of Arkansas Press, 2001.

Roberts, Gene, and Hank Klibanoff. *The Race Beat: The Press, the Civil Rights Struggle, and the Awakening of a Nation.* New York: Alfred A. Knopf, 2006.

Roberts, Gene, ed., and Thomas Kunkel, gen. ed. *Breach of Faith: A Crisis of Coverage in the Age of Corporate Newspapering.* Fayetteville: University of Arkansas Press, 2002.

Rosen, James. *The Strong Man: John Mitchell and the Secrets of Watergate.* New York: Doubleday, 2008.

Sabato, Larry J. *Feeding Frenzy: How Attack Journalism Has Transformed American Politics.* New York: Free Press, 1991.

Safire, William. *Before the Fall: An Inside View of the Pre-Watergate White House.* Garden City, N.Y.: Doubleday, 1975.

Sanford, Bruce D. *Don't Shoot the Messenger: How Our Growing Hatred of the Media Threatens Free Speech for All of Us.* Lanham, Md.: Rowman & Littlefield, 1999.

Schlesinger, Arthur M. Jr. *The Imperial Presidency.* Boston: Houghton Mifflin, 1973.

Schorr, Daniel. *Clearing the Air.* Boston: Houghton Mifflin, 1977.

Schudson, Michael. *The Power of News.* Cambridge: Harvard University Press, 1995.

————. *Watergate in American Memory: How We Remember, Forget, and Reconstruct the Past.* New York: Basic Books, 1992.

————. *Discovering the News: A Social History of American Newspapers.* New York: Basic Books, 1978.

Serrin, Judith, and William Serrin. *Muckraking! The Journalism That Changed America.* New York: The New Press, 2002.

Shapiro, Bruce, ed. *Shaking the Foundations: 200 Years of Investigative Journalism in America.* New York: Thunder's Mouth Press/Nation Books, 2003.

Shepard, Alicia. *Woodward and Bernstein: Life in the Shadow of Watergate.* Hoboken, N.J.: John Wiley & Sons, 2007.

Shirky, Clay. *Here Comes Everybody: The Power of Organizing Without Organizations.* London: Allen Lane, 2008.

Sloan, Wm. David. *The Media in America: A History,* 7th ed. Northport, Ala.: Vision Press, 2008.

Sloan, Wm. David, and Julie Hedgepeth Williams. *The Early American Press, 1690–1783.* The History of American Journalism, no. 1. James D. Startt and Wm. David Sloan, eds. Westport, Conn.: Greenwood Press, 1994.

Smith, Zay N., and Pamela Zekman. *The Mirage.* New York: Random House, 1979.

Smythe, Ted Curtis. *The Gilded Age Press, 1865–1900.* The History of American Journalism, no. 4. James D. Startt and Wm. David Sloan, eds. Westport, Conn.: Praeger, 2003.

Snyder, Louis L., and Richard B. Morris, eds. *A Treasury of Great Reporting: "Literature Under Pressure" from the Sixteenth Century to Our Own Time,* 2nd ed. New York: Simon & Schuster, 1962.

Sparrow, Bartholomew H. *Uncertain Guardians: The News Media as a Political Institution.* Baltimore: Johns Hopkins University Press, 1999.

Spear, Joseph C. *Presidents and the Press: The Nixon Legacy.* Cambridge: MIT Press, 1984.

Squires, James D. *Read All About It! The Corporate Takeover of America's Newspapers.* New York: Times Books, 1993.

Stephens, Mitchell. *A History of News: From the Drum to the Satellite.* New York: Viking, 1988.

Stone, I. F. *The I. F. Stone's Weekly Reader.* Neil Middleton, ed. New York: Random House, 1973.

Streitmatter, Rodger. *Voices of Revolution: The Dissident Press in America.* New York: Columbia University Press, 2001.

———. *Unspeakable: The Rise of the Gay and Lesbian Press in America.* Boston: Faber and Faber, 1995.

———. *Raising Her Voice: African-American Women Journalists Who Changed History.* Lexington: The University Press of Kentucky, 1994.

Sussman, Barry. *The Great Coverup: Nixon and the Scandal of Watergate.* New York: Signet Classics, 1974.

Sweeney, Michael S. *The Military and the Press: An Uneasy Truce.* Medill School of Journalism Visions of the American Press. David Abrahamson, ed. Evanston, Ill.: Northwestern University Press, 2006.

Teel, Leonard Ray. *The Public Press, 1900–1945.* The History of American Journalism, no. 5. James D. Startt and Wm. David Sloan, eds. Westport, Conn.: Praeger, 2006.

Thompson, Kenneth W., ed. *The Nixon Presidency: Twenty-Two Intimate Perspectives of Richard M. Nixon.* Lanham, Md.: University Press of America, 1987.

Tichi, Cecelia. *Exposés and Excess: Muckraking in America, 1900/2000.* Philadelphia: University of Pennsylvania Press, 2004.

Tracy, James F. *A Historical Case Study of Alternative News Media and Labor Activism: The Dubuque Leader 1935–1939.* Journalism & Communication Monographs 8, no. 4. Anantha S. Babbili, ed. Columbia, S.C.: Association for Education in Journalism and Mass Communication, 2007.

Ullmann, John. *Investigative Reporting: Advanced Methods and Techniques.* New York: St. Martin's Press, 1995.

Ullmann, John, and Jan Colbert, eds. *The Reporter's Handbook: An Investigator's Guide to Documents and Techniques,* 2nd ed. New York: St. Martin's Press, 1991.

Washburn, Patrick S. *The African American Newspaper: Voice of Freedom.* Medill School of Journalism Visions of the American Press. David Abrahamson, ed. Evanston, Ill.: Northwestern University Press, 2006.

Weinberg, Steve. *Taking on the Trust: The Epic Battle of Ida Tarbell and John D. Rockefeller.* New York: W. W. Norton, 2008.

———. *Telling the Untold Story: How Investigative Reporters Are Changing the Craft of Biography.* Columbia: University of Missouri Press, 1992.

Weir, David, and Mark Schapiro. *Circle of Poison: Pesticides and People in a Hungry World.* San Francisco: Institute for Food and Development Policy, 1981.

Weldon, Michele. *Everyman News: The Changing American Front Page.* Columbia: University of Missouri Press, 2008.

Wendland, Michael F. *The Arizona Project: How a Team of Investigative Reporters Got Revenge on Deadline.* Kansas City: Sheed Andrews and McMeel, 1977.

White, Theodore H. *Breach of Faith: The Fall of Richard Nixon.* New York: Antheneum Publishers, 1975.

Williams, Paul N. *Investigative Reporting and Editing.* Englewood Cliffs, N.J.: Prentice-Hall, 1978.

Williams, Walter, and Frank L. Martin. *The Practice of Journalism: A Treatise on Newspaper Making.* Columbia, Mo.: E. W. Stephens, 1911.

Wilson, Clint C. II, Félix Gutiérrez, and Lena M. Chao. *Racism, Sexism, and the Media: The Rise of Class Communication in Multicultural America,* 3rd ed. Thousand Oaks, Calif.: Sage Publications, 2003.

Woodward, Bob. *The War Within: A Secret White House History 2006–2008.* New York: Simon & Schuster, 2008.

———. *State of Denial.* New York: Simon & Schuster, 2006.

———. *The Secret Man: The Story of Watergate's Deep Throat.* New York: Simon & Schuster, 2005.

———. *Plan of Attack.* New York: Simon & Schuster, 2004.

———. *Bush at War.* New York: Simon & Schuster, 2002.

———. *Shadow: Five Presidents and the Legacy of Watergate 1974–1999.* New York: Simon & Schuster, 1999.

Woodward, Bob, and Scott Armstrong. *The Brethren: Inside the Supreme Court.* New York: Simon & Schuster, 1979; Avon Books, 1981.

Woodward, Bob, and Carl Bernstein. *The Final Days.* New York: Simon & Schuster, 1976.

Yochelson, Bonnie. *Jacob Riis.* London: Phaidon Press, 2001.

SELECTED NEWSPAPER, JOURNAL, MAGAZINE, AND WEB ARTICLES

Aftergood, Steven. "Classified Documents: Secrecy vs. Citizenship." *Nieman Reports* 62, no. 1 (Spring 2008): 19–20.

Allison, Bill. "Real-Time Watchdogs: Sunlight Foundation Bloggers Chip Away at Government Secrets." *IRE Journal* 31, no. 2 (March/April 2008): 20–22.

Andersen, Carrie, and Elizabeth McEvoy. "The Death of Journalism? Why the Plame Case Threatens to Undermine the Media." *Harvard Political Review* 32, no. 4 (Winter 2006): 24.

Arango, Tim. "Articles on Editor's Killing Made a Difference." *New York Times,* 23 February 2009, B1.

Armstrong, Scott. "Was the Press Any Match for All the President's Men?" *Columbia Journalism Review* 29, no. 1 (May/June 1990): 27–35.

———. "Friday the Thirteenth." *The Journal of American History* 75, no. 4 (March 1989): 1234–44.

Baker, Russell. "Goodbye to Newspapers?" *The New York Review of Books* 54, no. 13 (16 August 2007): 8.

Barlett, Donald L., and James B. Steele. "Reporting Is Only Part of the Investigative Story." *Nieman Reports* 62, no. 1 (Spring 2008): 50–52.

———. "Soaked by Congress." *Time,* 15 May 2000.

———. "America: Who Stole the Dream?" *Philadelphia Inquirer,* 22 September 1996, 1.

Baughman, James L. "The Transformation of *Time* Magazine: From Opinion Leader to Supporting Player." *Media Studies Journal* 12, no. 3 (Fall 1998): 120–27.

Baym, Geoffrey. "Strategies of Illumination: U.S. Network News, Watergate, and the Clinton Affair." *Rhetoric & Public Affairs* 6, no. 4 (2003): 633–56.

Becker, Lee B., Robin E. Cobbey, and Idowu A. Sobowale. "Public Support for the Press." *Journalism Quarterly* 55, no. 3 (1978): 421–30.

Berman, Paul. "The Watchdog." *New York Times Book Review,* 1 October 2006, 12.

Bernstein, Carl. "Watergate's Last Chapter." *Vanity Fair,* October 2005.

———. "The Idiot Culture." *New Republic,* 8 June 1992, 22–28.

———. "The CIA and the Media." *Rolling Stone,* 20 October 1977.

Borden, Sandra L. "Janet Cooke in Hindsight: Reconsideration of a Paradigmatic Case in Journalism Ethics." *Journal of Communication Inquiry* 26, no. 2 (2002):155–70.

Bowen, Ezra. "New Paths to Buried Treasure." *Time,* 7 July 1986, 56.

Brady, Kathleen. "Remembering Ida Tarbell: Standard Oil Investigation Set out to Capture an Era—and Readers." *IRE Journal* 31, no. 1 (January/February 2008): 12–13.

"Bribes Were Only Real Thing at Mirage." *Chicago Sun-Times,* 17 February 2008, A15.

Broder, David. "War on Cynicism: Politicians and the Media Badly Need a Dialogue about the Deterioration of Public Discourse." *Washington Post,* 6 July 1994, A19.

Brogan, Daniel. "Good Journalism Can Be Good Business," *Nieman Reports* 62, no. 1 (Spring 2008): 43–44.

Capo, James A. "Network Watergate Coverage Patterns in Late 1972 and Early 1973." *Journalism Quarterly* 60, no. 4 (1983): 595–602.

Caraley, Demetrios, Charles V. Hamilton, Alpheus T. Mason, et al. "American Political Institutions after Watergate—A Discussion." *Political Science Quarterly* 89, no. 4 (1974–75): 717–24.

Carlson, Scott. "In Jack Anderson's Papers, a Hidden History of Washington." *The Chronicle of Higher Education,* 16 March 2007, A16, A18.

Carter, Bill. "Television; Grit or Glamour? Time to Investigate." *New York Times,* 20 January 1991, B31.

Cattabiani, Mario. "The Sleuth." *American Journalism Review* 29, no. 3 (June/July 2007): 45–47.

Chamberlain, Sam. "Cuts Lead to New Interest in Indie Probes." *Editor & Publisher,* 1 August 2009.

Ciotta, Rose. "Baby You Should Drive This CAR." *American Journalism Review* 18, no. 2 (March 1996): 34.

Cohen, Noam. "Blogger, Sans Pajamas, Rakes Muck and a Prize." *New York Times,* 25 February 2008, C1.

Cohen, Patricia. "John Dean's Watergate Role at Issue in Nixon Tapes Feud," *New York Times,* 1 February 2009, A1.

Crain, Caleb. "A Star Is Born." *New York Review of Books* 49, no. 9 (23 May 2002).

Crewdson, John M. "Sabotaging the G.O.P.'s Rivals: Story of a $100,000 Operation." *New York Times,* 9 July 1973, A1, A22.

Culbertson, Hugh. "Veiled Attribution—An Element of Style?" *Journalism Quarterly* 55, no. 3 (Autumn 1978): 456–65.

Davis, Charles N. "Secrets in the Financial Sector Rescue Plan Test Obama's Call for Transparency." *IRE Journal* 32, no. 2 (Spring 2009): 21.

———. "Good News for FOIA." *IRE Journal* 31, no. 2 (March/April 2008): 15.

"Discretion Urged in Press Power; AP Manager Says Freedom Is Not a 'Hunting License.'" *New York Times,* 4 May 1976, 14.

Doig, Stephen K. "Reporting with Tools of Social Science." *Nieman Reports* 62, no. 1 (Spring 2008): 47–49.

Dorroh, Jennifer. "Statehouse Exodus." *American Journalism Review* 31, no. 2 (April/May 2009): 21–35.

Downie, Leonard Jr., and Michael Schudson. "The Reconstruction of American Journalism." *Columbia Journalism Review* (November/December 2009): 40.

Drogin, Bob. "Determining the Reliability of a Key CIA Source," *Nieman Reports* 62, no. 1 (Spring 2008): 12–14.

Dumenco, Simon. "The Last Hurrah of Hollywood's Hero Journalist?" *Advertising Age,* 13 April 2009, 16.

Eder, Steve. "Ohio Will Get $54.9M from Noe's Rare Coins." *Toledo Blade,* 25 July 2008.

Elliott, William R., and William J. Schenck-Hamlin. "Film, Politics and the Press: The Influence of *All the President's Men.*" *Journalism Quarterly* 56, no. 3 (Autumn 1979): 545–53.

Epstein, Edward Jay. "Did the Press Uncover Watergate?" *Commentary* 58, no. 1 (July 1974): 21–24.

Feldstein, Mark. "The Challenges and Opportunities of 21st Century Muckraking." *Nieman Reports* 63, no. 2 (Summer 2009): 50–53.

———. "A Muckraking Model: Investigative Reporting Cycles in American History." *Harvard International Journal of Press/Politics* 11, no. 2 (Spring 2006): 105–20.

———. "Watergate Revisited." *American Journalism Review* 26, no. 4 (August/September 2004): 60–68.

Fielder, Virginia Dodge, and David H. Weaver. "Public Opinion on Investigative Reporting." *Newspaper Research Journal* 57, no. 3 (January 1982): 54–62.

Fitzgerald, Mark. "Finances Seen Behind the Investigative Slowdown." *Editor & Publisher,* 1 July 1989.

Frank, Laura. "The Withering Watchdog." *Exposé: America's Investigative Reports,* 18 June 2009, http://www.pbs.org/wnet/expose/2009/06/the-withering-watchdog.html.

Frankel, Max. "The Washington Back Channel." *New York Times Magazine,* 25 March 2007, 40–47, 62, 66, 80.

Garber, Megan. "The Big Picture." *Columbia Journalism Review* 46, no. 4 (November/December 2007): 12–14.

Garment, Leonard. "The Guns of Watergate." *Commentary* 83, no. 4 (April 1987): 15–23.

Gartner, Michael. "First Amendment: Subpoena Madness." *Columbia Journalism Review* 37, no. 2 (July/August 1998): 45–47.

Genovese, Michael A. "The Lessons of Watergate: Thirty Years On." *Presidential Studies Quarterly* 34, no. 2 (2004): 455–57.

George, Kathy. "Nixon Plumber Who Went to Prison Tells Story." *Seattle Post-Intelligencer,* 15 September 2003, B1.

Georges, Christopher. "Confessions of an Investigative Reporter." *Washington Monthly* 24, no. 3 (March 1992): 36–44.

Gitlin, Todd. "An Unexpected Aeration: A Crisis of Conscience Breathed Life into American Journalism." *Media Studies Journal* 12, no. 3 (Fall 1998): 148–53.

Glover, K. Daniel. "The Future of Conservative Journalism." *Accuracy in Media,* 15 June 2009.

Graves, Florence. "Watchdog Reporting: Exploring Its Myth." *Nieman Reports* 62, no. 1 (Spring 2008): 32–35.

Greenberg, David. "Nabobs Revisited: What Watergate Reveals about Today's Washington Press Corps." *Washington Monthly* 35, no. 10 (October 2003): 45–48.

Gronke, Paul, and Timothy E. Cook. "Disdaining the Media: The

American Public's Changing Attitudes Toward the News." *Political Communication* 24, no. 3 (July 2007): 259–81.

Guensburg, Carol. "Nonprofit News." *American Journalism Review* 30, no. 1 (February/March 2008): 26–33.

Guthrie, Melissa. "Investigative Journalism Under Fire." *Broadcasting & Cable* 138, no. 26 (22 June 2008): 10–26.

Halberstam, David. "Justified Doubts: Reporters Underestimated the Strength and Resilience of America's Adversaries." *Media Studies Journal* 12, no. 3 (Fall 1998): 10–11.

Hamilton, Martha H. "What We Learned in the Meltdown." *Columbia Journalism Review* 47, no. 5 (January/February 2009): 36–39.

Hartmann, Anath. "Center of Attention." *American Journalism Review* 29, no. 26 (December 2007/January 2008): 10–11.

Hendler, Clint. "What We Didn't Know Has Hurt Us." *Columbia Journalism Review* 47, no. 5 (January/February 2009): 28–32.

Hersh, Seymour M. "Torture at Abu Ghraib." *New Yorker,* 10 May 2004, 42–47.

———. "The Debate Within: The Objective Is Clear—Topple Saddam. But How?" *New Yorker,* 11 March 2002, 34.

Hickey, Bill. "Money Lust: How Pressure for Profit Is Perverting Journalism." *Columbia Journalism Review* 37, no. 2 (July/August 1998): 28–36.

Hochschild, Adam. "The First 25 Years." *Mother Jones* 26, no. 3 (May/June 2001): 50.

Hohenberg, John. "Public Service: A 1964 Honor Roll." *Columbia Journalism Review* 3, no. 2 (Summer 1964): 9–12.

———. "New Patterns in Public Service." *Columbia Journalism Review* 1, no. 2 (Summer 1962): 14–17.

Houston, Brant. "Beacons of Hope: Investigative Journalism Centers." *Nieman Reports* 62, no. 1 (Spring 2008): 67–71.

———. "Consider the Alternative: Independence and Innovation Drive Nonprofits' Work." *IRE Journal* 31, no. 2 (March/April 2008): 17–19.

Huntington, Samuel P. "The Democratic Distemper." *Public Interest* 41 (Fall 1975): 9–38.

Hyde, John. "When a Few Dollars Make a Big Difference," *Nieman Reports* 62, no. 1 (Spring 2008): 38–39.

Johnson, Paul. "In Praise of Richard Nixon." *Commentary* 86, no. 4 (October 1988): 50–53.

Jones, RonNell Andersen. "Avalanche or Undue Alarm? An Empirical Study of Subpoenas Received by the News Media." *Minnesota Law Review* 93, no. 101 (17 November 2008): 101–85.

Kershaw, Sarah. "A Different Way to Pay for the News You Want." *New York Times,* 24 August 2008, WK4.

Kovach, Bill. "Report from the Ombudsman." *Brill's Content* 1, no. 2 (September 1998): 18–21.

Kraft, Joseph. "The Imperial Media." *Commentary* 71, no. 5 (May 1981): 36–47.

Kurtz, Howard. "Tightened Belts Could Put Press in a Pinch." *Washington Post,* 23 October 2006, C01.

———. "The Post on WMDs: An Inside Story; Prewar Articles Questioning Threat Often Didn't Make Front Page." *Washington Post,* 12 August 2004, A1.

Labunski, Richard E., and John V. Pavlik. "The Legal Environment of Investigative Reporters: A Pilot Study." *Newspaper Research Journal* 5, no. 3 (Spring 1985): 13–19.

Leadingham, Scott. "David Cohn." *Quill* 97, no. 6 (August 2009): 14–15.

Lears, Jackson. "Paper Trail." *New York Times Book Review,* 5 July 2009, 12.

Lemann, Nicholas. "Anchors Away." *Atlantic* 261, no. 5 (May 1988): 89.

Lewis, Charles. "Great Expectations: An Investigative News Network Is Born. Now What?" *Columbia Journalism Review* (September/October 2009): 17–18.

———. "The Future of Watchdog Reporting Brightens as Nonprofit Groups Organize a New Network." *Nieman Watchdog,* 3 July 2009.

———. "The Nonprofit Road." *Columbia Journalism Review* 46, no. 3 (September/October 2007): 32–36.

———. "Investigative Journalism Doesn't Win Many Friends." *Nieman Reports* 60, no. 2 (Summer 2006): 81–83.

Lieberman, Trudy. "In the Beginning: From a Consumer Movement to

Consumerism." *Columbia Journalism Review* 47, no. 4 (September/October 2008): 34–37.

Liebes, Tamar, and Shoshana Blum-Kulka. "It Takes Two to Blow the Whistle: Do Journalists Control the Outbreak of Scandal?" *American Behavioral Scientist* 47, no. 9 (May 2004): 1153–70.

Linzer, Dafna. "Lost in Translation." ProPublica, http://www.propublica.org/feature/alhurra-middle-east-hearts-and-minds-622.

"List of White House 'Enemies' and Memorandums Relating to Those Named," *New York Times,* 28 June 1973, 38.

Lule, Jack. "I. F. Stone: The Practice of Reporting." *Journalism and Mass Communication Quarterly* 72, no. 3 (Autumn 1995): 499–510.

Marder, Murrey. "The Press and the Presidency: Silencing the Watchdog." *Nieman Reports* 62, no. 1 (Spring 2008): 8–10.

———. "This Is Watchdog Journalism." *Nieman Reports* 53/54, no. 4/1 (Winter 1999, Spring 2000): 78–79.

Marro, Anthony. "A Larger-Than-Life Reporter." *Columbia Journalism Review* 40, no. 6 (March/April 2002): 18.

Maslin, Janet. "Absence of Malice." *New York Times,* 19 November 1981.

Massing, Michael. "Now They Tell Us." *New York Review of Books* 51, no. 3 (26 February 2004).

———. "The Libel Chill: How Cold Is It Out There?" *Columbia Journalism Review* 24, no. 1 (May/June 1985): 31–43.

Maurer, Paul J. "Media Feeding Frenzies: Press Behavior During Two Clinton Scandals." *Presidential Studies Quarterly* 29, no. 1 (1999): 65–79.

McQuaid, John. "Critical Mass: Crowdsourcing Projects Evolve at NewsAssignment.net." *IRE Journal* 31, no. 2 (March/April 2008): 24–26.

McWhirter, Cameron. "Saved by the Shield." *Columbia Journalism Review* 47, no. 1 (May/June 2008): 23–26.

McWilliams, Carey. "Is Muckraking Coming Back?" *Columbia Journalism Review* 9, no. 3 (Fall 1970): 8–15.

Metcalfe, Daniel J. "Sunshine Not So Bright: FOIA Implementation Lags Behind." *Administrative and Regulatory Law News* 34, no. 4 (Summer 2009): 5.

"More Ring Villainy." *New York Times,* 8 July 1871, 4.

Morrow, Lance. "Naysayer to the Nattering Nabobs." *Time,* 30 September 1996, 36.

Moynihan, Daniel Patrick. "The Presidency and the Press." *Commentary* 51, no. 3 (March 1971): 41–53.

Nelson, Jack. "Orangeburg Students Unarmed, Study Shows." *Los Angeles Times,* 18 February 1968, A3.

Nocera, Joe. "Self-Made Philanthropists." *New York Times Magazine,* 9 March 2008, 59–61.

Nomani, Asra Q., and Margo Humphries. "The Pearl Project: Wikis and Social Network Software Used to Track Daniel Pearl's Killers." *IRE Journal* 31, no. 2 (March/April 2008): 29–31.

Nordenson, Bree. "Overload! Journalism's Battle for Relevance in an Age of Too Much Information." *Columbia Journalism Review* 47, no. 4 (November/December 2008): 30–37, 40.

O'Brien, Sinéad. "Secrets and Lies." *American Journalism Review* 20, no. 7 (September 1998): 41–47.

O'Connor, John D. "I'm the Guy They Called Deep Throat." *Vanity Fair,* July 2005, 86–133.

Olmsted, Kathryn. "An American Conspiracy: The Post-Watergate Press and the CIA." *Journalism History* 19, no. 2 (Summer 1993): 51–58.

Palast, Greg. "U.S. Media Have Lost the Will to Dig Deep." *Los Angeles Times,* 27 April 2007, A33.

Peele, Thomas. "The Chauncey Bailey Project: Media Coalition Reinvests Arizona Project Model." *IRE Journal* 31, no. 1 (January/February 2008): 32–33.

Potter, Deborah. "Endangered I-Teams." *American Journalism Review* 30, no. 2 (April/May 2009): 58.

Priest, Dana. "CIA Holds Terror Suspects in Secret Prisons." *Washington Post,* 2 November 2005, A1.

———. "CIA Avoids Scrutiny of Detainee Treatment." *Washington Post,* 3 March 2005, A1.

Priest, Dana, and Joe Stephens. "Secret World of U.S. Interrogation: Long History of Tactics in Overseas Prisons Is Coming to Light." *Washington Post,* 11 May 2004, A1.

Pulliam, Myrta. "His Leadership Built IRE." *IRE Journal* 31, no. 3 (May/June 2008): 22.

Rector, Kevin. "Watchdogs with Teeth." *American Journalism Review* 30, no. 2 (June/July 2008): 10–11.

Reeves, Richard. "Lots of Footwork, No Footnotes: The Final Days." *New York Times,* 18 April 1976, 174.

Reiterman, Tim. "Journalists Press on for a Slain Colleague." *Los Angeles Times,* 6 April 2008, B1, B9.

Ricchiardi, Sherry. "The Oakland Project." *American Journalism Review* 30, no. 4 (August/September 2008): 30–37.

Risen, James, and Eric Lichtblau. "Bush Lets U.S. Spy on Callers without Courts." *New York Times,* 16 December 2005, A1.

Robertson, Lori. "Kind of Confidential." *American Journalism Review* 29, no. 3 (June/July 2007): 26–33.

Rolland, Asle. "Commercial News Criteria and Investigative Journalism." *Journalism Studies* 7, no. 6 (December 2006): 940–63.

Rozen, Laura. "Hung out to Dry: The National-Security Press Dug up the Dirt, but Congress Wilted." *Columbia Journalism Review* 47, no. 5 (January/February 2009): 33–35.

Rutenberg, Jim. "Anchor's Pay Package May Change Standards." *New York Times,* 20 December 2001, C5.

Safire, William. "Lancegate." *New York Times,* 11 August 1977, A17.

———. "Vic Lasky's Blockbuster." *New York Times,* 25 April 1977, A31.

Sandler, James. "The War on Whistle-Blowers." *Salon,* 1 November 2007.

Schaffer, Sarah. "Muckraking and Fundraising." *American Journalism Review* 24, no. 10 (December 2002): 16.

Schwartz, Barry, and Lori Holyfield. "Nixon Postmortem." *Annals of the American Academy of Political Social Science* 560 (1998): 96–110.

Segal, David. "Carl Bernstein, Back on the Beat." *Washington Post,* 20 June 2007, C01.

Shepard, Alicia C. "The Myth of Watergate, Woodward and Bernstein." *Poynteronline,* 7 August 2007.

Shogan, Robert. "Enemas for Elephants: A New Political Order Has Dumped New Responsibilities on Journalists." *Media Studies Journal* 12, no. 3 (Fall 1998): 50–56.

Sidey, Hugh. "An Interview with the President." *Time,* 8 December 1986, 43.

Sifry, Micah L. "A See-Through Society." *Columbia Journalism Review* 47, no. 5 (January/February 2009): 43–47.

Silverstein, Ken, and Chuck Neubauer. "Lucrative Deal for a Daughter of Politics." *Los Angeles Times,* 20 February 2004, A1.

Smith, Robert M. "Before Deep Throat." *American Journalism Review* 31, no. 3 (June/July 2009): 14–15.

Smolkin, Rachel. "Cities Without Newspapers." *American Journalism Review* 31, no. 3 (June/July 2009): 17–25.

Sokolove, Michael. "What's a Big City without a Newspaper?" *New York Times Magazine,* 9 August 2009, 36–43.

Starkman, Dean. "Power Problem." *Columbia Journalism Review* 48, no. 1 (May/June 2009): 24–30.

———. "Pulitzers a Triumph for Investigations." *Columbia Journalism Review,* 8 April 2008, http://www.cjr.org/the_audit/post_111 .php?page=all&print=true.

Steigerwald, Bill. "Sprigle's Secret Journey." *Pittsburgh Post-Gazette,* 2 August 1998, G10.

Stelter, Brian. "Was Press a War 'Enabler'?" *New York Times,* 30 May 2008, A18.

Stern, Marcus. "Digital Records Reveal Corruption on Capitol Hill." *Nieman Reports* 62, no. 1 (Spring 2008): 15–16.

Sussman, Barry. "Revealing the Disinformation Industry." *Nieman Reports* 62, no. 1 (Spring 2008): 45–47.

———. "Watergate, 25 Years Later: Myths and Collusion." *Watergate.info,* http://www.watergate.info/sussman/25th.shtml.

Swain, Bruce M., and J. Michael Robertson. "The *Washington Post* and the Woodward Problem." *Newspaper Research Journal* 16, no. 1 (Winter 1995): 2–20.

"The Times and Iraq." *New York Times,* 26 May 2004, A10.

Tyndall, Andrew. "Climbing Down from Olympus: 'CBS Evening News' from Walter Cronkite to Dan Rather." *Media Studies Journal* 12, no. 3 (Fall 1998): 134–41.

Umansky, Eric. "Failures of Imagination: American Journalists and the Coverage of American Torture." *Columbia Journalism Review* 45, no. 3 (September/October 2006): 16–31.

Weinberg, Steve. "Investigative Books of 2008." *IRE Journal* 32, no. 1 (Winter 2009): 6–10.

———. "The Accidental Icon: How Jacob Riis Went from the Muck to Muckraker." *Columbia Journalism Review* 47, no. 3 (September/October 2008): 61–62.

———. "Impeaching Woodstein." *Columbia Journalism Review* 32, no. 3 (September/October 1993): 57–59.

———. "Was Nixon Duped? Did Woodward Lie?" *Columbia Journalism Review* 30, no. 4 (November/December 1991): 88–94.

Weitzel, Pete. "Keeping Secrets." *The American Editor* (May/June/July 2004): 5–9.

Zimmer, Troy A. "The Impact of Watergate on the Public's Trust in People and Confidence in the Mass Media." *Social Science Quarterly* 59, no. 4 (1979): 743–51.

SELECTED SPEECHES, DISCUSSIONS, SYMPOSIA, AND RESEARCH PRESENTATIONS

Abrahamson, Jill, Andrew Donohue, Mark Katches, et al. "Doing Great Work in Tough Times." Panel discussion, Investigative Reporters and Editors Conference, Baltimore, 12 June 2009.

Agnew, Spiro. "On the National Media." Speech, Des Moines, Iowa, 13 November 1969.

Aucoin, James L. "Undercover Reporting, Hidden Cameras and the Ethical Decision-Making Process: A Refinement." Paper presented to the Qualitative Studies Division, Association for Education in Journalism and Mass Communication annual meeting, Chicago, 30 July–2 August 1997.

Barlett, Donald L., and James B. Steele. "Building the Story: From Getting Started to Knowing When to Stop." Panel discussion, Investigative Reporters and Editors Conference, Baltimore, 13 June 2009.

Bernt, Joseph, Marilyn Greenwald, and Mark Tatge. "Enterprise and Investigative Reporting in Three Metropolitan Papers: 1980 and 1995 Compared." Paper presented to the Council of Affiliates and

Investigative Reporters and Editors, Inc., Association for Education in Journalism and Mass Communication annual meeting, Anaheim, Calif., 12 August 1996.

Boardman, David, Leonard Downie Jr., and Manny Garcia. "Editors: Keeping Investigative Reporting Alive with Fewer People, Resources, Space and Time." Panel discussion, Investigative Reporters and Editors Conference, Baltimore, 13 June 2009.

Cox, Melisma. "The Development of Computer-Assisted Reporting." Paper presented to the Newspaper Division of the Association for Education in Journalism and Mass Communication, Southeast Colloquium, Chapel Hill, N.C., 17–18 March 2000.

Cuillier, David. "Access Attitudes: Importance of Community Engagement in Support for Press Access to Government Records." Paper presented to the Media Law Division of the Association for Education in Journalism and Mass Communication annual meeting, Washington, D.C., August 2007.

Demers, David Pearce. "Are Corporate Newspapers Less Critical of City Hall?" Paper presented to Association for Education in Journalism and Mass Communication annual meeting, Anaheim, Calif., August 1996.

Downie, Leonard Jr., and Bob Woodward. "Accountability Reporting and Digging Deep." Panel discussion, Investigative Reporters and Editors Conference, Baltimore, 12 June 2009.

Garrison, Bruce. "Newspaper Size as a Factor in Use of Computer-Assisted Reporting." Paper presented to the Communication Technology and Policy Division of the Association for Education in Journalism and Mass Communication annual meeting, Baltimore, August 1998.

Gilbin, Paul. "Journalism at the Crossroads: After Newspapers, Then What?" Panel discussion, Association for Education in Journalism and Mass Communication annual meeting, Boston, 6 August 2009.

Halper, Donna L. "Dangerous Ideas: Censorship in Broadcasting's First

Two Decades." Paper presented to Joint Journalism Historians Conference, New York City, 14 March 2009.

Killebrew, Kenneth C. "Don Bolles: News Martyr of the 1970s, Enigma of the 1990s." Paper presented to the History Division of the Association for Education in Journalism and Mass Communication annual meeting, August 1995.

Klein, Jon. Keynote address at the 2009 Investigative Reporters & Editors Conference, Baltimore, 13 June 2009.

Lanosga, Gerry. "'God Help Our Democracy': Investigative Reporting in America, 1946–1960." Paper presented to the Association for Education in Journalism and Mass Communication, Boston, 6 August 2009.

Lanosga, Gerry, and Jason Martin. "The Investigative Reporting Agenda in America: 1979–2007." Paper presented to the Association for Education in Journalism and Mass Communication annual meeting, Chicago, 6–9 August 2008.

Lewis, Anthony. "The Richard S. Salant Lecture on Freedom of the Press." The Joan Shorenstein Center on the Press, Politics and Public Policy, Cambridge, Mass., 1 October 2008.

Maguire, Miles. "Richard Critchfield: 'Genius' Journalism and the Fallacy of Verification." Paper presented to the International Conference for Literary Journalism Studies, Evanston, Ill., 15 May 2009.

Moyers, Bill. "Journalism Under Fire." Society of Professional Journalists Convention & National Journalism Conference, New York City, 11 September 2004.

Smith, Dean C. "Journalist Privilege in 1929: Sen. Arther Capper and the Start of the Shield Law Movement in America." Paper presented at the Association for Education in Journalism and Mass Communication annual meeting, Boston, 5 August 2009.

Sumner, David E. "Makers of the Modern Magazine Model: *Munsey's, McClure's* and *Cosmopolitan* in the 1890s." Paper presented at the Joint Journalism Historians Conference, New York City, 14 March 2009, 3.

"Watergate—35 Years Later." Panel discussion, Society of Professional Journalists Convention & National Journalism Conference, Washington, D.C., 6 October 2007.

DOCUMENTS AND REPORTS

"AIM Report: Treason, Plagiarism and The Washington Post." A report by Accuracy in Media, 4 December 2007.

"An Opportunity Lost: An In-depth Analysis of FOIA Performance from 1998 to 2007." Coalition of Journalists for Open Government, 3 July 2008.

Caulfied, Jack. Memorandum for John Ehrlichman, 31 July 1969. Released by the Nixon Presidential Library & Museum, http:// nixon.archives.gov/virtuallibrary/documents/jun09.php.

Colson, Charles. Memorandum for H. R. Haldeman, 4 November 1971. Released by the Nixon Presidential Library & Museum, http:// nixon.archives.gov/virtuallibrary/documents/jun09.php.

Department of Education—Contract to Obtain Services of Armstrong Williams. United States Government Accountability Office, no. B-305368, Washington, D.C., 30 September 2005.

Haldeman, H. R. Notes of 23 June 1971 and 15 May 1972. Released by the Nixon Presidential Library & Museum, http://nixon.archives .gov/virtuallibrary/documents/dec08.php.

Higby, Lawrence. Memorandum for H. R. Haldeman, 8 July 1971. Released by the Nixon Presidential Library & Museum, http://nixon .archives.gov/virtuallibrary/documents/jun09.php.

Hoover, J. Edgar. Letter to John W. Dean III, 20 December 1971. Released by the Nixon Presidential Library & Museum, http://nixon .archives.gov/virtuallibrary/documents/dec08.php.

Internet Sapping Broadcast News Audience. Pew Research Center for People & the Press, Washington, D.C., 11 June 2000.

Jones, Sydney, and Susannah Fox. "Generations Online in 2009." Data memo for Pew Internet & American Life Project, 28 January 2009.

Just, Marion, Rosalind Levine, and Kathleen Regan. "Investigative Reporting Despite the Odds: Watchdog Reporting Continues to Decline." Project for Excellence in Journalism, 1 November 2002.

Kaplan, David E. *Global Investigative Journalism: Strategies for Support.* Center for International Media Assistance, 5 December 2007.

The Pew Research Center's Project for Excellence in Journalism. *The*

State of the News Media 2009: An Annual Report on American Journalism. Washington, D.C., 2009.

Report of the Congressional Committees Investigating the Iran/Contra Affair. U.S. Senate Select Committee on Secret Military Assistance to Iran and the Nicaraguan Opposition and U.S. House of Representatives Select Committee to Investigate Covert Arms Transactions with Iran, 1987.

Schaffer, Jan. "New Media Makers." Institute for Interactive Journalism, May 2009.

Views of Press Values and Performance: 1985–2007. The Pew Research Center for the People & the Press, Washington, D.C., 2007.

Young, David R. Undated memorandum for Richard Nixon. Released by the Nixon Presidential Library & Museum, http://nixon.archives.gov/virtuallibrary/documents/jun09.php.

BROADCASTS

"How Secure Are U.S. Borders?" *ABC News,* 10 September 2003.

Nixon, Richard. Interview by David Frost. *Frost/Nixon: The Original Watergate Interviews,* originally broadcast as *The Nixon Interviews* by David Paradine Productions, Inc., 5 May 1977.

Ross, Brian, Rhonda Schwartz, and David Scott. "Customs Fails to Detect Depleted Uranium." *ABC News,* 11 September 2002.

"Wal-Mart." *Dateline NBC,* 22 December 1992.

WEB SITES

"The Black Press: Soldiers without Swords," http://www.pbs.org/blackpress/news_bios/index.html.

"The Encyclopedia of Television," Museum of Broadcast Communications, http://www.museum.tv/publicationssection.php?page=520.

Investigative Reporters & Editors, "IRE Celebrates Thirty Years of History," http://www.ire.org/history/30years/index.html; "The Arizona Project," http://www.ire.org/history/arizona

.html; and "The Desert Rats," http://www.ire.org/history/desertrats.html.

Project for Excellence in Journalism, http://www.stateofthenewsmedia.com/2009.

Reporters Without Borders. "Worldwide Press Freedom Index 2007," http://www.rsf.org/article.php3?id_article=24025.

INDEX

Jon Marshall is a lecturer at Northwestern University's Medill School of Journalism. He created the *News Gems* Web site and has reported for the *Tampa Tribune* and the suburban Chicago *Daily Herald*. His articles and columns have appeared in dozens of other publications including the *Christian Science Monitor*, CBS News's *Public Eye*, the *Chicago Tribune*, and *Quill* magazine.

Bob Woodward is an associate editor at the *Washington Post*, where he has worked since 1971. He and Carl Bernstein were the main reporters on the Watergate scandal, and the *Post* won the Pulitzer Prize for its Watergate coverage in 1973. He was also the lead reporter for the *Post*'s articles on the aftermath of the September 11 terrorist attacks, which won the National Affairs Pulitzer Prize in 2002. In the last thirty-six years, Woodward has authored or coauthored fifteen books, all of which have been national best sellers.